Voices & Visions

VOICES & VISIONS

A Journey through Vietnam Today

Carolijn Visser

Translated by Susan Massotty

SYCAMORE ISLAND BOOKS
BOULDER, COLORADO

The names of all but public figures have been
changed to protect their privacy.

Voices and Visions:
A Journey through Vietnam Today
by Carolijn Visser

Copyright © 1994 by Carolijn Visser and J.M. Meulenhoff bv, Amsterdam
(Translated from the Dutch version *Hoge bomen in Hanoi,*
Copyright © 1993 by Carolijn Visser and J.M. Meulenhoff bv, Amsterdam)
Translation © Susan Massotty 1994

Publication of this book was made possible with financial support from the Foundation for the Production and Translation of Dutch Literature.

Publisher's Cataloging in Publication
(Prepared by Quality Books Inc.)

Visser, Carolijn, 1956-
   [Hoge bomen in Hanoi. English]
   Voices & visions : a journey through Vietnam today / by Carolijn Visser ; translated by Susan Massotty.
   p. cm.
   Translation of: Hoge bomen in Hanoi.
   Preassigned LCCN: 94-65720.
   ISBN 0-87364-761-0
   1. Vietnam--Description and travel--1975-   I. Title. II. Title: Voices and visions.

DS556.39.V5713 1994   915.9704'44
                                              QBI94-453

Published by Sycamore Island Books, a division of Paladin Enterprises, Inc., P.O. Box 1307, Boulder, Colorado 80306, USA. (303) 443-7250

Direct inquiries and/or orders to the above address.
All rights reserved. Except for use in a review, no portion of this book may be reproduced in any form without the express written permission of the publisher. Neither the author nor the publisher assumes any responsibility for the use or misuse of information contained in this book.

Author photograph is by Harry Cock.
Printed in the United States of America

Contents

The Mekong Delta · 1
The Guru of My Tho   3
Sadec: The City of Marguerite Duras and Her Chinese Lover   13

Saigon · 27
Evenings in Apocalypse Now   29
Round Eyes   47
When the Snow Falls   53
Passion and Corruption   65
A Vietnamese in Amsterdam   73
Homesick for Long Xuyen   77
Under the Wing of a Vietnamese Family   85

The Central Highlands · 111
In Search of the Montagnards   113

Hanoi · 125
A French Wedding   127
Hanoi Hannah   141
A Tale of Two Fathers   147
The Battle of the Embargo   153

The Sorrow of War	165
Memories of the Wood of Crying Souls	173
Dreaming of a Vietnamese Village	183
Among Dissidents	195

HUE · 211
A Poet and a Princess	213

FAREWELL TO SAIGON · 239
New Memories	241

Preface

For me and my generation, the United States was not the defender of democracy that the Dutch government proclaimed it to be every Memorial Day. In our view, the Americans were conducting an unjust war against an innocent people. Demonstrations against "American imperialism" were held on practically a weekly basis in Holland. And, on a daily basis, we watched the suffering of the Vietnamese people on TV.

During my high school years in the small town of Middleburg, the Cold War was at its height. Then came detente, and the newspapers my parents subscribed to began to preach the end of the East-West conflict. We were admonished to show greater understanding of the USSR and the Communist system; it was not the evil empire the Americans claimed it was.

In the mid-1970s I cautiously began to explore the world beyond Holland's secure borders. My first trip took me to Eastern Europe. I wanted to see for myself what life was like behind the Iron Curtain.

It didn't take long for me to discover that the Dutch media hadn't painted an entirely accurate picture of Communist workaday reality. The lives of ordinary people seemed as drab and gray as the Socialist-style high rises in which they were housed. Long lines of dissatisfied people stood waiting for what the shops had to offer in the way of scarce and inferior goods.

After Eastern Europe, my first journey of any length took me to Communist China. The Socialist ideal may have died an ignominious death in the Soviet Union, but China was another story. There, it was said, "the new man" had arisen, and Chinese women had more rights than their European sisters. But in 1981 the Chinese people were still suffering the aftermath of a "Cultural Revolution" that had claimed the lives of millions. In my first book, *Gray China*, I described the unrelieved misery I encountered there. It never occurred to me that this travel book would unleash a flurry of angry reactions. Many members of the Dutch intelligentsia found it unseemly of me to have besmirched the name of their paradise in this way. From that time on, I was bound and determined to go to Vietnam as well.

The exodus of the boat refugees kept Vietnam in the international limelight for quite a while, but then the country seemed to disappear from the face of the earth. What had happened to all those Davids who had routed the Goliath, Uncle Sam? I had to go see for myself.

Flying into Hanoi, I couldn't help but notice the bomb craters still around the airport. Yet no one looking out the windows of our Boeing could see the scars that the "American war" had left on the Vietnamese people: the beautiful Tuyet, desperate to snag an American husband; the fragile Mr. Van Cao, the composer of the Vietnamese national anthem who fell into discredit; the Viet Cong veteran struggling with his war traumas — all of them attempting to give new direction to their war-torn lives. The one sings French *chansons*, the other dreams of a new life in Texas, and no one believes in Marx anymore.

Here, then, are their stories.

This book is dedicated to my grandmother, Gerda Demmink, who passed away when I was in Vietnam.

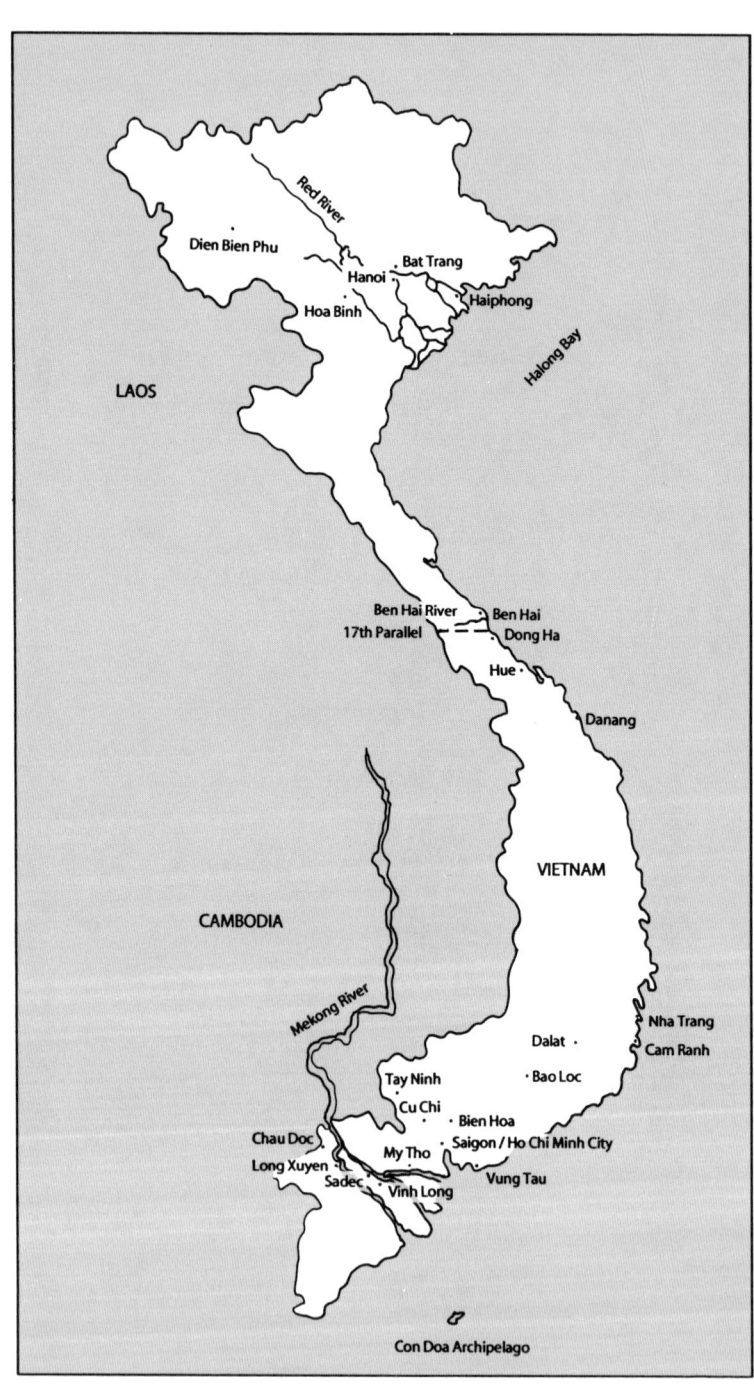

THE
MEKONG DELTA

The Guru of My Tho

Our boat is sailing serenely down a branch of the Mekong River, along a shore lined with lopsided palm trees. Fishing boats with huge eyes painted on their prows chug their way past us. Sampans seem to be plying endlessly from one side to another.

Seated in the bow, I take precise note of all I see around me. I've been in Vietnam for a few days and can think of nothing but the war. In my mind, helicopters keep skimming over the trees, and nightmarish films repeat themselves over and over in my head.

Back then, I ask myself as I cast my eye at the river, how did you know who might be hiding a machine gun in his boat? Or who was merely headed for the market and who was working for the Viet Cong?

Mr. Hanh, my Vietnamese guide, is also thinking about the past. "The Americans were scared here," he says, trailing a hand through the water. "Real scared."

Actually, Mr. Hanh is talking about himself, since he was in the South Vietnamese Army, fighting on the side of the Americans. He's paid for his collaboration ever since 1975. He spent a few months in a re-education camp, and after that no one would hire him. Four daughters were born, and the family found itself sinking deeper and deeper into destitution. For a time Mr. Hanh and his wife tried selling bread, but their customers had no money for bread. Then for several years he sold lard in the marketplace, but in a time in which everyone was as thin as a rake, his product bordered on the obscene.

A few months ago his luck changed. "That's because my father planted mulberry trees in my garden," he told me in all seriousness. "Mulberry trees bring good luck." Seeing my look of incredulity, he exclaimed: "It's not just the Vietnamese who believe that. The Chinese do too."

It must be true, since not long after that his next-door neighbor introduced him to one of the new travel agencies that have sprung up in the city, one that was looking for an English-speaking guide. Since then, Mr. Hanh has been constantly on the go, earning ten dollars a day, an amount of money that up to now would have taken him more than a month to scrape together.

Mr. Hanh talks about the future with great caution. He's constantly girding himself for a new disaster, since he's not an official guide. The travel agency merely acts as a go-between and arranges everything outside official channels. When he thinks he's not being observed, his face creases into an anxious frown: a tightrope walker who has to put all his energy into maintaining his mastery over the forces of gravity.

Despite his trials and tribulations, Mr. Hanh looks respectable, well-educated and gentlemanly, the type you would automatically assume earns a living as a civil servant. His nails are kept neatly filed and his hair slicked back, although at the moment, he's donned a blue cap to protect him against the rays of the sun bouncing off the water.

We're headed for the island of the Coconut Monk. According to Mr. Hanh it's a sight worth seeing; all his former clients enjoyed it. I agreed to go since I didn't want to disappoint him, and Mr. Hanh genuinely seems to relax once we're on the water. As the boat girl deftly secures the boat to the landing, he chuckles in delight, as if he's on an outing.

On the shore, a wrinkled old man is waiting for us, rubbing his

The Guru of My Tho

hands in glee. Mr. Hanh and he know each other from earlier visits, and the two men have grown fond of each other. Helping hands guide us out of the boat and onto land. The old man, Mr. To, was a policeman in the time of the Americans, Mr. Hanh explains. So things haven't gone very well for him since the war, although he's now leading a peaceful life on this tiny island and earning his living as a guide.

"*Bienvenue*," squeaks Mr. To. We follow him until he stops, gesturing broadly, among a dozen pillars entwined with plaster dragons attempting to wind their way to the top. "This is where the followers of the Coconut Monk stood while he sat on his throne — over there on top of that rock — and addressed the crowd." The followers prayed nonstop for hours, I'm told, until they fell into a trance. So that he could meditate in peace and quiet, the monk occasionally had himself hoisted by a rope to the top of a tall tower, an iron scaffold he dubbed Apollo in honor of the first moon landing in 1969.

The Coconut Monk dreamed of uniting South and North Vietnam. In the sixties and seventies, when the war was at its peak, he preached unity and tried to convince the high-ranking American officials he met, such as McNamara, of the truth of his vision. Wishing to express his ideas in tangible form, he ordered the construction of a huge map of Vietnam. And now, stretched out at our feet, is the country's elongated contour, cast in cement: two pillars rise up from Saigon and Hanoi and are joined together by a bridge. Mr. To implores me not to walk across the bridge, since it's on the verge of collapse.

I'm surprised that the Coconut Monk's empire was never attacked. After all, it lay right in the middle of the war zone. And he advocated disarmament, which was asking for trouble.

"No, no," says Mr. Hanh. "The Viet Cong found him useful. He called for disarmament in both North and South. But no one in the North had ever heard of him; nobody had ever written anything about him, and nobody ever talked about him. So actually he was supporting disarmament of the South. And naturally the Viet Cong had nothing against that."

Mr. Hanh and Mr. To shuffle their feet in uneasy silence. The Coconut Monk has suddenly become a sensitive subject.

"And the Americans then?" I ask. "They must have thought he was a troublemaker?"

"Well," replies Mr. Hanh, "the South Vietnamese government arrested him a couple of times and threw him in jail, but each time they had to let him go again. He was an idealist. He was peaceful and sincere. What could the Americans charge him with?"

Mr. To has walked on ahead of us and guides us into the cave where the monk received highly placed visitors. It's refreshingly cool inside. "Air-conditioned," remarks Mr. To.

I ask him what his personal opinion of the monk is. Grinning broadly, Mr. To replies, "He was an unusual man." He awaits my response in expectant silence.

"Yes, that's true," I agree. "And who were his followers? People from the island?"

Mr. To chortles and shakes his head. "No, the islanders never set foot in 'Paradise,' as they referred to it. His followers flocked to him from all over the Mekong Delta. There were also some Americans, people from the peace movement. They lived on coconuts like the Vietnamese and prayed for peace." Mr. To and Mr. Hanh chuckle in fond remembrance.

I was reminded of a friend of my parents. Living in a renovated farmhouse in the Dutch countryside, he had decided to let his beard grow. One day he took off for Ibiza. We heard that he'd joined a sect that gathered around the campfire every evening to chant their mantras. Babbling about a clear light, he wrote to his former wife, who read the letters, either roaring with laughter or choked with tears, to my mother over the phone. I can picture them here on this tropical island: lanky, hirsute Americans in tattered and scruffy garments. They pray, sing and smoke dope while the war passes them by.

Mr. To has saved the most interesting detail for the last. "The Coconut Monk was always surrounded by nine women. Nine naked women." Mr. Hanh comes to a halt in shocked surprise. That was something he hadn't heard during his previous visits. Nude? Mr. To repeats it solemnly in French. *"Totalement nue."*

It finally dawns on me: it was a hippie colony. The Age of Aquarius in Vietnam. The Coconut Monk was a guru.

The Guru of My Tho

The Americans, sailing their warships past the island, must have grinned in delight at the view through their binoculars. Naked girls with long hair, the monk high up in his tower in the lotus position. And music. The entire island must have reverberated with rock music night and day.

In 1975, when the last Americans had left Vietnam, the monk was rounded up by the new government. On second thought, the Communists decided he was a threat and placed him under lock and key.

After he was released, the monk returned to his native village to devote himself to contemplation. In 1990 he surfaced in My Tho, the city on the other side of the river, where he was planning to breathe new life back into his sect. But the police arrested him again. "And then he fell out of the second-story window of the police station," says Mr. Hanh in a neutral tone of voice.

Mr. To sells a book published by the government which sets about to disprove a variety of miracles attributed to the monk. The message to the readers is that he was an ordinary mortal, nothing more and nothing less. It contains a famous photograph of the monk — so emaciated he's almost transparent — surrounded by cats and mice eyeing each other in supreme tolerance. The caption reads: "This is a case of trick photography." In reality the cats presumably would have eaten the mice.

We study the page carefully. "I think it's real," I say.

Mr. Hanh and Mr. To prefer to remain noncommittal. "The question is no longer relevant," remarks Mr. Hanh, while Mr. To adds evasively: "It all depends on how you look at it." The two men allow a discreet silence to fall. The Coconut Monk is still a sensitive subject.

"Well," Mr. Hanh breaks the silence, "we've seen everything there is to see." Mr. To escorts us back to the dock. As the boat girl shoves off from the landing with an oar, Mr. To calls out something in his squeaky voice, but I can't make it out. Mr. Hanh laughs. "He said: '*Au revoir au paradis*, until we meet again in Paradise.'"

That evening at dusk, Mr. Hanh and I sit on folding chairs along the river. At first, Mr. Hanh had waved aside my offer: "No beer for me." But now he's sitting contentedly drinking a can of 333, brewed in Saigon. It's made him chatty.

"I can't say that my work as a guide has been blessed with good fortune," he begins. "I've only been doing this work for six months, but a lot of strange things have happened." One of the first groups he escorted came from Sweden. "The oldest one looked a lot like you. She could be your mother," says Mr. Hanh uneasily. One morning, when they were in the north of the country, she failed to wake up. Mr. Hanh turns pale as he recalls the cold corpse to whose bedside he was summoned.

In panic he called his employer. She told him: "Whatever you do, don't mention the name of my travel agency," and hung up. Mr. Hanh was obliged to do all the paperwork himself, while the police put him through the third degree. Didn't he know his client had a bad heart? Why hadn't he found her earlier? Mr. Hanh trembles at the recollection.

After that, two American veterans were entrusted to his care. The three of them traveled the length and breadth of Vietnam. "And every evening," recounts Mr. Hanh appalled, as if he still can't believe it, "they wanted a different woman. I had to scrounge them up for them. 'Mr. Hanh,' they said to me, 'where are the local beauties?'" He concludes gloomily: "Now they're sure to have AIDS."

Next, he set off with a group of Italians who were obsessed by the war. All they wanted to see were the remains of crashed helicopters and the tunnels in which the Vietnamese concealed themselves. Natural beauty or sunny beaches didn't interest them in the least. Halfway through the trip they were determined to take a look at the former American naval base in Cam Ranh Bay. After the war the base had passed into Russian hands. Even though most of the Russians have also left by now, the base is still strictly off limits. "It'll be hard to get permission," Mr. Hanh explained at great length.

"No problem," answered the Italians, "we'll simply climb over the fence."

Mr. Hanh could imagine how this adventure was going to end if they got caught: the Italians would be deported, and he, the former American collaborator, would wind up in jail. So when he had a free moment, he went to the local police and explained the situation. "I'm employed by a group of Italians who won't listen

The Guru of My Tho

to reason," he told them. "Tomorrow they're going to attempt to storm the base in Cam Ranh Bay. For goodness' sake, please stop them, before they get themselves killed."

The next morning, the group had just gotten started when their bus was stopped by plainclothes policemen. Where were the gentlemen going? Would they mind coming down to the station? Mr. Hanh pretended to be highly incensed and promised to do what he could. The Italians were ordered to leave the area and to drive to the North that very same day, and Mr. Hanh was saved from disaster in the nick of time.

"Don't worry," I say, in an attempt to reassure him. "I'm in perfect health, and I don't want to go anywhere I'm not allowed to go." Mr. Hanh regards me in silence, as if he still suspects me of having a hidden agenda.

In an attempt to clarify my motives, I add: "The reason I want to see the Mekong Delta is that twenty years ago I saw it almost every night on TV. I'm curious to see the area where all the fighting took place." Mr. Hanh nods and becomes cheerful again, since this is one wish he's capable of fulfilling.

Then I remove a book from my bag: *The Lover from North China*, written by the French writer Marguerite Duras. "Look," I say, "the author of this book grew up around here, in the city of Sadec. Tomorrow I'd like to go see Sadec." Mr. Hanh leafs through the pages but can't read a word since it's written in Dutch.

"Why Sadec?" he asks. "There's nothing special there."

"Oh there must still be traces of the French colonial past," I reply and add, to convince him further, that I'd also like to get an idea of what Vietnam looked like before the war, before the Americans arrived with their helicopters and napalm.

Mr. Hanh knits his brow. "There's probably nothing left from those days," he says fretfully. "The war has changed everything. For everyone in this country."

The next morning we resume our journey in a sweltering bus. We're surrounded by swarms of hawkers and beggars at every stop. "Madam, Madam," they beseech me, plucking at my arm through the open window. Old women and men with stumps hold up tin cups: "Madam, Madam."

Inside the ferry the misery is even worse. A man with a

burned face begs for alms, while another pushes himself along on a set of wheels, with a mob of raggedy children in his wake. When we reach the other side of the river, the mendicants remain on board. They only work the ferry, sailing back and forth all day long.

As the bus lumbers on through the green plains, Mr. Hanh broaches a subject dear to his heart: the widespread corruption in his country. He opens the conversation by stating unequivocally: "Everyone can be bought. If you have money, you can get whatever you want."

The border with Cambodia is about fifty miles away, and according to Mr. Hanh the area is rife with crime and mobsters. "TV sets, motorbikes and even cars are brought from Thailand, hauled through the jungles of Cambodia and smuggled over the Vietnamese border. The customs agents have all been bribed."

"Then what happens to all those things?" I ask out of curiosity.

"They're loaded into a truck and driven to Saigon or to the Chinese suburb of Cholon. Everything — and I mean everything — you see there in the marketplace has been smuggled into the country. And half the time it isn't what you think it is," he concludes enigmatically.

"What do you mean?" I inquire, intrigued.

"Well," he explains, "let's say you buy a Japanese motor scooter, a Honda, for two thousand dollars. And then what happens? You find out that it's not made of Japanese parts but that they've switched them all, and you're stuck with a scooter made out of cheap Chinese substitutes. It's been 'boiled,' as we say."

His stories surprise me. "I would have thought that in a Communist country like Vietnam the authorities would have cracked down on shady deals like that."

"Ha!" cries Mr. Hanh, warming to his subject. "But the authorities are the ones who are corrupt: the police, the politicians, the managers of state-run enterprises. They're all busy lining each other's pockets."

Looking out the window, I see a group of women in *ao dai*, the traditional Vietnamese garb, standing along the side of the road and chatting animatedly. In their fluttering yellow, pink and blue

The Guru of My Tho

tunics they look like butterflies. "A wedding," Mr. Hanh explains, following the direction of my eyes.

Everyone in the Mekong Delta seems to be getting married today. More than once I see a motorbike with a timid bride in pink tulle perched on the back race past us. "Today is the seventh day of the seventh month," observes Mr. Hanh. "It's an auspicious day."

As a black Citroën — a 1930's crank-up model filled to overflowing with wedding guests — overtakes the bus, Mr. Hanh launches into the story of his brother's marriage. It seems his brother married an Amerasian, a girl with a Vietnamese mother and an unknown American soldier for a father. Mr. Hanh's brother had paid the girl's family two thousand dollars (even Mr. Hanh had been obliged to contribute his share), because as the husband of an Amerasian, the brother was entitled to a visa and a free ticket to the U.S. This way the brother could leave Vietnam legally, without having to try his luck in a broken-down boat.

The brother divorced her directly after he arrived in California. "Didn't he like her at all?" I tease.

"Oh no," answers Mr. Hanh shocked. "She wasn't a decent girl. She had loose morals and had already had two abortions." In the camp where they went through all the red tape needed to emigrate to the U.S., they had been obliged to sleep in the same bed to avoid suspicion. "But my brother didn't lay a hand on her." Mr. Hanh is sure of that. Now his brother is living somewhere in California, by himself. Despite all his efforts, he can just barely eke out a living. He hasn't yet found a new wife. But, as Mr. Hanh concludes, that's hardly surprising, since as long as his brother doesn't have any money, no prospective brides are likely to present themselves. Reading between the lines of his letters, Mr. Hanh can see that his brother misses his family and Vietnam.

"Then why doesn't he come back?" I ask. Mr. Hanh clearly regards this as a stupid question. While fragments of music from yet another wedding waft into the bus, Mr. Hanh points out the obvious: "He has to have achieved something first."

SADEC:
THE CITY OF
MARGUERITE DURAS AND
HER CHINESE LOVER

Just before noon we arrive in the city of Vinh Long, where we're supposed to transfer to a bus that will take us to Sadec. I can't bear the thought of another jam-packed, stiflingly hot bus.

In her strongly autobiographical novel, Marguerite Duras describes how she once traveled, as a girl of fifteen, in the opposite direction, from Sadec to Saigon. On the ferry, she was offered a ride by a charming Chinese man in a chauffeur-driven limousine, a black Morris Léon Bollée.

I peer all around me. "Do you think maybe we could find a taxi?" I suggest.

Mr. Hanh trudges off towards the road and returns with nothing to show for his pains. "There aren't any taxis in Vinh Long. But," he offers by way of alternative, "we can take an *Xe Honda loi*. That's also a comfortable way to travel." He beckons a man with a motorbike, to the back of which a cart has been attached. We clamber aboard, sharing the cart with our luggage. It may not be as chic as a Léon Bollée limousine, but it's a lot cooler than the bus.

We zip along in our twentieth-century stagecoach. The road leads us through flat plains, past endless rice paddies and a garden dotted with fruit trees. Our driver stops at a roadside stand consisting of a table and three bottles of gasoline. The vendor has trouble getting to her feet: she has a wooden leg. She smiles, as if good fortune has fallen her way, carefully uncorks one of her bottles and pours the gas in our tank.

We push on. Remembering the area in which she grew up, Marguerite Duras wrote: "... the ocean of rice paddies in Cochin China... The overwhelming, motionless, Hades-like heat. The legendary silken flatness of the Delta, stretching as far as the eye can see." Later, she was to describe it as "an indeterminate land... a kind of tropical version of Flanders, barely wrested from the sea." And it does indeed remind me of the Low Countries.

In my thoughts, I race ahead to our destination. What will be left of the Sadec in which Marguerite Duras spent her youth?

It is an outpost in the south of French Indochina.
It is 1930.
It is the French district.
It is a street in the French district.
The night air is redolent of jasmine.
Mingled with the faint fragrance of the river...
It is a village of junks.
It is the beginning of the Delta. The end of the river.

More than sixty years ago, her mother was a teacher in Sadec. She had been widowed at a young age and left to care for her three children. But life had yet another disaster in store for Madame Duras: she was brought to financial ruin by colonial officials, who, under the guise of business, cheated her on a property deal. She never recovered from the blow. The poverty-stricken Duras family was shunned by the handful of other French people residing in Sadec.

We race over a bridge. The houses and huts on Sadec's riverfront look as though they might tumble into the river any minute. So this was the site of the opium dens where Marguerite's older brother racked up enormous debts to the Chinese owners.

Marguerite was barely fifteen when she had an affair with the owner of the bewitchingly beautiful Morris Léon Bollée: a Chinese man from Sadec with an extremely wealthy father. The

SADEC: THE CITY OF MARGUERITE DURAS

lovers met in secret until the father ordered his son to go through with the marriage to a Chinese girl which had been arranged in his childhood. He either had to marry her or risk being disinherited by his father. Years ago, Marguerite Duras wrote an earlier version of this story, entitled *The Lover*. The book was made into a movie, in which the city of Sadec provided a breathtaking backdrop.

Mr. Hanh and I stroll by a French villa desperately in need of paint. Did the young Marguerite stand outside this house, peering in at a garden party in which a dazzling French woman in a red dress held every eye in thrall?

Our walk takes us to the marketplace, which used to have a roof resting on iron supports. But, as Mr. Hanh is told by a woman selling a gleaming fish, the original French construction was burned to the ground. While rain beats down on the faded fabric stretched across the merchandise, business continues as usual. Like everyone else, we wade through the black mud.

In the middle of the market a woman is brandishing a big stick, screaming and chasing away any terrified children who happen to cross her path. Everyone makes way for her. The eyes of the thin women selling their wares are filled with gentle compassion rather than anger. It's as if they merely hope the evil spirit possessing the raging woman will soon wear itself out.

Mr. Hanh and I come to a halt at the river and watch sampans glide back and forth over the brownish water. We stare out in silence over Sadec's shabby harbor. "Hmm," remarks Mr. Hanh, "it's a very interesting city."

"Tomorrow," I suggest, "let's go see if we can find the house where Marguerite Duras' Chinese lover lived. In her book she describes it as the most beautiful house in Sadec, decorated with blue tiles."

Mr. Hanh nods in ready anticipation. "Okay," he replies, "I'll go see if I can find us some rooms in Sadec's best hotel."

Standing on the balcony of the hotel, Mr. Hanh surveys the city. Below us I hear female voices calling out to him. Embarrassed, he goes back inside. "Bad women," he mumbles, flustered. "Wearing lots of makeup."

Sometime later, the word "massage" lights up in neon on the building next to the hotel. I ask the reception desk if women are also welcome. "Sure," answers the desk clerk, "forty-five minutes costs ten thousand dong." Less than a dollar.

After my massage, I ask Mr. Hanh if he might want one too. "Oh no" is his shocked reply. "In Vietnam a massage means sex, and you can get AIDS from that."

"I've just been there," I respond, "and there was nothing going on."

Mr. Hanh sticks to his guns. "I don't want to have anything to do with that kind of thing," he states in no uncertain terms.

Escorting foreigners on trips must be a real trial for him. As far as I can tell, Mr. Hanh would much rather be sitting at home with his family under the mulberry trees. But this is the only way he can save his family from the clutches of poverty, and he seems determined to make a go of it. His eyes take on a wishful glow when he talks about money.

At seven o'clock I knock on the door to his room, one floor below mine. The door flies open. Apparently Mr. Hanh is under the impression that he has to be ready to grant my every wish at any hour of the day or night. "Are you hungry?" I ask. "Shall we go and get a bite to eat?"

I steal a glance into the room over his shoulder and see on top of the bed the *Time* magazine I loaned him. No doubt he'd been reading the cover story on AIDS in Thailand. Next to the window, a white shirt has been hung up to dry. "Where would you like to go eat?" asks Mr. Hanh. At my suggestion we decide to dine in the hotel.

We may be the restaurant's only dinner guests, but there's a legion of waiters bustling around. They haul in crate after crate of beer and disappear up a stairwell bearing trays of bottles. "There must be another room upstairs," Mr. Hanh notes, while carefully following their movements with his eyes.

In the middle of the night I'm awakened by a loud commotion in the hall. I look out to see what's going on and notice that one of the doors is open. Inside, a man looking somewhat the worse for drink is bellowing into the ear of a woman in a tight skirt snuggled up next to him. From behind another door I hear

SADEC: THE CITY OF MARGUERITE DURAS

giggling. Someone walks unsteadily down the hallway and staggers into the room across from mine.

Who are these people, I wonder. Are they Vietnamese, or are they tourists from Korea or Singapore? And how can I tell, standing in a dark corridor in the middle of the night? Crawling back into bed, I conclude that it must be a busload of tourists since they all seem to have appeared at the same time. My last thought before drifting off to sleep is one of surprise that a state-run hotel in a Communist country like Vietnam would allow so much hanky-panky among its guests. In China the hotel staff would have nipped such goings-on in the bud ages ago.

The party-goers depart in high spirits early in the morning. Several hours later, sitting on my balcony and rubbing the sleep from my eyes, I think back to last night's events. Suddenly I realize how naive I've been. How could I have thought there was a tour bus! This isn't a tourist hotel; tourists don't come to Sadec. Mr. Hanh's numerous innuendoes finally begin to dawn on me. And besides, hadn't he told me a slew of stories about corrupt managers? Mr. Hanh had explained to me that many managers of state-run enterprises owe their appointments to their loyalty to the Viet Cong during the war. Consequently, when they get out of line no one dares to lay a hand on them. Putting two and two together, I conclude that this hotel is teeming with corruption. How was I to know that Sadec's tourist hotel was merely a cover for one of the biggest brothels in the Mekong Delta?

At breakfast the hotel is so quiet you can hear a pin drop. Mr. Hanh's hair is neatly combed back with water, but his face looks haggard. He doesn't look as though he's had much sleep either, but I don't say anything since I know that if I were to complain about last night's noise Mr. Hanh would feel obliged to take action. Besides, there's nowhere else to go. There's only one hotel in Sadec that will take foreigners, and I want to stay another day so we can track down the house of the Chinese lover. So feigning innocence, I inquire of Mr. Hanh: "Are you enjoying your fried egg?"

"Yes," he replies affably, "but the French bread is far from fresh."

Sometime later he heads outside to see if he can find out where the Chinese lover used to live. One of the drivers of the bicycle-driven carts who hang around the hotel says he knows which house we mean. But, he warns us, it's a long way over a very bad road.

We quickly reach the outskirts of town and keep going, over an unpaved path alongside a busy canal dotted with boats. Fishermen standing along the shore lower large square nets into the water. The other side of the path is lined with wooden houses which have a great variety of tropical fruit trees growing in their gardens. Many of the occupants are busy filling enormous earthenware crocks with cassava, which Mr. Hanh informs me has to be soaked before it can be turned into flour.

We bounce our way past a wondrous world: no scraps of plastic, no throwaway bottles, no empty boxes. Disposable packaging is a luxury that hasn't made its way here yet. There's only organic waste, and anything that can't be reused is fed to the pigs. Such zealous recycling gives me a great feeling of satisfaction, even though I know that the friendly people who smile at us are impatiently awaiting the day that they too can switch on their TV sets.

The driver peddles patiently on, even when the path opens onto a deeply rutted valley. From time to time he dismounts and pushes us over a rise. I finally understand how, during the war, the Viet Cong managed to transport food, weapons and even tanks through the jungle.

In the meantime an hour has gone by and I'm beginning to worry. Did the Chinese man live so far out of town? It's beginning to seem as if the driver hasn't the faintest idea of where to go. At every crossing he stops to confer with passersby.

A woman whose mouth has been stained red from chewing betel nuts points the way: it's on the other side of the canal. The three of us push the bicycle cart over a bridge which is arched like the back of a hissing cat. After five hundred yards we come to a much smaller bamboo bridge. "The Americans called these monkey bridges," remarks Mr. Hanh with a grin. "They used to collapse when the fat GIs tried to cross them."

We're obliged to proceed on foot; the cart and its driver remain behind. After walking for half an hour, we suddenly see it: an enormous house with a verandah resting on ebony pillars.

Mr. Hanh politely addresses a thin man in a ragged T-shirt,

SADEC: THE CITY OF MARGUERITE DURAS

who hospitably invites us to take a seat on a carved bench. Mr. Hanh plunges into his story and I see the old man shaking his head. No, he's not Chinese. No, he's never heard of Marguerite Duras, much less had a father who was her lover. No movie crew has ever been on his property. He does live in this house, that he can answer in the affirmative. Yes, his father was a large landowner, but Vietnamese, not Chinese. No, there's nothing he can do about it either.

A throng of men, children and dogs has flocked around us and is watching us expectantly. "Now that we're here, may we take a look at the house?" I ask Mr. Hanh. Two sons are instructed to open the heavy doors. A glare of light falls into a dusty interior that nevertheless twinkles and glitters like a cache of jewels. "Don't mind the mess," apologizes the elderly father as he leads the way over the high threshold. We find ourselves standing among inlaid mother-of-pearl black-lacquered chests, tables and chairs. The walls are covered with scenes of flowers, trees and birds likewise done in mother-of-pearl.

"There's a whole story written in Chinese characters," I whisper. "Maybe they're Chinese after all."

Mr. Hanh shakes his head. That doesn't mean anything, he explains. Before the French came, the Vietnamese also used Chinese characters, and the custom was kept up for quite some time in classical poems and proverbs.

We follow the old man through the rest of the house. Except for a few colorful wall calendars, the other rooms are devoid of ornamentation. Everywhere we go we see large beds draped with mosquito nets. The old man has umpteen sons, and they all live with him, along with their wives and children. The family no longer has much land. "We used to own about fifteen hundred acres of rice," he tells us. "A few years ago they gave us back seven and a half acres."

From the verandah, I can look in at the beautifully preserved front room. My eyes fall on a portrait of a venerable grandmother in an embroidered silk gown, sitting with her head erect like a queen. Her grandchildren, in worn-out T-shirts or pajamas, follow my gaze. They smile genially. The father remarks with great dignity: "We live in different times."

Mr. Hanh takes one last look at the antiques inside and then turns to the sons. "I told them," he translates for me a moment later, "that they ought to fix the place up and sell it to foreign tourists." His eyes have taken on their special glow.

The oldest son stares at him in bewilderment. A few minutes ago he was the satisfied occupant of a run-down farmhouse, and now it seems he's sitting on a fortune. He fires a barrage of questions at Mr. Hanh, wanting to know how to make the most of his assets. "Fix it up and sell it to some foreigners," repeats Mr. Hanh. "To help with repairs you might be able to get some financial aid from the United Nations. Provided the Americans lift the embargo, of course." The son nods, his eyes open wide.

Mr. Hanh taps his watch; we mustn't keep the driver waiting any longer. It's time to say good-bye. Turning around when I reach the garden gate, I see the sons in animated discussion. The father watches in silence while the children jump up and down beside him, curious to know what's going on. "Mr. Hanh," I say in a tone of reproach, "we're leaving that family in a state of utter confusion."

He shakes his head. "They can become very rich," he declares, with a note of undisguised envy creeping into his voice.

Back in the city our driver gathers fresh information. It seems the house of the Chinese lover isn't located on the plains outside the city but in the middle of town. He brings us to the gate of a majestic edifice sorely in need of paint. "This isn't a Chinese house, but a French one," cautions the discouraged Mr. Hanh to avoid raising my hopes. Inside, in the semi-darkness, we stare in surprise at dozens of school desks until the janitor appears.

"Well, they did make a movie here," Mr. Hanh translates, relieved. "A Chinese wedding was filmed out front." But the Chinese man actually lived somewhere else, on the other side of the river. The janitor is willing to show us the house in return for a small remuneration, but no amount of money could tempt him to go inside: these days it's the headquarters of the security police, and he prefers to keep his distance.

"Anyway, you'd be better off visiting the people who live next door," the janitor advises, "since they're related to the Chinese man."

SADEC: THE CITY OF MARGUERITE DURAS

After crossing the river in a rocking sampan, we scurry past an enormous house with a courtyard in the front. I steal a glance at it, but there's not enough time for me to see whether there are any blue tiles under the layers of dirt. "No pictures. Please don't take pictures," Mr. Hanh implores me.

The janitor gestures for us to follow and enters the imposing house next door. Feeling our way through the darkness, we manage to maneuver through piles of baskets. The building is clearly being used to store goods for the market. There are a couple of shacks in the backyard, presumably the servants quarters in days gone by. The janitor points to a door. Mr. Hanh hands over the agreed-upon amount of money, and the man disappears.

After knocking on the door a few times we hesitantly step inside. Light reflects off the recently polished tile floor and gleaming wood furniture. A distinguished-looking man appears from behind a curtain and welcomes us with great dignity. Mr. Hanh no longer has to translate: our host teaches English. And what's more, his wife turns out to be the niece of Marguerite Duras' lover. We don't catch so much as a glimpse of the wife, as she modestly remains behind the curtain.

"Her uncle died in 1969, when the family was living in Saigon. He had a stroke. In 1975, just before the fall of Saigon, his widow and children left Vietnam. They're now living in France."

He speaks slowly, as if he's standing before a classroom of children. "One of his daughters was married to South Vietnam's last president, Tran Van Huong. There was no way they could stay here. And of course it was better for the rest of the family to leave as well."

He sounds embittered. Is that because he was left behind, I wonder. "And you?" I ask.

"I'm fine," replies the man tersely and shoots a look of hatred at Mr. Hanh. When the Americans were here he taught at a school. Now he merely gives private lessons to students who come to the house. That's all he wishes to reveal about his past.

"You weren't sent to a re-education camp?" I insist.

"Fortunately not," he retorts succinctly.

"Is life getting better these days?" I ask in an attempt to shift the conversation to more neutral territory.

"Most assuredly," he says sarcastically, "our government is developing the country at a rapid pace, isn't that right, Mr. Hanh? The country is moving forward by leaps and bounds."

Mr. Hanh lowers his eyes. "He thinks I'm a spy," he says. Although the teacher must have heard his remark as well, he doesn't respond. An icy silence descends on the room.

"Mr Hanh doesn't work for an official travel agency," I explain. "He used to work for the Americans and is absolutely not working for the present government."

"Oh indeed," sneers the man.

It's gotten darker and darker and suddenly rain begins to pound on the roof. The electricity goes out. Almost immediately a young woman appears from behind the curtain with a candle. "My daughter," says the teacher. "You can't leave now. Have another cup of tea," he says and refills our cups.

It's true, we can't leave. I can see the rain coming down in torrents outside the front door and we haven't got an umbrella or rain gear, but I no longer know what to talk about.

Something about children, I think frantically. "Do you have any other children?" I ask.

"I have just two daughters," the man replies. "The oldest one lives in Sydney, Australia. Last spring a former neighbor came for a visit. He left the country on a boat ten years ago. Before his departure, he told my daughter he'd come back and marry her. She waited for ten years and he came."

"What a romantic story," I say. "She must really miss her family."

He shoots me a look of disapproval. "So she wrote. I answered: 'It's useless to think about that. You now belong to your husband's family. Make the best of it.'"

Even though the rain hasn't let up, I announce that we're going. I thank him for having received us. Once again he gives a dignified nod. He mumbles something in Vietnamese to Mr. Hanh.

I feel cold, and not just because I'm soaked to the skin. "What on earth was going on?" I ask Mr. Hanh.

"The teacher thinks every guide is working for the government," explains Mr. Hanh grimly. "He thinks I have to report everything he says, since that's how the system worked up until a few years ago. He doesn't realize that lots of things have changed

SADEC: THE CITY OF MARGUERITE DURAS

in Saigon, that there are now privately owned enterprises. Apparently everything has stayed the same here."

We sprint to the hotel in the pouring rain. I have trouble unlocking the door to my room. It feels strange inside, as if I'm being watched by an invisible being. I inspect the closet, the balcony and the bathroom. No one.

Then I check the bag holding my computer; it's empty. My camera is also missing, along with an envelope containing my money. I've been robbed. I rush down to Mr. Hanh's room, and he comes immediately to take a look. Then he dashes off to get the hotel manager, the desk clerk and the chambermaids. All of whom hurl reproaches at me. "Why did you leave those things lying in your room?"

"Why doesn't your hotel have better security?" I shout back angrily. "Call the police!"

Half an hour later a young man in uniform reports at my door in the company of Mr. Hanh, who is wringing his hands. He's afraid I'll be impolite to the authorities, since that's how his other clients reacted when they were struck by disaster. And the results were terrifying. Apparently one has to tread lightly with the authorities in Vietnam. I offer the policeman a chair and a cup of tea.

The matter doesn't fall within his jurisdiction, he informs me, so that we'll have to go to the station. There we will be received by the Head of Interrogations in Sadec. As the interrogation techniques of the Vietnamese were notorious on both sides during the war, I'm not exactly thrilled at the prospect.

The police station consists of a tumbledown shack across from a lake. In the middle of the lake are two cubicles which can be reached by a small bridge. "Toilets," Mr. Hanh indicates, "so the fish will get their share of precious food."

The "Chief Interrogator" wants to hear a detailed version of the story from my own mouth. Someone takes notes. No, he hasn't the faintest idea who could have done it. I'm not really getting a whole lot of cooperation. His eyes are filled with suspicion, as if he thinks I had something to do with the theft. "How do we know for sure you really had those items with you?" he asks.

"Mr. Hanh has seen my computer and my camera," I reply. Mr. Hanh doesn't look particularly happy at this disclosure.

"But not the money?" the interrogator shoots back sternly.

"No," I admit. "I never showed that to Mr. Hanh. Why should I?"

"My point exactly," the man replies unpleasantly. Clearly reluctant, he writes out a statement. Pen and paper are supplied by me since these items seem to be in scarce supply in his office. The interrogator announces that my statement has to have an official stamp and that we'll have to wait until morning; only his superiors can do that, and they're out of the office at the moment.

Little by little, my suspicions are aroused. Why don't the police want to have anything to do with the case? Is there any truth to all those stories I heard in Saigon about corrupt policemen working hand in glove with the city's pickpockets?

That evening I stop by Mr. Hanh's room and, much to my surprise, find him chatting away with the hotel manager, the man I've secretly dubbed the "Head Pimp." Mr. Hanh smiles apologetically; they're discussing a plan for a mutual project involving tourism. "Oh," I say crossly, "luring tourists to Sadec to be robbed?" Mr. Hanh coughs, and the manager makes himself scarce.

The next morning I wait in my room after breakfast for the document with its official stamps to be delivered. My plans to travel to the southern tip of the Mekong Delta have to be canceled, since I only have a few dollars left. We'll have to return to Saigon as soon as possible.

At eleven o'clock I take a stroll around the hotel out of sheer boredom. In the lobby, I once again find Mr. Hanh and the manager in a tête-à-tête. Just what do Mr. Hanh and this sleazy character have to discuss? Are the two of them in on the plot together? Did Mr. Hanh deliberately lead me outside the city yesterday so that my room could be thoroughly searched?

The manager excuses himself. "He's going in person to inquire if anything's happening at the police station," explains Mr. Hanh. I watch while the manager charges off on a brand-new motor scooter. A "boiled" one, I presume.

"Why didn't the crooks take my passport?" I ask Mr. Hanh. "It was lying there right next to the other things."

"Because," he explains, "when someone steals a foreign passport, the embassy has to be notified. Both the embassy and the authorities in Hanoi put an enormous amount of pressure on the

Sadec: The City of Marguerite Duras

local police to solve the case. The thieves know that as well and try to avoid it. If they do happen to take a passport by mistake, they usually send it back to the hotel in the mail. Then they don't have to worry."

My eyes are stinging with tears of rage. "I've also lost all the information in my computer," I note indignantly. "Everyone gives me such friendly smiles and talks to me, but suddenly I suspect them all of having ulterior motives."

Mr. Hanh is quiet for a moment. Then he says: "People act nice to you so they can get closer to your wallet. In this country, you can't trust anyone, not even your best friend."

SAIGON

Evenings in
Apocalypse Now

It's ninety miles between Sadec and Saigon. Mr. Hanh and I say very little to each other during the four-hour bus ride. In the bus station, I promise to pay him as soon as I've picked up my traveler's checks from the friends who were keeping them for me. Mr. Hanh extends an invitation to me to visit his family. His house, thatched with palm leaves, is located just outside the city. I make a vague promise to come. We say good-bye, and I check into a hotel.

Once upon a time it was called the "Saigon Palace," but these days the flaking stucco exterior doesn't even reveal so much as the trace of a name. The elevator is a metal cage reminiscent of swank Parisian apartment houses. No one can remember the last time any guests used it to make their descent. Now the only way up or down is by a marble staircase with missing steps.

My room resembles the wing of a palace; there's a spacious sitting room which I can use to receive guests and an enormous bedroom which can double as a study. Except that the walls are covered with mildew and the windows are black with soot. The bathroom is lined with lovely tiles, all of them cracked. To add insult to injury, the sink hasn't got a drainpipe. Not that it matters anyway, since the water flows right out of the wall and not out of a faucet. The electrical wiring juts menacingly out of the sockets, and while the air conditioner is prominently displayed, it maintains a stubborn silence.

Outside, the afternoon heat holds sway. All is quiet in the street below. Peddlers are dozing beside their fruit-laden baskets and not a soul is stirring in the stores.

Downtown Saigon was built by the French during their heyday. This includes the City Hall, my hotel and the street on which it is located. The French called it *Rue Catinat*, after a French hero no one remembers anymore. Then the Vietnamese dubbed it *Tu Do*, Freedom Street. In 1975, after the fall of Saigon, it was renamed the Street of the Revolution. Saigon residents wryly joke: "After the revolution, there was no more freedom."

Later in the day, when it gets a little cooler, the Western tourists emerge to stroll under the trees on Tu Do Street. Sailors on leave cruise the streets in search of excitement and hefty Russian matrons, whose husbands work on the offshore oil platforms, doggedly scour the city for bargains.

In years gone by it was American soldiers looking for a good time. Saigon, now Ho Chi Minh City, still exudes the atmosphere of the war, since nothing has changed since then. The city is in decline, and Saigon has been waiting for nearly twenty years for a prince to come and awaken it with a kiss.

In my youth, the war in Vietnam was daily news and a constant topic of heated debate. Nevertheless, it remained an abstraction to me since no one in Holland had fought there. In 1975, while traveling through Mississippi, I met a Vietnam veteran for the first time in my life: a truck driver named Fred who gave me and the Danish girl I was traveling with a lift. He drove us through Mississippi's hot, humid mangroves with one hand on the wheel and the other rolling a joint. When I looked surprised, he assured me he always drove stoned. He talked very slowly, one word at a time, the way blood wells up, drop by drop, in a wound. He was from the south, and he came from a religious family. Before the war, he admitted, he was a redneck. He went to Vietnam to teach the Commies a lesson; it was as simple as that, and later he seemed astonished by his own naivety.

Evenings in Apocalypse Now

He could still remember with crystalline clarity the day he arrived in "Nam." Someone picked him up at the airport and brought him to a camp. He was introduced to his commanding officers and fellow soldiers, who had just returned from some kind of mission. They all lay on their beds, recovering, listening to music played at full blast and kind of smiling at each other. Only then did Fred smell the heavy pot fumes, and he was shocked. The way he saw it, a drug user was some kind of anarchist. He didn't join in but stuck to beer, drinking maybe twenty cans a day. Then one day he was granted leave to visit his brother, who was stationed somewhere else in Vietnam. It was then that the two boys smoked their first joint, with heroin. "Us, two Seventh Day Adventists," commented Fred in a tone as if it had all happened in another life.

He then launched into a story whose authenticity I'm still not sure of. As he tells it, he became part of a group that was highly critical of the war. They felt that the soldiers were being exploited. Their superiors issued inhuman orders while keeping their own hands clean. Obsessed by this thought, the young men devised a heinous plan. One dark night they tossed explosives into the tent of a couple of higher-ups, who were killed instantly. Since it was thought to be the work of the Viet Cong, Fred was never caught. "They called it fragging," he explained to us two innocent Europeans, "short for fragmentation bomb."

We two girls stared at each other in amazement. Was he just saying this to impress us? Or was he making the whole thing up? We didn't have a clue. I shivered when he confessed, at the end of the ride, that he was homesick. Homesick for Vietnam.

Here in my decrepit hotel room, I try to imagine what kind of boy Fred was when he arrived in Vietnam. I've brought with me a stack of *National Geographic* and *Life* magazines from the sixties and seventies, the issues with photographic essays. In the accompanying text it sounds as if victory is just around the corner. The possibility of defeat never seems to enter anybody's mind. Interspersed between the photos were full-page ads. For example, one for the Pontiac Grand Prix, a car with fins. And another in which a blond with a bouffant hairdo is casting an adoring glance at a similarly elegant Lincoln Continental. On the next page a happy family is eating Kellogg's Cornflakes. The mother looks like Jackie Kennedy, the father like JFK. The son is still too young to be sent to the front.

I look out my hotel-room windows. Several panes have been heavily criss-crossed with adhesive tape to keep the glass from shattering during a bombing raid. Twenty-year-old adhesive tape.

Downstairs, the tattered drivers of the bicycle-propelled rickshaws known as cyclos hang around near the entrance to the hotel, leaning against their vehicles while waiting for customers. The oldest cyclo driver speaks a little English. He used to work for the Americans, he told me this morning while driving me to my destination. After the war, he said, Saigon was transformed into a city without cars.

As darkness falls, a stream of motorbikes and motor scooters is set in motion. The drone gradually intensifies. Everyone makes the same round: boys with their girlfriends perched sidesaddle on the back seat, single girls and entire families on one scooter. They drive down the Street of the Revolution to the Saigon River and then head down Nguyen Hue Boulevard to the yellow stucco City Hall. Around and around, talking and laughing. In the pale light of the headlights you can catch only a glimpse of the latest styles in clothing, sent by relatives who fled to the U.S. The beautiful dark tresses of the young women flutter freely in the wind. They let their hair grow so long I keep expecting it to get caught in the spokes. Their lips are covered with lipstick, and their slender legs have been thrust into short shorts. A few male tourists are standing still on the sidewalk, watching the ongoing traffic. No wonder some Americans still dream of the women of Saigon.

The scooters and motorbikes outside my hotel make me feel I'm missing something. I get dressed, chat with the desk clerk, who complains that she's always on duty because she's the only one who speaks English, and gesture to the cyclo drivers lined up in a row outside the door that no, I'm going to walk, I don't have far to go. Disappointed, they let me through.

A few dark streets from the hotel is a bar blazing with light. I like bars; a good bar is like a living room in which anything goes. You don't find bars in China. The Chinese don't like to drink

Evenings in Apocalypse Now

with total strangers. They distrust each other too much for that, and besides, they probably think people could occupy themselves doing something more useful. In Saigon there's a bar or café on practically every street corner. Most of them serve only coffee, but that's merely because there's no money for anything else. Vietnamese like to talk, to anyone and everyone. If you're willing to listen, they'll tell you their whole life story within five minutes. In that respect, they're a lot like Americans. Most of the customers are males, as in bars everywhere. In some Saigon bars there are hostesses, young women who talk with the customers in exchange for a drink and a tip. If I order something for them I'm given the same service. They tell me, swearing with their hands on their hearts, that they don't sleep with the customers.

I would never like to live in a place bereft of bars. Saigon has lots of them. It's a city that takes you in its embrace. You can plunk yourself down anywhere and before long someone will come over and ask: "Where are you from?" You can stay an hour, you can while away a morning or an afternoon, or you can take a nap if you're so inclined.

The bar I prefer going to in the evening is frequented by foreigners and *Viet Kieus*: overseas Vietnamese who are visiting their homeland. There's a large oval window overlooking the street, so that the cyclo drivers and cigarette hawkers outside appear to be enclosed in a frame. I seat myself on one of the tall stools at the circular bar in the middle of the room. Tuy, the bartender, immediately sets a bowl of peanuts in front of me, while his assistant ferrets out the coldest bottle of beer from an ice-filled chest.

It's not busy yet. John, a New Zealander who lives in Saigon and owns a small furniture factory, is playing pool with one of the bartenders. The bartender lets him win, and I play the next game with John.

"This country's really going to make it big," he says, while concentrating on the ball. "Once the doors open up, things will start hopping. Let me tell you something: ten years from now you won't recognize this city. Ten years! What am I saying? Five years!"

I ran into John a while ago, before my trip to the Mekong Delta, and visited him in his apartment on Dong Khoi Street. His Vietnamese girlfriend, Miss Snow, served us sweet coffee while he regaled me with stories of how he'd earned his living up to now.

Once upon a time he'd been the biggest marijuana grower in New Zealand. "And I never got caught." In those days he had shoulder-length hair and was stoned all day long. After that he became an itinerant building contractor. He showed me pictures of trucks and bulldozers with his name painted on them. At a certain point he got involved in a fraudulent business deal. Rather than face a long prison sentence, he left the country. First he lived in Australia, then he moved to the Philippines, and now he's been in Saigon for a year. He's rented a shed where carpenters make furniture out of tropical hardwood. Three years from now, the statute of limitations will run out on his case and he can go back home again, to see his six children, who have done a lot of growing up in the meantime.

"How's Miss Snow?" I ask.

John grins. "I'm afraid she's walked out on me." He chalks his cue and continues: "She was getting too demanding."

"So what did she want?" I inquire.

"Oh, money," he says vaguely.

"So you're back to being alone?"

"Well, not really," laughs John. "Besides the four casual relationships I already had, I'm currently sleeping with my landlady's daughter, without her mother's knowing it, of course."

"Let's hope she doesn't find out."

"Oh well, I like living dangerously," he replies.

He doesn't look like a Don Juan. Instead, he looks exactly like the farm boy he is. As I recall, he only saw a city for the first time in his life when he was fifteen. And now he's forty.

A slender woman comes in and writes her name on the blackboard: Tuyet. That means she wants to play the winner. Seated on a stool near the pool table, she watches our movements. It's hard to place her. She looks a little like Yoko Ono. Might she be Japanese? No, she's speaking Vietnamese to the bartender. They know her here, she's a local. She has wavy hair and is exquisitely dressed. I figure she must be in her late thirties or early forties. She speaks English with a French accent. She works as a guide, she tells us. Today she helped a French customer purchase a generator. He's busy building a ship in the harbor but isn't making enough progress because of the constant power failures.

In the past she used to find apartments for foreigners temporarily posted to Vietnam. She can arrange whatever you want. "Do you need anything? Do you have any problems? Have you seen the War Museum?" she asks. "And the former American Embassy, where the helicopters landed on the roof to evacuate the last Americans?"

"Yes," I reply, "I've been there."

"Then I can't make any money off you," she laughs.

"Well," I say, "I've been hoping to find an American who fought here in the war and has come back for a visit."

She inhales one last time on her Dunhill cigarette; there's a circle of lipstick on the filter. Her fine-shaped fingers stub the cigarette out with unexpected ferocity. "I've got another appointment tonight," she says professionally. "But tomorrow evening, at seven o'clock, in this bar, I'll bring you a GI. His name is Mark."

After she leaves, I ask John: "Do you know her?"

He grins. "Not yet, but I wouldn't mind getting her between the sheets."

The next evening, just before seven, I'm waiting in the bar. The music of The Doors is blasting away; overseas visitors like to hear music dating back to the war. A bottle of beer has just been fished out of the chest for me when a huge uproar erupts at the door. The bouncer, who can usually be seen squatting on the sidewalk among the waiting cyclo drivers, is poised like a fighting cock in front of the woman I've arranged to meet. She parries with a shrill reply, pushes him aside and charges into the room. The bouncer trots after her and shouts to the waiters behind the bar. Since the woman has come to a halt behind me, the bouncer's rage is now directed at both of us. He jabs his finger in our direction.

Tuy the bartender comes towards me. "Is it true that you have an appointment for seven o'clock with this person?" he asks.

"Yes, yes," screams the woman next to me. She slams a couple of documents on the bar. Some kind of ID with her picture.

"Yes or no?" the man beside me insists.

"Yes," I reply, with little enthusiasm. The bouncer slinks off like a terrier who's been made to relinquish its bone.

"Have something to drink," I say to the woman. "And for goodness' sake stop shouting. Besides," I add, remembering what brought us here, "where's the GI?"

"He'll be here soon," she says, dragging on her cigarette. Her eyes are filled with tears. "They're crazy," she sniffs. "All Vietnamese are totally out of their minds."

"All except you," I say.

"No," she laughs. "Me too, especially me."

Once she's calmed down, she explains what was going on. The police have started cracking down on prostitution, so that every woman who goes to a bar alone is under suspicion. But she's an official guide, she maintains, showing me her license. She also hands me a business card with the address of the travel agency she works for.

Seeing that I'm convinced, she shows me the snapshots she keeps in her wallet. "That's me," she says, "twenty years ago in my school uniform." I see her posing on a street corner in a white *ao dai*. In the background an American jeep happens to be passing by.

The next picture shows a man in his fifties with a stylish haircut and a trendy pair of glasses. "My oldest brother," she explains. "He's living in Boston now. He used to be an officer in the South Vietnamese Navy. He's very rich," she proclaims proudly. "During the war, well-to-do Vietnamese families didn't want their sons fighting at the front. For a million piasters, my brother arranged a safe desk job for them." She looks at me with a smile, delighted at her brother's financial wizardry. "He used those piasters to buy gold, and then he buried the gold. After four years in a re-education camp, he got a visa for the U.S. So he dug up the gold and took it with him to start his new life."

"A man with foresight," I respond. Tuyet and I are momentarily distracted by a man and a woman who take a seat at the circular bar. The man is a tall Westerner, and the woman a tiny Vietnamese. "I've seen her before," I say to Tuyet, "but with another man, an Australian."

Tuyet nods angrily. "They let her in without a question," she fumes. "Of course she paid them off."

We order another beer and I ask Tuyet to continue telling me the story of her family. She digs around in her wallet for something. "This is all that's left of my youngest brother," she says, laying on the table an aluminum dog tag embossed with a Vietnamese name and birth date. Tuyet looks past me in the direction of the couple at the bar, not for dramatic effect, but simply because it's her way of talking. "He was a pilot," she resumes. "His plane crashed when my sister-in-law was six months pregnant." She also has a snapshot of her nephew, now a grown young man, standing with his arm around the shoulder of her own son, a spindly eleven year old.

"And your husband?" I ask.

She shrugs; he's not included in her portrait gallery: "One day he took off, just like that."

Then her face lights up. Suddenly he's standing beside us, Mark. I hadn't seen him come in. It's as if he floated in. He has a magnificent, angular face and green eyes that look into ours with total innocence, like an angel. How can he have fought in the war, I wonder: he's not old enough. Then I notice the sharp lines around his mouth.

"Hi," says Mark languidly. No, he doesn't drink beer, he'd like orange juice. He seats himself with slow deliberation, as if he's come to the end of a long journey. He doesn't say anything, perhaps because he's stoned; his eyes have that telltale glow.

Tuyet observes with satisfaction: "Mark is the quiet type, a quiet American." I look at her in surprise, since *The Quiet American* is the title of Graham Greene's novel about Vietnam. But it must be sheer coincidence, since it doesn't look like she's making an allusion. Apparently Vietnam makes more than one American quiet. Tuyet excitedly tells Mark about her recent contretemps with the bouncer.

"Oh well," says Mark, not at all surprised, "Vietnamese are always fighting."

While I try to figure out which movie star he looks like, Mark looks at Tuyet. He seems to like her a lot. There's something odd about him. He's breathtakingly beautiful, but it's as if he's not real. As if he might vanish in a cloud of smoke.

"Let's go to Rhythm and Booze," suggests Tuyet. We head for the dark street, to another bar, which is actually a patio on top of a roof. It's quiet here. We also have a great view of the city's monumental mosque. Many Moslems used to live in Saigon, but most of them left the city after 1975. The mosque is lit up inside. Through the windows we can see a pool of blue water where the few remaining faithful can wash their feet before saying their prayers.

All around the patio are potted plants and statues of voluptuous Cham women, reminders of an ethnic minority that originally came from India centuries ago. Tuyet and Mark are sitting on the other side of the table, totally wrapped up in each other. Maybe I shouldn't have come along. They probably prefer to be alone. Tuyet complains to Mark about the incident in the other bar. It upset her more than I thought; she was apparently keeping herself under control before he arrived. "People are always creating problems for me, no matter where I go," she sighs. "They're forever keeping tabs on me and sticking their noses in my business. They should have shot me in 1975. This is slow torture. Every day I die a little bit more." She savagely stubs out her cigarette.

Mark is not impressed by her morose musings. He massages her shoulders and neck and remarks enigmatically to me: "She tries to keep the world out, while I'm trying to let everything in. Two sides of the same wall."

I ask him if he's visited any old friends. He grins. "I didn't get to know any Vietnamese back then. People weren't exactly glad to see us enter their villages in full battle gear. Besides, they didn't dare be friendly because they might be punished afterwards by the Viet Cong. No, we weren't welcome here. Only the whores were willing to talk to us. And they still want to talk to me." We say nothing. Tuyet lights another cigarette.

I had hoped that Mark might be able to explain something about this country to me. I had hoped that during the war he might have caught a glimpse of the old Vietnam, which now seemed to be obliterated. But he saw nothing. The country in which he fought was nothing more than a scenic backdrop to him.

It's dark on the patio. Sometimes the stone images around us seem to be moving. Strange creatures with elephant trunks and

Evenings in Apocalypse Now

bird beaks. Hostesses wearing gobs of makeup have joined the men at the table next to ours.

Mark arrived in Saigon a month ago. He met Tuyet the same way I met her: in a bar. Since then, they spend every evening together. During the day, Mark usually stays in his hotel room, smoking joints with a few friends. Sometimes he goes outside and has a look around.

"Some of the cyclo drivers who drive me around," Mark begins, "fought in the South Vietnamese Army. They complain that that's why they're having such a hard time now. 'Why did you leave?' they ask me. 'Well,' I say, 'I'm sorry, but we shouldn't have ever come here in the first place. You should have tried a little harder, fought a little better.' Dammit, what do they expect? I came from an entirely different culture; I didn't even look like them. I was twenty years old! Wasn't it a bit much, expecting me to feel responsible for their fate?"

He's lost in thought. "My god," he continues, "the cyclo drivers. Back then, they were the soldiers who stole your rations if you let your guard down for a minute. Or who sold your ammunition to the Viet Cong."

Then he falls silent again for a while. Tuyet smiles sweetly. Mark's green eyes search her face. Is he really in love with her? Why not. She's beautiful, witty and intelligent and shares the memories of the war with him. I take a look at the magnificently lighted mosque below us. Just one more beer, I decide, and then I'll be moving on. This couple is not exactly dying for my company.

"I was wet for three months," I hear Mark say. "It was the rainy season, and you never got dry. Sometimes it was so cold that in the evening I peed in my pants, wrapped myself in my rain poncho to keep warm and then went to sleep."

Tuyet roars with laughter. "How awful," she comments.

I think back to the picture of her in her white *ao dai*. In the period Mark is talking about, she was attending an expensive school.

"I was sent into the mountains as a medic," he resumes. "The guys were all real nice to me." He laughs while looking at Tuyet. "I was always allowed to serve myself first; I got the best food. They were all scared they'd be hit one day and I'd say 'tough shit.'"

One of the heavily made-up hostesses comes and stands next to our table. My glass is empty. "Can I get you anything?" she asks. Tuyet orders another Seven-Up and Mark his umpteenth glass of orange juice. It's after midnight, but they don't look a bit sleepy. In the dim light, they remind me of two night owls sitting side by side on a branch, keeping watch through the night.

"No more for me," I say, suddenly exhausted. "I'm going home."

Walking back to my hotel through a dark street, I'm suddenly accosted by a man with blond hair. "Accosted" isn't exactly the right word: he mutters something and wraps his arm firmly around my neck. A Russian, I decide, who's had one too many. "Do you speak English?" I ask.

"Yes!" he spits out. "Yes!" I make an attempt to slip away, but he's clamped himself to me. He beats himself on the chest. "Sportsman," he exclaims. "Me sportsman." Side by side like Siamese twins, the two of us proceed down the street.

"Gogol," I giggle, far from sober myself, "you're like someone from *Dead Souls*." All of a sudden, the man loses all interest in me: we're standing before the bar with the oval window and he's staring longingly inside. He lets go of me, and three flapping steps later he's inside and out of sight.

Early the next morning I walk down Dong Khoi Street and see Tuyet sitting in Café Brodard. It's cold inside — the air conditioner is turned up full blast — and it exudes an atmosphere of faded French glory. The waiter, wearing a red vest, asks: "*Que prenez-vous, madame?*"

"Mark's not all that bad looking," I tease Tuyet.

She laughs and then turns serious. "He's also polite and intelligent."

"Well," I reply, "what more do you want?"

Tuyet shakes her head: "He's the type who's always on the go." She pulls something out of her purse and shows it to me. "His passport. I'm going to get an extension on his visa." Curious, I leaf through it until I find the information I'm looking for. Birthplace: New Orleans. Birth Date: December 10, 1945. "He looks a lot younger."

Tuyet shakes her head. "He's an old GI," she laughs.

Evenings in Apocalypse Now

"Can you also get an extension on my visa?" I ask.

"Twenty dollars," she nods, and carefully tucks the two passports in her handbag.

Not far from our table, a little boy taps on the window and holds up a selection of foreign newspapers. Another kid presses his wares, old coins, against the glass. Once they see me looking outside, a couple of beggars go stand next to them. A thin woman holding a child in her arms taps against the windowpane. An armless man stares at me. "Madam," they all call, "Madam, Madam, Madam."

Tuyet ignores the hapless throng. She stands up. "Tonight Mark and I have agreed to meet at Apocalypse Now," she says. "At eight o'clock. I'll see you there." When the waiter brings me the tab, I see that her order has been put on my bill.

The bar's steel shutter is just being slid open when I come walking up. Zip, the young owner, turns on the evening's first music: the soundtrack of the well-known war movie, *Good Morning, Vietnam*. Zip knows the words by heart and shouts along with the tape: "Today I'd like to talk about Charlie. I'd like to talk about the enemy and what they're wearing. They're wearing black. I say you can fight in the jungle in it and at night put on some pearls and you're ready for formal wear."

It surprises me that he can laugh at the war that destroyed his country. "Oh well," he says matter-of-factly, "it all happened so long ago."

Okay, it all happened long ago, but still the war is the theme of his bar. In it, he has made an attempt to recreate the movie *Apocalypse Now*. The walls have all been painted black and the blades of the ceiling fans whirl round and round over our heads, not so much to cool the customers as to evoke the image of hovering choppers. After all, helicopters are the symbol of the Vietnam War.

"Look," says Zip, "I'm going to hang these on the wall," and he shows me two pictures from an old American magazine. In the first one, John F. Kennedy is riding in a limousine and waving to the crowd. In the second one, he's been hit and is lying with his head back, while Jackie, in her pink Chanel suit, turns to him.

"The war only really got started after that," I say.

"I know," replies Zip cheerfully, "that's why I'm going to hang it up."

When Mark and Tuyet arrive, they don't want to sit inside in the dark bar but outside on the sidewalk in comfortable beach chairs. Mark is in need of a new stash. For five dollars he buys a bag of marijuana so big he can barely get his hands around it from a young cyclo driver with only one tooth in his mouth. "Is the dope as good as it used to be?" I ask.

A grin slowly appears at the corners of his mouth. "It seems to be." After a short silence, he adds: "But I'm not the kind of guy to go chasing after the hashish harvest. I didn't come to Vietnam for the dope."

"Why did you come?" I ask, all ears.

"Oh, I've traveled all over the world," he replies vaguely, to fend off my question, "so why on earth shouldn't I come here?" He smokes, I drink beer and Tuyet sips her Seven-Up and stares intently at her feet.

"I need new shoes," she notes. There's no reaction from Mark.

"What else do you want to see," I ask, "except Saigon?"

It doesn't take him long to find an answer. "The road between Danang and Hue," he responds without a moment of hesitation. "It goes through some beautiful mountains. I drove there once with a truckload of lukewarm beer. We'd organized a party in our camp."

Tuyet breaks into the conversation. "If you ask me, you're not going anywhere," she says. "Most of the GIs who come back here don't go anywhere outside Saigon. Leaving town is too much of a bother." Mark laughs, as if he understands it all too well.

"What do the GIs do all day?" I ask in surprise.

"Well," mumbles Mark, "today I tried to buy a book, but I couldn't find one. Maybe tomorrow I'll write a letter." Then he takes a deliberate drag on a new joint. "The Saigon blues again," he sighs.

Tuyet, sunk as usual in her own thoughts, suddenly remembers: "The passports!" To me she says, "Your visa has been extended for two weeks, but the head of the Immigration Police has written something stupid on it." She shows me the document, to which a

Evenings in Apocalypse Now

note has been appended in minuscule Vietnamese writing. At the end of the last sentence, there's a huge question mark.

"What's it say?" I want to know.

Tuyet glares at the paper. "The damn police here," she fumes. "Making all kinds of trouble for everyone. They say they want to promote tourism and foreign investment, but all they do is drive everyone so crazy they leave the country."

"But what did they write?" I insist.

Tuyet squints at the paper. "The bearer of this tourist visa has not come to Vietnam for the purposes of tourism. The Immigration Police are wondering: What is this person actually doing in our country?"

"No!" I exclaim. "You must be making that up!"

Tuyet jumps up flustered from her chair. "I'm not crazy enough to make up something like that," she cries. "Only the Saigon police are capable of pulling off a stunt like this." She lifts her hands dramatically in the air.

"Calm down," I say soothingly, afraid she's going to make a scene here as well. "There's nothing we can do about it."

Mark regards us calmly; no words have been added to his visa. "They're probably following you," he says. "They must have figured out that you're gathering information for a book."

Tuyet creases her brow in thought. "Maybe we can arrange for a whole new visa," she says, "but that'll cost a lot of money. The VC don't do something for nothing."

"We'll see," I reply, leaving the problem to be dealt with later, and I order another round.

A little girl selling combs and nail files has seated herself on the arm of Mark's chair while her companion shows me some postcards. "You buy, Madam," she pleads. "You help me." She's twelve, she tells me, but she looks more like eight. "You buy postcards, Madam. Me buy food."

"How much are they?" I ask.

Mark buys an ear scratcher and is then lost in thought. When I ask him what he's thinking about, he says: "Uh, well. I was thinking about the night it occurred to me that we were never going to win the war."

As he tells it, he was sitting beside some guy who was badly wounded, waiting for the sun to rise. The kid was deathly pale from the loss of so much blood. Mark had to make sure the guy didn't lose consciousness, as otherwise he didn't have a chance. Suddenly, Mark thought that he heard some noise underground, that he felt something moving. The Viet Cong, he thought. They're digging tunnels. "I was imagining it," says Mark, taking a drag on his joint, "but strangely enough, that didn't seem to matter. Because of that vision of the Viet Cong, digging tunnels under your butt even in the middle of the night, I knew from then on that it was a lost cause."

In those days, the air was rife with rumors of Viet Cong tunnels. Even so, virtually no one had any idea of the extent of the existing network. Mark had a vision, and he sensed that it was based on fact. Somewhere, though it might not be right underneath him, the Viet Cong were busy making tunnels. Ceaselessly, night and day.

"Have you been to Cu Chi?" he asks.

Yes I had. I had looked around in astonishment at what is currently Vietnam's biggest tourist attraction: less than an hour away from Saigon, one hundred and twenty-four miles of tunnels, about which the Americans knew absolutely nothing. I had imagined it to be a kind of huge cellar, partially or maybe even totally underground. In reality it's like a subterranean apartment house, with tunnels on three different levels. Under normal circumstances, the people lived in the upper level. In times of danger, they dived down to the second or third levels through shafts only big enough to accommodate a skinny Vietnamese. A nightmare for anyone with claustrophobia. The guide who gave me a tour reported with a chuckle that foreign tourists often fainted down in the lower level because there was so little oxygen. "Vietnamese people need less air," he added apologetically.

I preferred to view the model of the network, which showed how they would have been able to escape from the deepest level if the Americans had pumped the tunnels full of poison gas. You had to wriggle on your hands and knees through a tunnel that kept getting narrower and narrower until you came to a well. Then you had to dive into the well, in total darkness, guided only by your sense of touch. If you dived deep enough, you came out via a U-shaped curve in a ditch. If the enemy was around, you could stay hidden under water for hours at a stretch by breathing through a reed. The Vietnamese lived for months at a time in these tunnels. Children were even born there.

"I would have given up the fight," I remark. "I couldn't live like that. I'd rather be dead."

Tuyet looks up. "The Vietnamese are capable of it," she asserts firmly. "That's something you don't understand. We're very patriotic. That's why we can do that."

"But you and your entire family were on the other side!" I exclaim in amazement.

"That doesn't matter," Tuyet contends, defending her former enemy. "I know how a Vietnamese thinks. They were able to do it because it was for their fatherland."

Mark nods. He understands what she means.

At the end of the street we spy a brightly lit cart that is slowly pushed in our direction until the vendor brings her stand, filled with dried octopus, to a stop directly in front of us. A tangy sea smell fills the air. The sea creatures have been suspended by strings so that they look more like extraterrestrial beings jubilantly throwing their arms in the air. Tuyet and I adore these delicacies. "One or two?" she asks.

"Two," I decide and give her the money. We tear the octopus in strips and dip it in a miniature cup fashioned out of folded newspaper, which is filled with hot sauce.

"Later, when you're back in your own country," muses Tuyet, "you'll have a craving for these."

I nod and ask Mark what happened after his "tunnel revelation." He got wounded, he relates. A triple fracture in one leg. He was sent back to the U.S., where he spent three months in a hospital, and then he let his hair grow down to his waist and threw himself headlong into flower power. He never thought about the war. "On the rare occasions when I ran into someone I knew from Nam, we both looked the other way. Out of shame. We preferred to forget what we'd seen each other do. What you discover during a war is that there's a Nazi inside you," grins Mark. "Ordinary people don't know that. Only the people who have been there know it, and that's why you avoid them."

Tuyet looks at him without emotion. She probably knows exactly what he means. After all, she lived in the midst of the war. But she says nothing. She inspects her polished fingernails.

Round Eyes

One hot afternoon Mark, Tuyet and I have agreed to meet in Restaurant Thirteen, which consists of a handful of tables under a frayed awning. To reach the bathroom, you have to walk through the kitchen, a veritable inferno in which huge fires rage under a blackened ceiling and perspiring cooks labor over their woks.

A horde of shoeshine boys has gathered around our table. A spastic boy shoves them aside. He plunks down on the table a cage with dozens of frightened birds flapping around inside. Anyone who pays him some money is allowed to set one free. "Flee," the boy lisps, "flee." I can't help noticing the trampled birds lying dead on the bottom of the cage. When I point an accusing finger at them, Tuyet translates: "You can have those for free."

She continues, very practical: "What do you want to eat?" I decide on noodle soup, Mark wants to eat a vegetarian dish and Tuyet orders steak and French fries. "Like in France," she says with gusto. This afternoon, we've agreed, we're going to go on an excursion.

Tuyet hails two cyclos. Mark takes one, and she and I take the other. We cross through the city, passing the track where horse races are held every weekend. After forty-five minutes we draw up to the gate of the Amerasian Transit Center, a processing center for the children of American fathers and Vietnamese mothers. Until just a few years ago, these children were considered the scum of the earth. They were left to scrounge around on their own, since their families had often disowned them. In the intervening years, most of them have left for the U.S.; I haven't seen even one in the streets of Saigon. All the Vietnamese I questioned about this said they were not sorry to see them go. In their opinion, Amerasians were without morals, and the girls were all prostitutes. The mothers had collaborated with the enemy, they told me, which explains why the children had such bad characters. A depressing line of reasoning, but one that has been applied down through the ages. For that matter, after World War II, I don't think the Dutch could bring themselves to shower much affection on the offspring of the German occupiers. But perhaps this is not an apt comparison, since in Holland the children of German fathers and Dutch mothers have no distinguishing features, whereas Amerasians are clearly of mixed race. Might racism also be a factor?

    The cyclos aren't allowed on the grounds, although we are permitted to take a look around in the company of the gatekeeper. The Amerasian Transit Center looks like an army base, with row after row of barracks. A green-eyed teenager saunters past. "He looks like you, Mark," both Tuyet and I exclaim at the same time.

    According to Tuyet, a lot of Amerasian children have been adopted in recent years. "When it was announced that Amerasians and their families would be allowed to immigrate to the States and that the plane tickets would be free, everyone said: 'Hey, come join our family.'"

    We stroll past rooms crammed with bunk beds. "These people will be leaving this month," the gatekeeper informs us. Then those in the next group of barracks will be flown to the States. "These days they're coming from further and further away. The first Amerasians in this processing center came from Saigon, but now they're coming from more remote areas, from

ROUND EYES

the Mekong Delta or high up in the mountains. These are more or less the last."

Two boys with noticeably kinky hair, sons of African-Americans, smile shyly at us. All the other people walking around here look like ordinary Vietnamese. "Relatives," the gatekeeper explains.

If we stop for a minute, a group forms around us. A woman grabs me by the arm. She says something in what sounds like English, but it's hard to understand her since she hasn't got any teeth. She pulls a pouch out from under her blouse and carefully removes a snapshot of a young man and a young woman in a bar. The girl is wearing a petticoat, her eyes are lined with black mascara and her hair is done up in a beehive. I look at the picture and then back at her, and only then do I realize she's the one in the snapshot. A uniformed soldier with short hair has flung his arm around her shoulder. "Husband," she points. "His name Lizmore." She pulls out another creased snapshot, this one of an American family: father, mother and two grown daughters wearing cat's eye glasses seated around the dining room table. The whole scene is so outdated that I burst into laughter, but it doesn't seem to perturb her. "His family," she says. She bore the soldier three sons, and after he left she had seven children by someone else. "Me ten babies now," she concludes. The three oldest are already in the U.S., and now it's her turn to follow with the rest of her brood. She can't be more than fifty, but she looks like she's eighty. She tucks her possessions away with great care. In a few days, she'll be in America, she mutters indistinctly with her toothless gums. Maybe she'll find Lizmore there.

And what if he doesn't want to have anything more to do with her, asks Mark. What if he's got himself another family in the meantime? Her mouth stretches in a broad toothless grin. "Nevu mind," she mumbles indulgently.

Tuyet is not impressed by her story. "She's nothing but a cheap bar girl," she says contemptuously. "You can hear by the way she speaks English that she's never been to school."

Tuyet leads me to a young woman she's discovered in the meantime. She has light skin and round eyes. "She's a good example of an Amerasian," according to Tuyet. The woman is surrounded by her three sons, and her seven in-laws are sitting in their room. Their house recently caught fire, she relates, and all their possessions went up in flames. That disaster was their ruin. The only trump they could produce was her mixed blood. Her father had been a pilot, she remembers. She no longer knows his name, but she does know his serial number. Her primary objective in the New World is going to be to locate her father. She's not going to leave any stone unturned.

"My god," says Mark, scratching his head. "After so many years he may not be exactly happy if she turns up with her entire family on the doorstep."

Tuyet translates his remark, but the woman doesn't budge from her plan. She's going to find her father, even if it takes her twenty years. Mark sighs.

A woman standing in the doorway of one of the rooms on the other side of the hall beckons in our direction. She has an odd look in her eyes, but she does seem to be extending a cordial invitation to me to step inside. I head her way and she nods, yes, I've understood her correctly. As soon as I'm within reach, she grabs me by the arm, pulls me into the room and points to one of the beds with the sleeping figure of a girl on it.

The girl wakes up, turns around and sits up. She has a beautiful face with regular features, almond-shaped eyes and a thick head of hair. In the semidarkness I can make out a man and four boys sitting on the other beds. One of the boys goes to get Tuyet to translate.

"This is a Chinese family," she says. "They come from the Mekong Delta, where the father grows rice. Fifteen years ago, when he was in the city he saw this girl roaming around the market. She was filthy and had nothing to eat. He could see that she was very beautiful, and he took her home with him. She was about four years old at the time." Tears trickle down the girl's cheeks.

"Why is she crying?" I ask.

"Because she's reminded of the time when everyone despised her and threw rocks at her."

Fate took a happier turn after she moved in. She became the oldest child: since her arrival, her adopted parents had a series of sons. Namely the bright-eyed adolescents who are following our conversation with animated expressions on their faces. The books they're using to learn English are lying on the table.

"What nice children you have," I tell the man through Tuyet.

"But we have a serious problem," the man replies. Everyone turns towards the mother. "She's ill. Mentally ill." Their plan to leave Vietnam has completely thrown her for a loop. She doesn't appear to understand what we're talking about and keeps looking around the room with a wild look in her eyes. Until the mother is declared sane, the family won't be allowed to leave. After this story, the beautiful girl starts weeping again.

"There's no way out," states the father. They sold their modest farm and have been living here for three months. Food and lodging are free but, as everyone knows, five children cost a lot of money. Little by little, he's reaching the end of his savings, and what will they use to start a new life in America? The man tells his story with dignity. He doesn't want pity, and he's not asking for a handout.

"What kind of work do you want to do in the States?" I ask the girl.

"It doesn't matter," she replies with a sniffle. "I'll do whatever they want me to do. Wash dishes, clean, whatever."

"Have you heard about those big hamburger restaurants they have there?"

She nods: "McDonald's."

"Yes," I nod, "maybe you can get a job at one of those. They give you a uniform, and you have to wear a cap."

She laughs. Her brothers laugh. "She'd really like that," Tuyet translates.

"And," I suggest, "maybe you'll meet a nice American boy."

"That'd be nice too," she responds. She looks uncertainly at her adopted mother, who gazes in incomprehension from one to the other.

Mark has come inside. "The gatekeeper has to get back to his post, and we have to go," he announces. Then he looks around, raises his hand by way of greeting and proclaims to everyone in the room: "Welcome to America."

That evening we find ourselves once again on Rhythm and

Booze's rooftop patio. A cooling breeze is wafting over the roof. I ask Mark if the war has changed him. "Oh, yes," he responds with characteristic deliberation. "Since the war, I always think: it's a miracle I survived. The rest of my life is a kind of gift. Since then I only want to do things that are fun. I don't want to do anything because I have to. I don't want a career. I don't want to be tied down by responsibilities, for anyone or anything. No family, no house. In the U.S. I work as a carpenter until I get fed up and then I split." If he hadn't been through the war, Mark suspects, he would have turned out like his sister, a woman with a good job and a new car every five years.

I continue to wonder about Mark. To me he remains a shadowy figure, hard to pin down. From the stories he tells me, he seems to realize just what the war destroyed within him. But he doesn't appear to be aware of the damage he inflicted on this country. As if none of it really happened. As if it's nothing more than the memory of a long-ago nightmare.

Suddenly Mark interrupts my train of thought: "What's your book about?"

"It's a love story," I reply, "about the love between a Vietnamese woman and a GI who goes back to Vietnam." Tuyet shoots him a sardonic look. A smile glides over his angelic face.

"Count me out," he declares. "I come and go with the tide."

Tuyet stubs out her umpteenth cigarette and matter-of-factly sums it all up: "Men are all the same. They sleep with you and then leave you behind like an empty glass of beer."

WHEN THE SNOW FALLS

In the courtyard of the Continental Hotel, I imagine myself to be on the Côte d'Azur. I seat myself at one of the white cast-iron tables and read *Le Monde*, which was for sale in the lobby. The menu promises croissants and *café glacé*.

During my first weeks in Vietnam, my thoughts kept straying to the "American war," as the Vietnamese refer to it. Now it occurs to me more and more that Saigon actually resembles an old-fashioned French provincial capital: an enormous cathedral, the Notre Dame, towers above all the other buildings, and a sprinkling of French *deux-chevaux* cars ply their way down the cool, tree-lined avenues. The yellow stucco City Hall would be more at home in Cannes, and the imposing post office, a beehive of activity, could easily serve as the backdrop in an historical French movie.

On the sidewalk cafés along the boulevards, people drink coffee, an unusual beverage in this part of the world. The coffee is filtered right at the table, with aluminum filters which I'm told are made from downed American helicopters. Still, the coffee tastes no less French because of it.

A couple of days ago, when there were floods in France, an old man could tell me exactly which area was affected:

"*L'Ardèche, madame.*" Like many Vietnamese, he studded his speech with "*ooh la la*" and "*bon.*"

But the strangest thing of all is that the Vietnamese look French, even those who swear there isn't a drop of European blood coursing through their veins. Their particular brand of charm and their habit of talking with their hands remind me of Avignon and Aix-en-Provence.

In Saigon I sometimes forget for hours on end that I'm in Asia, and I'm apparently not the only one: at the table next to me I notice a young woman and her daughter, both Vietnamese by the looks of them, but speaking French to each other. "*Alors, ma petite,*" says the mother, "drink your Coke."

Before long the child's newly acquired ball lands on my table. The mother sternly calls her to task: "Go say you're sorry." And in flawless French, the girl murmurs: "*Excusez, madame.*"

The mother stands up and comes to sit next to me. "Are you from Paris?" she inquires, hopefully.

"No," I respond, "from Holland."

"Oh, I must have made a mistake."

"Are you French?"

"No," she replies, "I was born in Saigon; I'm from here."

Why she's so fascinated by France is a mystery to me. I make a stab: "Surely you've been to France. Are you familiar with Paris?"

"*Ah non.*" A shadow of gloom crosses her face. "Paris is a dream of mine." Then she smiles, and her mouth resumes its cheerful expression.

She's quite an arresting sight: she's clad in tight jeans and a brightly colored print blouse, and her eyes are dancing constantly. She's gorgeous. Only the lines around her nose and mouth disturb the regularity of her features and betray the fact that she hasn't had an easy life.

"I'm a singer," she declares. "I sing in this hotel, every evening."

"May I come and listen?" I ask.

"But of course. You're welcome to come, every evening at nine. Ask for Thi Phuong; that's my name."

The disco is as dark as a coal mine. A woman in an *ao dai* leads me to my place with a flashlight; when I bought my admission ticket, they showed me a diagram and asked me to point to which one of the tables in front of the stage I wanted to sit. Some Asian businessmen are also seated there, and when the band strikes up the first notes of the next number, they start dancing with the girls in pink *ao dai* who have been hovering around in the back of the room like a flock of flamingos. The band plays without any vocal accompaniment, and the pink-clad girls, slender as reeds, dance deftly and dutifully in the arms of their fat dance partners. Each girl has a large number pinned to her chest.

Thi Phuong comes on stage in a cloud of glitter and makeup, her jet-black eyes gleaming out from a layer of white pancake. She sings a song, in French of course, which I recognize, since Adamo used to sing it years ago on the Dutch radio: *Tombe la Neige*. "I'll leave you when the snow falls." An odd text in this room, where the air conditioners strive audibly to cool the air. Thi Phuong nods at me, her face a white mask. She sings the song in a low, husky voice, with a great deal of dramatic sostenuto. And she looks as if she means it, that she'll leave when the snow falls. After two more songs, she steps down from the stage and comes to sit beside me.

"Beautiful," I exclaim. "You sing so well."

"Well," she retorts, "if you like it you can come here every evening to listen to me." She performs seven days a week in this hotel.

"Don't you ever take a vacation?" I inquire. She shakes her head. Getting someone else to rehearse a few numbers with the band just so they can take over for a couple of evenings is too complicated.

"What happens when you get sick?"

She laughs. "Then I sing anyway. This is my life."

The vocalist who came on after her has already left the stage and a young woman appears in his place. "New talent," Thi Phuong laughs.

The music is played in a specific order, I realize. First there's a waltz, then a tango, and after that a rock 'n' roll number, followed by a paso doble. Then it begins all over again. "It's like that in every disco in Saigon," declares Thi Phuong. "We call it 'musical rotation.' There's something for everyone. It's always been like that. It was the same during the old regime." She refers to it as the "old regime," I note. Since everyone is officially supposed to talk about before and after "liberation," my guess is she's not a supporter of the Communist Party.

After the waltz there's another tango. Only one couple is striding, with practiced movements, across the dance floor. The drunken businessmen don't dare attempt a tango. They've let the girls in pink return to their corner.

Thi Phuong nods towards the two dancers. "They used to have a dancing school," she explains. "One day he fled the country, on a boat. After a couple of years in a refugee camp, he was allowed to go to the U.S. She was supposed to join him, but she had second thoughts. So they divorced, and both of them remarried. But he couldn't live without her, and now he's back."

"What a tragedy," I sigh.

"Not really," she says. "This kind of thing happens all the time in Vietnam."

The girls in pink are once again gliding over the dance floor. "Anyone can buy a ticket," Thi Phuong explains. "One dance costs about a dollar." In Vietnam, you don't ask a woman you don't know for a dance. Not, at any rate, a decent Vietnamese, since decent women don't dance with total strangers. So men without partners have to resort to taxi dancers.

"Are the customers allowed to take the girls with them to their rooms?" I ask. Thi Phuong laughs.

"That's not what they're for. Officially, they're only dance partners. But who knows what happens after closing time?"

Glancing at her watch, she remarks: "I have to head for my next performance." It seems she has another engagement tonight. "Would you like to go with me?"

Her motor scooter is parked in the hotel parking lot. Mounted on the back is a chest in which she transports her clothes and makeup: a mini road show. There's enough room for me too, and she heads for a traffic circle at a sedate speed. We get swallowed up in the stream of motorbikes, motor scooters and bicycles which always fill the streets in the early evening. We whirl past the towering cathedral and the former residence of the colonial government

When the Snow Falls

and zoom over boulevards framed by tall trees. From time to time a fan races past us and exclaims in amazement: "Thi Phuong!" Even though it's dark outside, it's still hot. Everyone is wearing short sleeves and letting the warm evening air caress their bare arms.

We arrive at a theater consisting of little more than a giant umbrella, under which the audience is engrossed in the show that's already begun: several young women are parading across the stage in striking attire, the kind of clothes you'd expect to see in Miami rather than Saigon. "A fashion show," Thi Phuong explains. A regular feature of a night out in Vietnam. The people in the audience, seated on uncomfortable wooden benches, are of quite a different sort than those in the disco: here they're poor and thin, and many of the young women are holding children on their laps.

Sitting in a cluttered area behind the stage, where a couple of vocalists are lounging around, Thi Phuong arranges her hair. They see each other every night, since they do the same shows every night. "Only in Saigon can you earn your living this way," says a young singer with a crew cut.

"Not in Hanoi?" I ask. They glance at me in surprise.

"No," the young man responds, "I sang in Hanoi once, but things are very different there." The others nod and look restrained. "Very different," they echo in confirmation.

"Not much of a night life in Hanoi?" I persist.

They cough. "No, in the North everyone goes to bed early."

I look questioningly around, but no one is prepared to explain why Hanoi is so obviously different. Thi Phuong joins in the conversation. "There are people who like Hanoi," she says, in an attempt to smooth things over, "but we artists prefer Saigon." After that no one ventures to say anything more on the subject.

It's her turn to perform, and without a trace of nervousness she climbs on stage, where she's met with a roar of applause. Afterwards, dropping me at my hotel, she says: "Tomorrow I'll be performing for the female workers in a factory. If you want, you can come with me."

An entire bus has been rented to transport the company: musicians, instruments, sound equipment, vocalists and a photographer. Thi Phuong is dressed simply. She probably knows it's going to be a long, hot day. We arrive at a huge textile factory located at the edge of town, and the girls in the band go off to change while the rest of us are led to an enormous room with easy chairs and proffered cups of tea.

In the weeks I've been in Vietnam I've seen countless pictures in the newspapers and on television of people staring into the camera from reception rooms like this one. Anyone who pays an official visit to Vietnam apparently winds up sooner or later in this entourage.

One of the singers seated beside me tells me in halting French how much he adores Russian literature. It seems he visited the former Soviet Union years ago. Outside we can hear them testing the sound equipment, but it's not yet in working order. We are given more tea, and then the show can finally begin.

Thi Phuong directs me to a place in the front row, next to the factory's general manager. "She's from the North," explains Thi Phuong. The woman says something to me in Russian, but unfortunately I can't understand a word. At one time she was a student in Leningrad, I'm told, and she's been managing this company since 1975.

I've heard a lot of talk about those "Northerners" who were given important posts in the South after the war. The Saigonese look upon them as colonialists, foreigners usurping power. The big shots from Hanoi are frequently not very competent: they were given these plum positions as a reward for their services to the revolution. After that, the Southerners complain, they did little more than run the Vietnamese economy into the ground.

Looking at the general manager beside me, I wonder what intrigues are going on in this factory. Did she actually know anything about textile, or was she given the job because of her brave exploits during the war? And what does the future hold in store for her? These days, state-run enterprises are being put up for sale to foreign investors. Will the Northerners continue to pull the strings during this period of liberalization?

My reverie is interrupted by the all-girl band, which starts off on an upbeat number at full volume. All five of the girls are dressed in identical tight shiny-blue costumes. One of them has a boyfriend in tow. He carries her instrument and her suitcase, which contains a change of clothes. He nods in encouragement as she plucks the strings of her electric guitar.

The general manager stares straight ahead. She's dressed simply, and her gray hair has been cut short and neat. Thi Phuong, seated next to her, looks like a sophisticated woman of the world. You might even say flashy. Sitting side by side, the two women seem to form a symbol: the manager representing the puritanical North and Thi Phuong the flamboyant South.

Thi Phuong had told me before that she'd gone to a French school. During the old regime, her father ran a delicatessen, together with a French partner. After Saigon fell the French man was forced to go home, and the business was confiscated by the new government. Even though this ruined her family, Thi Phuong still managed to go to a conservatory and to build up her career. One evening, a man in the audience showed a lot of interest in her. He had come to live in Saigon after '75 and spoke with a Northern accent. His father, it seems, was a retired general from the North Vietnamese Army, and the family was part of the city's new elite. Eventually they got married. I didn't dare ask how their respective families reacted to the marriage. Surely her father, who had lost all he had, wasn't pleased with a son-in-law from Hanoi. And the general, shaped by years of Communist discipline, would more than likely regard his heavily made-up daughter-in-law as a sure symptom of Southern decadence.

The blue-costumed band members fall silent and bow shyly towards the audience. One of the factory workers presents each of them with a flower. "It's a must," Thi Phuong explains. "Singers and musicians always get flowers."

Next, the general manager ascends to the stage to give a welcoming speech. She addresses the workers: thin women with bad teeth and hairpins in their hair. Thi Phuong translates without comment. The speech is about the fatherland, the revolution and the future shimmering on the horizon. Thi Phuong is apparently used to these kinds of speeches.

The atmosphere only picks up after she installs herself in front of the microphone. She kicks off her set with a French number: *Non, Je Ne T'aime Plus* resounds over the factory grounds. After the first few verses, she descends from the stage and strolls through the audience. From time to time she comes to a stop, and the women next to her cling giggling to each other's necks. Back with the band, she begins a rock 'n' roll number and plucks one of the workers from the front row to dance with her. Frolicking like a colt in a pasture, the young woman keeps glancing over her shoulder at her fellow workers, who cheer her on, screaming with pleasure.

On the way home, it's quiet in the bus. The performance has tired everyone out. "You did that so well," I say to Thi Phuong, who is examining her smeared mascara in a mirror. "The audience is not at all like the one in the disco, and yet you know just how to reach them." She shrugs her shoulders. She often performs in factories, she remarks, so she's used to them. The Musicians' Union, of which she's a member, encourages her to accept these kinds of engagements. It doesn't pay well, but it would be unseemly to refuse.

The Musicians' Union orchestrates a lot of her activities, I gather. They provide the words to new songs and arrange TV performances. "I'm not allowed to sing French numbers on TV," complains Thi Phuong as we approach downtown Saigon. "Every song has to be in Vietnamese, and I can't wear what I want. If I want to appear on TV, I have to wear an *ao dai*." She stares gloomily at the cathedral as we drive by. Does she see herself as a puppet, I wonder. Does she feel hemmed in by this lack of freedom? She looks at me, with a smile on her face. "Oh well," she says deprecatingly, "that's the price you have to pay for success."

Thi Phuong and I have been hanging around together for several days, and everyone's beginning to notice. Thi Phuong is having to answer more and more questions about me, and it seems to be making her nervous. One morning, after an early performance in a coffeehouse, her husband comes and picks us up in his car. While the two of them confer, their eyes keep turning in my direction. It looks like he's issuing Thi Phuong a warning. "It would be a pleasure for me to introduce you to the executive committee of the Musicians' Union," Thi Phuong says to me. She makes it sound like a favor, but I'm afraid it'll be more of an interrogation.

When the Snow Falls

Her husband drops us at the gate of the run-down French villa housing the Musicians' Union. Anyone who is active in the world of music is a member. I reluctantly step inside. The reception room holds a group of men, including the union's chairman. Thi Phuong acts as interpreter. How long have I been in Vietnam and how long am I planning to stay, the gentlemen inquire. What part of the country have I already seen and where am I planning to go next? "What organization has invited you here?"

I look around in noncomprehension. "Well," explains Thi Phuong, "you're here to write a book, right? So maybe you're here at the invitation of the State Department? Or perhaps your visa has been arranged by the Writers' Union? That's how we do things here," she concludes a little impatiently. "Every foreigner who comes to Vietnam is linked to some official body."

I break out into a sweat. "I simply went and bought a ticket at a travel agency," I finally manage to utter. "I don't have any contacts with the authorities here." I get the impression this admission doesn't improve my case any.

"So you have a tourist visa?" the tenacious chairman says.

One of the men around the table asks if he may see what I've written. My heart starts pounding in my throat. Are they going to inspect my notes? Will I ever get them back? "I'm sorry, but I write in Dutch," I stammer.

"That doesn't matter," Thi Phuong replies. "This gentleman is psychic. He just wants to analyze your handwriting."

I quickly leaf through my notes to find a page without any names or phone numbers. The man scrutinizes my scrawling script. Then he asks to look at my hand. "You've lost your hat," he says.

My mouth falls open. A couple of days ago I forgot and left a cherished sun hat in a bus. "That's right," I say.

"Then you've missed a big opportunity," he adds, then continues, "you nearly drowned once when you were a child."

"Yes," I acknowledge. And that too is true. Once, when I was learning how to swim, I was thrown into the deep end of the pool. The boy next door dragged me, choking and sputtering, out of the water.

"Of course," remarks a man I'd noticed earlier because his hair was pulled back in a fashionable ponytail, "there's so much water in Holland that I bet almost every kid nearly drowns at some time or another." He roars with laughter, and his laughter sounds like music to my ears.

Undeterred, the other man proceeds to predict my future: "There's an important figure in your life who was born in 1941." Everyone turns questioningly towards me. My heart pounds in my throat. Is this how they want to find out who I'm hanging around with?

"John?" Thi Phuong suggests, since she's also met the New Zealander.

"No, he's a lot younger," I reply. "It must be someone in Holland." My remark is greeted with looks of skepticism by those on the other side of the table. Apparently they all suspect I'm trying to hide something.

"You should wear purple, white and red," the fortune-teller continues. "Those colors will bring you luck. When you're forty-one you'll be awarded a prize or win some money, and four years after that you'll divorce your husband."

I withdraw my hand. "I'll write all this down," I declare, "and I'll let you know if it comes true."

The chairman nods: we may go.

"Did it go all right?" I ask when we're standing outside.

"What do you mean?" asks Thi Phuong.

"Oh, nothing," I reply. Apparently there are no official objections to our friendship.

With me clinging to the back of her motor scooter, she drives us to her apartment: a huge white apartment building done in the austere style currently so popular in Vietnam. As we climb the stairs, I notice that everything is new and white. Thi Phuong, her husband and her daughter live on the fourth and top floor. They share the apartment with her husband's parents and his brothers and their families. Thi Phuong mutters that she pretty much stays out of their way, without saying why.

The living room is ultra-modern: black imitation leather furniture and a lot of glass and chrome. We continue on to the bedroom, so I can admire her costumes. There's a second television in the bedroom. Thi Phuong explains that she prefers spending her spare time playing video games. She demonstrates this by dexterously manipulating the remote control, plucking bricks out of the air and stacking them in a pile. She can spend hours a day at it, she confesses. In the morning after she wakes up and in the evening after she's finished with her performances.

Why the great need to lose herself in a mindless game? I contemplate this and conclude, while following the action on the screen, that Thi Phuong and Tuyet are alike in a lot of ways. They are roughly the same age, both their families were on the wrong side in the war, and afterwards neither of them let themselves be thrust aside, but kept on striving to take an active part in life.

We hear the door slam. Thi Phuong's husband has come home. We go to greet him and discover he's brought a friend. The two men are flushed with drink. The friend proudly displays his ID: he works for the secret police. Laughing, he asks if I'm afraid of him.

"No," answers Thi Phuong in my place. "She has a clear conscience." In an aside to me, so that the two men can't hear her, she gripes that they reek of beer. "That's all they do all day: drink beer."

It seems her husband speaks German, since he studied mechanical engineering in East Berlin. At the time, that was a privilege accorded to children of high-ranking cadre members. After that, he accepted an interesting job aboard a Vietnamese freighter and spent the last ten years traveling all over the world.

He takes a photo album from a cupboard in a modern wall unit and starts thumbing through it. "That's me in Paris," he points, and I can see him, somewhat younger, standing in front of the Eiffel Tower with his arm around a blonde.

"His girlfriend," says Thi Phuong, piqued. She had just finished telling me how jealous he is and how she has to make sure she doesn't give rise to any gossip, as otherwise he would retaliate in some awful way. Her husband laughs off her anger and, searching for a picture of himself in Rotterdam, bumps his hand against an envelope lying on the table, which opens to reveal a thick stack of American dollars. The two men are apparently involved in a business deal.

The husband's boasting begins to irritate Thi Phuong. "Come on," she says, "let's go back to our video games."

While various strange objects float over the screen, I ask her when her husband will be heading out to sea again. "Oh, he's on vacation," she answers vaguely.

"Until when?"

She shrugs. "He's been home for a year."

"So what's your husband doing now?" I insist.

Thi Phuong explodes dozens of little men on the screen. "Oh, he's doing some business with his brother and his friends."

"What kind of business?" I press her.

She stares evenly at me: "I don't want to know, and you don't want to know either."

Why did she marry him, I wonder. Because of his family's beautiful apartment? Was she seeking protection because of her capitalist origins? Did marrying him make it possible for her to perform wherever she wanted? Had she ever loved him?

When a suitable occasion arises, in between the video games, I ask: "Are you happy together?"

She sighs. "No, not really. Or rather, sometimes. For a few brief moments."

Passion and Corruption

It's still dark when I hear the slow scrape of the streetsweeper; every move brings him closer. Peeking outside, I see that the waiters from Restaurant Thirteen are astir. At night they sleep on the tables they serve by day. They brush their teeth, spit in the gutter and comb their hair. Then, while the first shoeshine boy of the day horses around in their midst, they adjust the awnings.

Some time later, when the sun is glaring into my room, I wake up again. Once I'm up and moving, I notice that the clothes I took off last night are nowhere to be found. Since a lot more is missing from my wardrobe, I decide to ask the chambermaid what's going on. I wrap myself in a sarong and step into the corridor which ushers me into the hotel's labyrinth.

Rain spatters down into the inner courtyard day and night, regardless of the weather, and moss and ferns cling to the walls.

The chambermaid's room, which she shares with her husband and child, is like a cave. A pan of rice is steaming in a corner. Behind her, my clothes are hanging neatly on a hanger to dry. She must have come and got them this morning while I was asleep. Every time I see her, she inquires in sign language if I have any laundry for her; this additional income makes her job very lucrative. She spends all of her spare time washing and ironing. Except that now, as I come in, she's reading a book.

She springs to her feet, hands me my clothes and, to indicate the price, holds up two five-thousand dong bills, less than a dollar. With one customer like me a day, she earns three times as much as a teacher. Her hands are covered with calluses, and half her teeth are missing, though she's not a day past thirty.

I take a look at the book she's reading. The cover shows a man with a sword and in the background a woman in a floor-length dress longingly awaiting his return. The laundress smiles and makes a thumbs-up sign. "Number one," she says; it's a good book.

In other countries as poor as Vietnam, a woman like her wouldn't be able to read. Here, to my great amazement, I'm constantly running into salesclerks reading when business is slack, or cyclo drivers awaiting their fares with a book in hand. They'd rather earn money, but if that's not in the cards, they're likely to be engrossed in a good story. The tales are usually about Vietnam's glorious past, in the days when, centuries before the Americans ever arrived on the scene, wars were fought by long-haired men in silken robes. The same heroes whose sculptures adorn the city.

I'm curious about Vietnam's contemporary writers, about how they depict life in Saigon today. The only problem is: how do I come in contact with a writer? Of course everyone who publishes in Vietnam is a member of the Writers' Union. But if I approach this august body, I'll find myself facing the same problem as with the Musicians' Union. They'll want to know which organization invited me and who is responsible for me during my stay in Vietnam. Without a "sponsor," as it's called, I am accountable to no one. If problems should arise, there is no official body they can turn to. Being without a sponsor in Vietnam is like being stateless.

The best solution would be if I just accidentally happened to run into a writer, but it might take a while for that to happen. I'd heard a lot of good things about the magazine called *Tuoi Tre*, "Youth," whose editorial board consists of several known writers. *Tuoi Tre* was said to be progressive, so I reasoned that they might be prepared to talk with me without an official introduction.

I ask the desk clerk at my hotel to write in Vietnamese: "May I please speak with a young writer?" I then hop into a cyclo and at the office of *Tuoi Tre*, present the note to the doorman. His eyes move from the paper to me and back to the paper. He disappears from sight and returns shortly, accompanied by the head of the literature and art section, Nguyen Dong Thuc, who is also a writer. Mr. Thuc speaks halting English.

He leads me to a reception room, switches on the overhead fans and knits his brow in thought. "If you've come to discuss our magazine," he says, "I will be obliged to ask our superiors for permission."

"And if we talk about something else?" I inquire.

"As long as we talk about my books, that won't be necessary."

"Thank goodness," I reply, "because that's exactly what I'm interested in."

Mr. Thuc, I gather, is a popular writer, even though he's modest about his accomplishments. Almost all of his books have been made into movies. "My books are only read in the South," he notes diffidently. "Only Southerners go to my movies, because my stories are always situated in Saigon. No one in Hanoi is interested in knowing how we live, and besides, they wouldn't understand. Things are quite different there. A lot simpler, poorer, less . . . how shall I put it? North and South, they're two different worlds."

One of his most recent books, entitled *The Lonely Star*, is about the life of a famous singer. Another one, called *Farewell, Summer*, deals with a schoolgirl who has problems at home and at school. In his books, says Mr. Thuc, he portrays present-day Saigon without idealizing it. He writes about such things as corruption, prostitution and crime in no uncertain terms.

Mr. Thuc was born in Saigon. His family didn't take part in the resistance movement, and during the war he took an English course from the Americans. Yet in spite of all this he's a member of the Writers' Union.

"I didn't know that was possible!" I remark with surprise.

"It has been for the last couple of years," Mr. Thuc replies neutrally.

Farewell, Summer was recently made into a movie, he informs me. The premier is going to be in a couple of days, and I'm welcome to come see it if I want to.

Sunday morning Mr. Thuc comes to get me on his motor scooter. As we drive away, he grumbles: "The security man at your hotel is very interested in my license plate."

"I know," I say. "I think they're keeping tabs on me. I hope I'm not getting you into any trouble."

He shrugs. "I'm not worried," he shouts above the roar of the engine.

We're headed for the headquarters of a youth organization, which turns out to be a huge complex consisting of two theaters, a coffee shop and sports facilities. One of the hallways houses an exhibition of photographs. Several of the pictures on the wall are familiar to me from my visit to the War Crimes Museum: a group of American GIs grinning sheepishly around a heap of arms and legs of a number of Vietnamese. Another of a man with misshapen arms, the result of cruel torture. And a picture of the young man who attempted to assassinate Robert McNamara, the U.S. Secretary of Defense. The next photograph shows the man being executed, and one of his garments is on display in a glass case.

"One of Vietnam's greatest heroes," comments Mr. Thuc tonelessly. I gulp; I was not prepared for this horrible reminder. Can displays like these really persuade young people to toe the line?

Apparently no one is meant to linger in the hall; instead, the pictures seem to serve as a kind of historical backdrop. And so everyone scurries off to a tennis tournament or to Mr. Thuc's movie. My escort wants to sit in the back of the theater so that no one can observe his reaction to his own story.

The movie begins with shots of Saigon: the Saigon River and a traffic circle with a statue of a horseback rider in the middle. The action begins on a rooftop patio dotted with tropical plants in flowerpots, where a man is doing his exercises. A girl who looks like she's about sixteen brings him a cup of coffee. We look in surprise, as does the girl, at the man's bare back, which is crisscrossed with red welts clearly made by a woman's fingernails.

Next to me, Mr. Thuc explains in a whisper: "The man is a friend of her father's. He's currently staying with them."

We follow the girl to her modern bedroom, which is larger than the living quarters of most Vietnamese families.

"How come this family is so rich?" I ask Mr. Thuc.

Passion and Corruption

"The father is the general manager of a state-run import-export firm" is the reply. Everyone in Vietnam knows that these kinds of government jobs don't pay high salaries, but that there's a lot of extra money to be made in kickbacks.

"How did the father get such a good job?" I ask.

"He used to be a revolutionary," Mr. Thuc explains.

I'm surprised at the overt criticism. This family truly lives in a palace. We are shown the spacious guest bedroom, where the guest, to the consternation of the audience and the daughter, is now seen to be lying in bed with the mother. This couple is actually breaking all the rules of an orderly Communist society.

"Yes," Mr. Thuc concurs, "but also those of Confucianism. We in the South attach great importance to those rules. After all, Communism is a fairly recent development. Family relationships in the South are much more old-fashioned than those in the North. Our daughters and wives are supposed to serve men and guests, while in the North . . ." His words get drowned out by the audience's audible reaction. The screen dialogue is repeatedly greeted with loud laughter, but Mr. Thuc's halting translation can't keep pace with the jokes.

We've now arrived at the girl's school. One of the teachers clearly has his eye on her. One evening she and her girlfriend attend a poetry reading, where the teacher reads a poem. When the girl responds enthusiastically to someone else's verse, the jealous teacher vanishes into the dark night.

A few weeks ago, I wouldn't have understood why, but in the meantime I've had ample opportunity to observe at first hand the surprisingly vehement jealousy of the Vietnamese. It crops up at the strangest moments: let's say you're sitting with someone, either male or female. If you start talking to someone else, he or she is bound to throw a jealous fit. So I'm on my guard today, with Mr. Thuc.

Now that the teacher has disappeared from view, we learn that the girl is friends with one of the boys in her class — all very platonic. Alas, it seems that he is of humble origins, and her father, the former revolutionary, forbids her to have anything to do with him.

We see her walking down the street one day, beautifully dressed, and she calls for a cyclo. As the cyclo driver draws near, she recognizes him: it's her classmate, doing what he can to help the family finances. The shame is unbearable, and the boy pedals furiously away on his cyclo. The girl starts walking home, filled with shame on his behalf. Then, to top it all off, she sees her father walking through the park, hand in hand with a young woman.

"And now," concludes Mr. Thuc with a note of satisfaction, "her whole world has collapsed."

Just then the film breaks. "No problem," Mr. Thuc assures me, "it'll be fixed in no time."

We wait half an hour, an hour, and then the electricity goes out. "No problem," repeats Mr. Thuc. "Everything will turn out okay. It's only a local power failure. Apparently the electricity is still working in the city."

The theater gets hotter and hotter, since the fans have also stopped. The heat finally becomes unbearable. This particular Sunday morning, the problem in the movie theater is never going to be resolved.

Drenched with sweat, we find ourselves some time later drinking coffee at a sidewalk café.

"How does the story end?" I ask to satisfy my curiosity. I'm fascinated by the theme of the total moral collapse of this family in a Communist country.

Well," begins Mr. Thuc, "the mother leaves, since she can't possibly stay after this disgrace." The girl's classmate also disappears from the story: one night, while he's driving a rich foreigner around in his cyclo, the poor kid is attacked by bandits and stabbed to death.

"And what happens to the girl?" I want to know.

"She volunteers to work in the mountains with a youth group," replies Mr. Thuc.

So there's a moral after all, I gather. Her schoolmates come to visit her in that primitive, remote area of the country and find her transformed into a wise young woman who knows the difference between good and evil.

"Just what is the author's message?" I ask Mr. Thuc, to be on the safe side.

"That adults should set a good example for young people," is the reply.

"Okay, but is anything done about the corruption shown in the movie?"

Mr. Thuc snorts scornfully. "No, you can't lay a finger on people like that."

A Vietnamese in Amsterdam

One evening Mr. Thuc picks me up and we drive on his motor scooter through the badly lighted streets of Saigon en route to a restaurant to meet one of his fellow writers, Nguyen Quang Sang, who also happens to be the chairman of the Writers' Union, the man who decides what may or may not be published in Saigon. I didn't think it was such a good idea at first because I was afraid of getting ensnared in a web of officialdom. But Mr. Thuc swore up and down that I wouldn't be. "He knows you're here as a tourist, but that doesn't matter," he insisted. So here we are, with Mr. Thuc parking on a busy street near a small restaurant which doesn't seem to have a front wall; the tables are practically on the sidewalk.

Mr. Sang is halfway through his meal. He turns out to be a small, shy man, seated beside a beautiful woman in a spotless white blouse whose hair reaches below her waist. "This isn't Mr. Sang's wife," says Mr. Thuc jovially. The young woman's face radiates a sense of goodness.

"She's our Maecenas," Mr. Thuc translates for Mr. Sang. She's married to a wealthy businessman, and from time to time she invites writers to dine with her.

The fourth person at the table is introduced next: a French-speaking man who doesn't look the least bit Vietnamese. I thought I caught the word "Israel," and wonder if he works for an Israeli company or for the Israeli Consulate in Saigon.

"Not *Israel*," Mr. Thuc corrects me, "but *Islam*." The man is a Muslim.

But where does he come from then? I'm now more confused than ever. Mr. Thuc patiently explains that the man is descended from the Chams, an ethnic minority that was almost entirely wiped out by the Vietnamese. The largest group of Chams still in existence, a few thousand souls, lives in the city of Chau Doc, near the Cambodian border, and in Central Vietnam. The Chams were originally Hindus, but a few centuries ago they were converted to Islam.

I've barely had time to digest this complicated story when the Cham addresses me solemnly in French: "How are things in Dam Square?"

At first I think I didn't hear him correctly. "Dam Square?" I say incredulously. "In Amsterdam?"

"Yes, the square with that big white monument in the middle. Is it still there?"

"The war monument. Yes, it's still there."

"Oh," the man laughs, "is that what it is. I didn't have the faintest idea what it was when I was there." And he launches into a strange story that seems hard to believe, except that Mr. Sang swears as head of the Writers' Union that his friend is telling the truth, the whole truth and nothing but the truth.

In the sixties, when the war was at its height, the Cham, then a teenager, met a Dutch sailor in Saigon Harbor. The sailor didn't have any children and, wanting to surprise his wife with a foster child, he took the boy on board with him. Unfortunately, the wife didn't think it was such a good idea; after one week, she heartlessly threw the Cham out on the street. The boy drifted around for awhile, finally winding up in Amsterdam, where he ran into hippies from the U.S., Canada and all of Europe, living on the steps on the monument. He quickly become one of them. They gave him bread, beer and hashish. He already knew a little French and could manage to make himself understood, except that no one believed he came from Vietnam. After all, he looked like an Arab. He lived there for two months, without a penny to his name, until one day a passing Vietnamese heard his story and alerted the authorities. To his great relief, the Cham was repatriated to Vietnam, where he picked up the threads of his former life.

"That's why," the man concluded, as if his was the most ordinary story in the world, "I wondered how things were in Dam Square."

"I'll send you a postcard of it as soon as I get home," I promise.

And then a new round of beer is ordered: ten green cans of Heineken, in honor of the fact that I come from Holland. We're also drinking shot glasses of whiskey.

When Mr. Thuc begins to spout a series of speeches which are incomprehensible to me, Mr. Sang makes attempts to calm him down. The restaurant's other guests, who likewise have a forest of empty beer cans on their tables, good-naturedly shout encouragement. Only the beautiful woman with the long hair who has confined herself to Coke is still totally sober. She smiles benignly at everyone.

Not long afterwards, she helps me into a cyclo. Her pale face, with its regular features, hovers above me, and I feel like a baby in a baby carriage. It has started to rain. The cyclo driver produces a sheet of plastic that covers me from head to toe, and I find my buggy being propelled through the deserted streets of Saigon. No one can see me; I'm invisible under the improvised canopy. The cyclo driver pedals slowly, as we're not in any hurry. Peeking through a crack, I see the cathedral and the post office. We glide over the Boulevard of the Two Sisters, two legendary women who nearly two thousand years ago sacrificed their lives to free Vietnam from foreign domination. The occasional night watchman who crosses our path has no way of knowing that this cyclo harbors a foreigner. I'm a mere shadow in this ravaged city. I suddenly realize that it's the first time I really feel at home in Saigon.

Homesick for Long Xuyen

In the morning, after waking with a crashing headache, I find a note in my purse. "Lunch with Mr. Sang. Twelve o'clock," with an address jotted underneath it. Mr. Sang is, so I gathered last night, a real Communist, which is why I don't feel like spending the entire afternoon in his company. Exactly what was his role in the past? I can understand his initially wanting to free his country of foreign domination. But what was he doing after 1975, when thousands of people were thrown in jail and tens of thousands took to the seas to escape the hell? He must have remained loyal to the party, as otherwise he wouldn't have such a high-level job now.

I also don't know whether I feel up to having a serious discussion about Vietnamese literature with Mr. Sang today, as we agreed last night. By way of briefing, he had handed me a photocopy of one of his stories, which had been translated into Spanish. Scanning the manuscript, I note that the story takes place in 1956, though I could have guessed that without knowing a word of Spanish. I decipher one sentence: "They tortured him for three months, but he didn't say a word."

The story is about a young man's struggle against French

colonialism. It might have been Mr. Sang himself. Last night, I remember now that my headache is on the wane, he told me that he became a member of the Viet Minh, the outlawed anti-French independence movement, when he was fourteen years old. His father, a jeweler from Long Xuyen, a city in the Mekong Delta, was a wealthy man. Even in the 1930s he owned a car. Like all children of well-to-do families in that period, Mr. Sang was sent to a French school where he read Balzac and Baudelaire and was reared as a strict Catholic. The largest cathedral in the entire Mekong Delta was located in Long Xuyen; sometimes more than a thousand Catholics came there to worship.

There were numerous religious sects in the area, which meant that in their search for eternal bliss the people of Long Xuyen had the pick of the bunch. One of these was Cao Dai, a religious movement that still has thousands of adherents. Some time ago I had visited their headquarters in Tay Ninh, arriving in the hush of a sweltering afternoon. Shimmering in the heat, the temple looked like a mirage that might be swept away on the next breath of wind. Just as I was about to enter the light-yellow temple, a procession of dozens of young men, marching solemnly with a rowboat, passed me by.

An obliging French-speaking nun explained that Cao Daism is a combination of Buddhism, Confucianism and Christianity. On the way to the prayer room, she pointed out a portrait of the French writer, Victor Hugo.

"What's he got to do with Cao Dai?" I asked.

"His spirit often appears to us during seances," the nun explained and led me into a vast sanctuary, where pale-pink dragons smiled benignly at each other while winding their way around row upon row of pillars. We walked in the direction of the altar, towards what appeared to be a globe, more than three feet in diameter. As we got closer, I realized that it was actually a huge eyeball. The Eye of God cast me a weary glance through a half-open eyelid.

If Mr. Sang had wanted to rebel in his youth, he might have left the Catholic church and embraced Cao Dai's version of salvation. But he became a Communist instead.

I had asked him last night how a family arrived at such a deci-

Homesick for Long Xuyen

sion. Did they all get together at a certain moment and reach a group decision? What about aunts, uncles, nephews and nieces?

"It was a personal decision," explained Mr. Sang, "depending entirely on how the seeds of personality were sown in each individual. For example, my brother opted for the other side, later on becoming a major in the South Vietnamese Army. Even though we had the same parents and were raised the same way."

At the age of sixteen, the young Sang was a hardened guerrilla. He knew how to handle weapons and how to survive in the jungle. For years he was always on the move, hiding in villages or with his comrades in the forest.

"Was it exciting?" I asked him.

"Oh, I don't know," replied Mr. Sang. "I was always homesick for Long Xuyen."

I looked at him in surprise, but he seemed to mean what he said: he was genuinely fond of the city where he was born.

The French disappeared and the Americans took their place. Mr. Sang stayed in the resistance movement. In the meantime, he had become a reporter for the Viet Cong. "I wrote about our heroes, about the victory that was sure to be ours." At times he lived in a so-called "liberated zone," usually a desolate area where the Viet Cong held sway. Occasionally he traveled for weeks through "enemy territory" where he was dependent on the help of Viet Cong sympathizers. Once, when he was in a very remote area, he was visited by one of his relatives, who came to see him in the greatest of secrecy.

Thinking back on our meeting last night, I realize that I do like Mr. Sang. He has an engaging air of vulnerability. He seems to me to be someone who is capable of having doubts, even though he's a confirmed Communist.

I get dressed and show the cyclo driver at the door of my hotel the note with the address. "Very long," he says. "One dollar."

"Five thousand dong," I answer, driving a hard bargain by offering half.

"Okay," he says, "let's go."

Mr. Sang lives, as I soon find out, just around the corner, across from an old French colonial building.

"Shall I wait?" the cyclo driver grins.

"No," I reply crossly, "I can manage those five hundred yards by myself."

A young woman is waiting in the entryway: Mr. Sang's daughter, who speaks English. The Sang family's apartment looks out on an inner courtyard, where a table has been set. Mrs. Sang, a practicing engineer, has already laid the table for lunch. Looking inside through the open windows, I can see that the living room is furnished sparsely; the TV is the only luxury item. That puts my mind at ease, since I was prepared to find the family living in the lap of luxury, like the characters in Mr. Thuc's movie.

While Mrs. Sang serves homemade egg rolls and her husband reverently fills my glass with Heineken beer, the daughter translates the conversation.

"I wrote my first book in 1954," relates Mr. Sang. "The story takes place in Long Xuyen. I wrote it out of homesickness." Due to a variety of circumstances, *Land of Fire* was only published ten years later.

"The story is a little complicated," Mr. Sang resumes gloomily. It's about a simple peasant in the beginning of the 1940s. Oppressed by the French regime, he decides to join the Viet Minh. But he becomes disillusioned and converts to Hoa Hao, a strange religious sect whose male followers let their hair grow long and tied it in a topknot.

"The peasant is a good man with a good heart," adds Mr. Sang. "He loves his country. He's a patriot."

"Yes," I nod, "he's a good Vietnamese."

At a certain point in the novel, the main character begins to wonder what the difference is between good and evil. Is there a heaven and a hell? The peasant comes to the conclusion that only death can provide the answer, and that unfortunately, the dead can't talk. At the end of the novel, fate strikes: the Hoa Hao sect suspects that the peasant is spying for the Viet Minh, and he's killed by his fellow believers. Mr. Sang sighs deeply. "That's the tragedy of the Mekong."

It's also the drama of his own life. Like the peasant in his story, he will spend the rest of his life suffering the consequences of his one-time choice.

In 1954, when Mr. Sang was nineteen, the warring factions

Homesick for Long Xuyen

in Vietnam signed the Geneva Agreement, officially dividing the country in two: North and South Vietnam. Ho Chi Minh rose to power in the North, while the French continued to rule the South. The Catholics in the North who couldn't reconcile themselves to Ho Chi Minh were given the opportunity to move to the South, and Communists, like Mr. Sang, were allowed to leave for the North.

"I traveled in a Polish ship," recalls Mr. Sang, "the *Silensky*. And so I went further and further away from Long Xuyen," he concludes dejectedly.

He wound up in a totally different world. The North was oriented towards the Soviet Union; many North Vietnamese spoke Russian. Mr. Sang threw himself into a study of whatever translated literature was available, reading Tolstoy, Paustovsky and Dostoyevsky. In 1966 he was ordered to return to the South, this time as a reporter. He made the journey of roughly eighteen hundred miles on foot, crossing through the jungle on the Ho Chi Minh Trail. After working for a few years as an undercover reporter in enemy territory, he returned to the North, once again traversing the eighteen hundred miles on foot.

By the time he was back in Hanoi, Mr. Sang had turned forty. In the meantime a good friend of his had died, leaving behind his wife and little girl. Mr. Sang married the widow, the friendly engineer who is nearing with another platter of egg rolls. She smiles shyly. The two of them then had two sons. Mr. Sang notes with satisfaction: "She comes from Long Xuyen, just like me."

In 1975, when the Americans had been vanquished, the family returned to their beloved South. They arrived too late to be able to bid farewell to Mr. Sang's brother, who had just departed for the U.S. in one of the last refugee-laden planes.

"Were the stories you wrote after the war any different?" I inquire.

"Yes, they were," Mr. Sang nods. "During the war, we wrote about heroes and about the coming victory. Afterwards, we mostly wrote about the pain caused by the war."

In a collection of short stories I had seen examples of war stories, supercharged with emotions and inflammatory language. There is no room for despair and no sacrifice is too great to achieve the glorious goal on the horizon. Exaggerated, inflated prose. But then, moderation never won a war.

When I ask Mr. Sang if he still enjoys reading that type of writing with pleasure, he replies: "Of course it doesn't represent all that life has to offer. These days people want to forget the war and read about love. But I don't have much time for writing now. I've passed the torch to the younger generation. Mr. Thuc is a young writer whom I greatly admire."

I get the feeling that Mr. Sang is trying to change the subject. Of course we could comment at great length on Mr. Thuc's talents, and that would fit in nicely with the atmosphere of politeness that reigns at this food-laden table. But I ignore the hint, since I'm curious as to what Mr. Sang's views might actually be. I press on.

"So every period in history has its own style?"

"Yes," Mr. Sang answers, somewhat curtly. "Every situation requires a certain type of literature."

"And in looking back, is any of it of lasting value?" The obliging smile has been wiped off the interpreter-daughter's face.

"What was necessary then doesn't have to be so now," Mr. Sang avers.

"So no book in Vietnamese literature is of lasting value?"

"Oh no," Mr. Sang retorts. "There's one book that continues to influence us, in times of war or peace. That book is as important to us as the Bible is for you. I'm referring to the masterpiece, *The Tale of Kieu*, written in the middle of the last century by the incomparable Nguyen Du."

Mr. Sang's voice takes on a tone of respect. *The Tale of Kieu* is a wonderful story about a beautiful and intelligent girl named Kieu who, under normal circumstances, would have married the boy next door. But fate decides otherwise. When her family finds itself in financial straits, she is married off to a pimp. She spends years working in a "green house" until she meets a man who idolizes her. He buys her and makes her his concubine, but his jealous wife takes revenge by treating poor Kieu like a slave.

The plot takes several turns, and Kieu finally winds up in another brothel. Interestingly enough, she remains the heroine of the tale, even as a "fallen woman." No Confucian admonitions are forthcoming; we all know that Kieu's soul remains as pure as the driven snow.

Once again, she meets a customer, a wild adventurer, who falls madly in love with her and wants to marry her. He and his rebel army conquer a large territory. He then proclaims himself king and Kieu queen, and sees to it that anyone who has ever harmed his beloved wife is punished. After he dies, Kieu returns to her family and to the love of her youth, who has faithfully waited for her all these years. They live happily ever after, even though Kieu insists, given her tainted past, that she "doesn't think it necessary that we share the same blanket or the same pillow."

Gravely, Mr. Sang states: "If we Vietnamese have problems, we open *The Tale of Kieu* at random, and view what is written on that page as our horoscope." His daughter nods; she does it too.

Amazing, I think, that someone raised on Marx and Lenin should attach so much importance to the randomly opened page of a book. Still, I find it touching that a whole society could view life as a novel and see itself as the characters.

This time Mr. Sang has managed to steer the conversation into safer waters. Anyway, I no longer feel the urge to pose thorny questions like: Why didn't you rebel against the authoritarian character of the Communist Party? Or: Why did you stand by and watch the country being brought to economic ruin? I have the feeling I would be overstepping my bounds, and I don't know how Mr. Sang would react. Just what is the extent of his power? For example, can he urge the Immigration Police to deport me because I ask impertinent questions? With that long comment tacked on to my visa, my presence here is already hanging in the balance.

Besides, what right do I have to call him to task? I wasn't faced with the choices the Vietnamese were. Mr. Sang strikes me as a man of integrity. He hasn't been tempted into corruption as so many of his colleagues have. At least he possesses that kind of courage.

In the meantime, the conversation has turned to more recent events. In 1989, much to his great surprise, Mr. Sang was invited, as chairman of the Writers' Union, to visit the United States. "A group of Vietnam veterans invited me to come and paid for my entire trip."

Mr. Sang went to see the country he had fought against for so many years. He wasn't so ignorant that he thought all Americans were monsters. Still, he hadn't expected his hosts to be admirers of Ho Chi Minh, and yet they were. "Ho's portrait was hanging in the house where I stayed, occupying the most important place in the room."

"In the U.S.?" I ask dumbfounded.

"In Boston," Mr. Sang corrects me.

As for his other impressions, he keeps it short: "It's just like it is here. Some people are good and some people are bad."

"Were you able to talk to your brother?" I ask.

Mr. Sang looks past me as he says, "Unfortunately, I didn't have his telephone number with me."

With respect to the future of Vietnam, Mr. Sang still sees the light at the end of the tunnel: the new era of openness will ensure the country's development. And if that takes longer than hoped, there's no need to worry. "Whatever isn't achieved in my lifetime," he intones, "will come to pass during the lifetime of my children." And so the history of Vietnam will ultimately have a happy ending.

We eat the last of the egg rolls and drink the last of the beer. The daughter's cheeks are flushed from having to translate. As we say goodbye in the entryway, she translates, with her last ounce of energy, the final thought her father wishes to impart to me: "There's one important rule in warfare: He who knows himself and his enemy is invincible. That's why the Americans never should have occupied our country; they didn't know who we were."

Under the Wing of a Vietnamese Family

After years of traveling through China, there are only two inhabitants of that vast land I can call my friends. Chinese people rarely took me into their confidence. Things are different in Vietnam; here, people routinely invite me to their homes, take me out to eat, tell me stories and come visit me in my hotel.

One hot morning, I walk into one of the antique stores on Dong Khoi Street, which are packed with wares. Little did I know it was to be the beginning of a new friendship.

I let my eyes wander over a display case full of a popular Vietnamese souvenir: cigarette lighters formerly belonging to American soldiers. Identical Zippo lighters, engraved with a variety of dates and places. Kontum 66-67, or Long Binh 68-69. Etched on the backs were messages the owners must have considered good-luck charms. "You never really lived until you almost died," I read, along with "There is no gravity, the world sucks." A young woman rummages in a cupboard and produces more examples of soldierly doggerel. "Death is my business and business has been good."

The next one I pick up I've read before, in a book written by an American psychiatrist treating Vietnam veterans: "Though I walk through the valley of the shadow of death, I fear no evil, for I am the evilest son of a bitch in the valley." According to the psychiatrist, this symbolized the beast that the patients saw in themselves.

"Did these really belong to Americans?" I ask intrigued. "Why did they leave so many behind?"

The woman smiles shyly; her English isn't up to an explanation. She calls to an old man, barely visible in the semidarkness at the rear of the store. He steps forward, dressed simply in white underwear.

"Do you know how many Americans were stationed here?" he asks in fluent English. I have the impression that he's not merely after a sale, but that he wants to make a point, like a teacher. "Millions!" he continues. "And they all had a lighter. These have come from all over the country. All over the South, I mean. People find them, save them and sell them, and they eventually wind up here."

"Have the GIs, the owners of these lighters, all been killed?"

The old man pauses for a moment before replying: "Not necessarily." He adds, with a fleeting smile: "They also gave them to their girlfriends. Or if they were wounded and transported somewhere else, they lost their gear. And of course, sometimes the lighters were stolen." He throws his hands in the air as if to say: that's life.

The old man has an animated face. He speaks not only English, but also French. It seems he was once in Paris. "In the old days, under the old regime."

Even though the heat is at its worst at this time of day, it's bearable in the store, especially in the back where a collection of vases is displayed. The sun is filtered thousandfold by the leaves of a tree that towers protectively over the building. A ceiling fan churns round and round above our heads, and black chairs with an inlaid mother-of-pearl design look so invitingly cool that it's all I can do to keep from sitting down on one of them.

"Would you like a cup of tea?" the old man offers. He calls out a few words and before long someone comes shuffling up with a glass. "This store is owned by my family," he explains. All of his

UNDER THE WING OF A VIETNAMESE FAMILY

daughters and sons, except for the oldest one, work here. He points to where his sons are sitting behind a curtain repairing antiques. The term "repair" needs to be interpreted loosely in Saigon, since according to experts the antiques here are mostly fakes. The man follows my gaze as I direct a searching look at his vases, lamps and tea sets. He makes a gesture of resignation. "I have old antiques and new antiques," he confesses openly. "One person wants one thing, another wants something else." I laugh and suddenly realize that I like him.

He introduces me to his wife, the gray-haired woman sitting behind a tall desk, where she can keep an eye on the entire store. She nods. She's quite a bit younger than her husband, but a lot more serious. "She's the boss," he whispers. "She controls the cash register."

Next, he introduces himself. His name is Trang. I may guess how old he is.

"Sixty-five," I say, after a moment's thought.

"Seventy-five," he proudly chuckles.

"Since you're from Holland," he says in a conspiratorial tone while glancing at his wife, "I'd like to treat you to a Heineken." He issues an order, and one of his daughters reaches into a rumbling refrigerator and takes out two green beer cans. We take minute sips, as if we're drinking expensive wine.

"Doesn't taste bad today," Mr. Trang observes.

Behind us, a large crucifix is hanging in a prominent place in the store. Every time I look up, I catch sight of a pierced foot of Jesus.

"Various customers have offered me astronomical sums of money for that," says Mr. Trang, "but I'll never sell it. It's brought me good luck my entire life."

Mr. Trang is a Catholic. "I was born in Hanoi," he explains. "We came here in '54." Every Vietnamese knows what that means: that was the year the Geneva Agreement was signed, dividing Vietnam in two. At that time, Mr. and Mrs. Trang had eight children, and they jumped at the chance to emigrate to the South. "As a Catholic, I knew I couldn't expect much from the Communists," he says by way of clarification. The family boarded a ship and sailed to Saigon. "Together with this crucifix," laughs

Mr. Trang. His face has the gentle look of someone who is satisfied with his existence. "For whatever reason, the good Lord has always seen to it that I had everything I needed."

Mr. Trang's store quickly becomes one of my regular stops in Saigon. I drop in for a visit almost every day and drink a cup of tea with one of the daughters or a Heineken with Mr. Trang. If I want to buy something in Saigon, one of the daughters goes with me to do the negotiating since, as she indignantly explained, foreigners are always being cheated. Because Mrs. Trang is sure the city is teeming with thieves, she takes my traveler's checks into safekeeping.

"She hasn't lost anything in her entire life," Mr. Trang swears, "not so much as a button."

I enjoy the calm, old-fashioned atmosphere exuded by the family. Before the war, all Vietnamese families were probably like this, with the father as the undisputed head of the family, even though the mother makes the major decisions in league with the children. In all the history books about Vietnam, emphasis is placed on the role of the family. Anyone who ignores the importance of the family, we are repeatedly told, fails to understand the past. Nowadays many families have been torn apart and have been scattered all over the face of the globe. But here in this antique store, everything is the way it used to be, or at any rate that's what it seems like to me. Despite the store's handsome profits, they hardly live a life of luxury, with the possible exception of Mr. Trang's Heinekens.

"We're Northerners," explains Mr. Trang. "We're used to living frugally." He adds, darting a quick look around before continuing, "If people from Saigon earn ten thousand dong, they spend ten thousand dong, while we save at least half that amount."

The Trangs may be Northerners, but they're of the old school, from the pre-Communist era. Even though he's Catholic, Mr. Trang has a high regard for Confucian values. As for Mrs. Trang, though her family has lived in cosmopolitan Saigon since 1954, the Americans hardly made a dent in her value system: the entire neighborhood throbs to a disco beat, but her daughters — not one of whom is under twenty — are not allowed to go to a

UNDER THE WING OF A VIETNAMESE FAMILY

disco. They stay at home, without demur, and gracefully pour tea in my cup. The sons, working into the night, remind me of the old illustrations of Vietnamese students preparing for the Imperial Examination.

One day Mr. Trang invites me to join them for a day in the country. His brother and his wife, likewise born in Hanoi, are visiting from Paris and staying in a nearby hotel. "Today we're going to visit a beautiful sight," Mr. Trang promises. "We can drink our Heinekens while enjoying the view."

We set off on motor scooters, with the sons doing the driving and Mr. Trang, his wife, his brother and his sister-in-law in the passenger seats. Since even Mr. Trang doesn't have an infinite number of sons, I've hired a motorbike and driver. We race through the outskirts of Saigon, where it's crowded and dusty. Mrs. Trang, sitting side-saddle, is wearing a conical straw hat. We turn on to Vietnam's only four-lane highway, built by the Americans during the war. The divider in the middle forms a huge obstacle, since people are continuously having to lift their bikes, children and bags over it to cross to the other side. We turn off the highway and follow a dirt road under an archway. Ahead of us is an oasis of peace and quiet: a lake surrounded by a park. While we stroll over the well-maintained paths, Mr. Trang points out the various flowers which are in blossom. The sons rent boats shaped like swans and float out over the water. The rest of us follow their movements from a wooden table under the trees.

"And now it's time for a cool drink," announces Mr. Trang, opening a picnic basket and passing out the cans.

The shore is lined with rows of chairs, wider than normal and covered with a canopy. Mr. Trang explains their purpose in a whisper. "Young couples who don't want to be seen can rent one of those chairs." Now I understand why we're about the only guests this morning; the park receives most of its visitors after dark.

Mr. Trang and his brother don't look like each other. It's as if years of living in Paris have smoothed away the brother's Vietnamese features. "He's become a Frenchman," concurs Mr. Trang as we head towards the restaurant by the lake. His brother and sister-in-law live a quiet life in a Paris suburb. "A rather boring life," Mr. Trang can't resist adding. His brother is retired and his children have moved away from home. That's how people do things in the West. One son lives in Brittany, and the other on the Côte d'Azur. As a result, the parents are usually alone.

"They have a garden," says Mr. Trang. "I've seen pictures of it. Very orderly. I have to admit, they do a perfect job of maintaining the garden."

We gather around the table that has the best view of the park, and Mr. Trang beckons the waiter. The two of them confer at length, and Mr. Trang finally places his order. "We'll have lots of specialties," he promises us in the best of spirits.

We begin with two platters of crispy egg rolls, which are to be dipped in fresh spices and wrapped in lettuce leaves. There is also Chinese soup, French steak sliced in bite-sized pieces that can be picked up with chopsticks, and French fries. I'm not familiar with the last dish, a whitish blob with a strong flavor, like octopus.

"What is this?" I ask Mr. Trang.

"The uterus of a cow" is the answer. He places another piece in my bowl and, like a good host, turns his attention to his guests of honor.

"My brother's children have all turned out very well," he begins. "They're both educated, and one works for the post office while the other works in a hospital."

The sister-in-law is visibly flattered, but the brother humbly demurs: "One of our boys drinks like a fish."

"Oh it's not as bad as all that," his wife responds, piqued. "Besides, he earns good money."

"They're both very successful," Mr. Trang placatingly interjects.

Satisfied, the sister-in-law observes: "All over the world, Vietnamese are said to be hardworking and intelligent."

Mr. Trang sighs. His sons are seated on the other side of the table, talking to each other since they can't follow our conversation in French. Mr. Trang had grumbled to me once about their not having gotten much of an education. Since he had worked for an American company during the war, his children weren't allowed to go to college and were also excluded from government jobs.

Walking back to the parking lot after lunch, Mr. Trang expands on his regret at not being able to offer his sons a better education. But while the two of us are waiting for the rest of the group to catch up, his eyes regain their conspiratorial sparkle.

"My sister-in-law is from a good family. Her father is a professor. She's what you'd call the dominating type. In that respect, I'm very pleased with my wife's humble origins." And with a flourish, he seats himself on the motor scooter behind his son.

We head sedately home in a column. Suddenly, a child darts across the road in front of Mrs. Trang's motor scooter, which swerves in the direction of an oncoming vehicle. Just when I'm sure she's about to go flying through the air, the son surprisingly manages to get the scooter back on course. Mr. Trang, who has likewise observed the near-accident, merely looks like he's enjoying the wind blowing through his hair. "Don't worry," he shouts in my direction, "anyone who lives in Saigon has to be an acrobat."

One evening, when the rain is gushing through the downspouts, Mr. Trang and I are sitting in the middle of his store, surrounded by dusty antiques. Because of the tropical storm, there's a power failure, and the city has been plunged into unfathomable darkness.

"Oh well," Mr. Trang sighs in resignation, "there's always something. During the dry season they complain that there's no electricity because the reservoir is empty, and when it rains everything breaks down and we also wind up sitting in the dark."

Mr. Trang has lighted candles here and there, and in the flickering light I notice a bust of a thin man with a wispy goatee that I'd never seen before. "Ho Chi Minh?" I inquire.

Mr. Trang nods. "I met him once. At one time I was even in his service." Noticing my look of amazement and curiosity, he shifts into a comfortable position and launches into his story.

"In 1945, I was working for the French as a bookkeeper in the palace in Hanoi." He pauses momentarily to refresh his memory. "I wore a good suit. Every day I had to look neat and tidy."

It was a strange time. During World War II, Vietnam was occupied by the Japanese, but governed by the Vichy French. After the capitulation, while Mr. Trang was still conscientiously keeping his books, there was a power vacuum. Ho Chi Minh made a brief bid for power.

"We heard that the Viet Minh Army was approaching Hanoi and we knew that Ho Chi Minh would be arriving at our government building at a certain time. As a sign of respect, all of the government workers were lined up outside the building to greet him, arranged in order of importance. The highest-ranking official was closest to the door, while the lowest-ranking one — that was me — was at the end of the line. Ho Chi Minh came driving up in a car. He stopped, got out of the car and began shaking hands at the wrong end of the line, so that I was the first one to greet him." Mr. Trang laughs with pride; it was a moment of great honor.

A voice calls out something through the darkness. Mr. Trang answers, turns to me and says: "My dinner is going to be served any moment. I've asked them to set an extra place."

As head of the family, Mr. Trang usually dines alone. His wife and two daughters shuffle towards us. They set the table, dish up some rice and cover it with meat and vegetables. They give me an amiable smile. "Eat, eat," they motion me.

"You have a good life," I say to Mr. Trang, and he nods.

"My wife is always thinking of my welfare. The only thing we're missing now are a couple of Heinekens." And before long, they too have arrived.

"What happened next in the palace?" I ask, wanting to hear more about the legendary Ho Chi Minh.

Between bites, Mr. Trang continues his story: "I knew that as a Catholic I wouldn't be acceptable to Ho Chi Minh, but I didn't dare turn in my resignation or simply stay at home." So he kept on punctually showing up for work. "And the last month, I also shared a room with Vietnam's last emperor, Bao Dai."

Mr. Trang notes with satisfaction that I'm very impressed by this revelation. He explains the situation: Bao Dai had collaborated with the Japanese. Therefore, in a face-saving maneuver, the emperor was offered a job as a government adviser after the war.

"But there wasn't any work for him to do," Mr. Trang recalls. "Nor did he have an office. They didn't even have a desk for him. All day long, he sat on a chair across from me, on the other side of the room."

"And what did you talk about?" I inquire breathlessly.

UNDER THE WING OF A VIETNAMESE FAMILY

Mr. Trang shoots me a reproachful look. "I was merely an assistant bookkeeper. How could I initiate a conversation with the emperor?"

I gather that Mr. Trang's civil service career didn't exactly end with a bang. One morning, he simply stayed home, hoping no one would order him to show up. For years afterwards, he earned his living giving private lessons. One of his students was the woman he later married. "She wasn't my best pupil. It wouldn't be an exaggeration to say she was the worst, but she's an excellent wife," Mr. Trang philosophizes while chewing his food with audible satisfaction.

Then came the day he and his family and the crucifix boarded the ship that would take them to the South. "If you ask me," remarks Mr. Trang, "everything in life is predestined. Up there," he concludes, pointing towards the ceiling.

The streets are quiet tonight. Because of the rain, nearly everyone has stayed home. I walk back to my hotel, skirting around the dark puddles. Even the beggars have called a temporary halt to their activities and are stretched out in doorways. A young child extricates himself from a dark shadow and clings to one of my legs. "Madam," he begs while letting himself be dragged along, light as a feather. "Madam, dollar, dollar."

The next day, as I enter the store Mr. Trang is engaged in serious conversation with a customer. A Frenchman, I judge by the accent. And one who lives in Hanoi, I conclude by eavesdropping. They're bargaining over a crystal chandelier, which according to Mr. Trang was made in Czechoslovakia and probably once graced a French villa. I inspect inlaid lacquer boxes until they conclude their deal.

Mr. Trang's face lights up when I inform him that I've come to replenish his supply of Heinekens. Taking his customary seat, he sighs: "It's too bad I gave up smoking, as otherwise I could have lit up a cigar right now."

That reminds him of an event that happened years ago when he was a photographer.

"A photographer?" I exclaim. "Have you also been a photographer?" It sometimes seems as if the Vietnamese have nine lives, like cats.

As it turns out, after the boat trip that brought him from North to South, Mr. Trang became the South Vietnamese government's official photographer. "I followed President Diem wherever he went. And of course I was on hand to record all official receptions."

This was how he got to meet Lyndon B. Johnson, then Vice-President of the United States, when he came to Vietnam. He also photographed Prince Sihanouk of Cambodia. But his favorite head of state during that period was President García of the Philippines. "He gave me a fat cigar, as big as your thigh."

"And," Mr. Trang recalls with a note of vexation, "I was frequently obliged to photograph Madame Nhu." Interestingly enough, Vietnam's First Lady was not married to the President; Diem was a bachelor. Instead, she was married to his brother. Madame Nhu was reputed to be an avid schemer.

"I have observed her through the lens of my camera on many an occasion," remarks Mr. Trang with a knowing air, "and I can assure you that she wasn't as beautiful as she was said to be."

"May I take a look at your photographs sometime? Do you still have them?"

"Oh no, oh no. I burned them all. In 1975 I got a good fire going, and I made sure all of my photographs, negatives, books and papers went up in smoke."

One hot morning Mr. Trang invites me out for breakfast. We head for the restaurant on his motor scooter. "I don't like driving slowly," he shouts over his shoulder, and we zigzag through the traffic at forty miles an hour.

"Look," says Mr. Trang, putting the motor scooter on its kickstand, "this isn't exactly a classy restaurant. But the service and the soup are the best in the city. And believe me, I've done exhaustive research."

A steaming bowl of chicken and noodles is placed before me. On the table are bowls of fresh mint, coriander and bean sprouts, which you can add to the soup if you like.

Still recovering from the drive over here, I conjecture: "Traffic accidents must really take their toll in Saigon."

"Not at all," cries Mr. Trang, dismissing my anxiety-ridden

reflections. "Nothing has ever happened to me." He pauses for a moment, apparently pondering all the dangers he's been through, because he continues: "One day in 1973 I did have a close brush with death."

At the time, Mr. Trang was working for a New York news agency. One day he was out on a story with an American journalist and a Vietnamese driver. They were driving around in the vicinity of the 17th Parallel, the border between North and South Vietnam.

"Then we heard that there was a squad of Viet Cong about twenty miles ahead of us." Mr. Trang, it would seem, preferred to keep his distance, but the American wanted to get close to the action.

"Late in the afternoon, we got stuck in the middle of a deeply rutted path. That means . . ." Mr. Trang's eyes open wide at this point in the story, "that it would soon be dark." The three men were unable to get the car going. Mr. Trang and the driver were beginning to panic, but the American seemed pleased. "He was hoping the Viet Cong would capture us during the night," Mr. Trang exclaims indignantly. "They'd give him some information and then release him, and he'd have a great news story. You can just picture the headline, can't you? *A night with the Viet Cong.*"

I nod. I would have been seventeen at the time, and a story like that would have interested me greatly. But Mr. Trang was well aware that he and the driver wouldn't have gotten off so lightly. He would have been forced to confess that he was a Catholic who'd left the North. He threw his hands in the air: "They would have killed me."

After sitting around for an hour, a passerby offered to tow the car out of the rut. "For five dollars," adds Mr. Trang in great agitation. "Five dollars, and the American refused to pay." So Mr. Trang forked over the money himself, for which the American never forgave him. But Mr. Trang is not the only one capable of carrying a grudge: "He didn't think twice about sacrificing me for a good story," he concludes highly incensed.

Sometimes I wonder if Mr. Trang carefully selects his stories, dividing them into those he's willing to tell me and those he wants to keep to himself. Since he's asked me not to mention his name to anyone, I can't verify the stories. "In this country, it's always better if you don't use names," he explained.

But I still don't get it. Were there things I wasn't supposed to know? Is he being held under surveillance?

I try to imagine Mr. Trang twenty years ago, as a photographer. He must have been youthful and charming in those days, since he still is. At that time, he lived in a fifteen-room house and owned his own car. His numerous children had their every want attended to, since their father was swimming in money. Or at any rate until 1975, when the curtain fell.

Having finished my soup, I ask: "Why didn't you go to the States?"

"I'll tell you that story another time," says Mr. Trang, wiping his mouth with a napkin he had brought from home, "over a couple of Heinekens. I've got to get back to the store now, or my wife will be furious."

That evening I go to Rhythm and Booze, alone. I want to chat with the owner who, like Mr. Trang, was a photographer during the war. The rooftop patio is closed because of the rain. It's still early; the hostesses are sitting at the bar, watching video clips.

Mr. Vuong, they point in answer to my query, is in his office. I find him sitting motionlessly behind a desk. Though I've met him before, I'm again surprised by his air of serenity. He's a devout Buddhist, that I know. He greets me with a calm smile.

"Some time ago you told me you had a file with pictures of the war." He nods.

"May I have a look at it?" I'd like to be able to tell him hello from Mr. Trang, but I keep my promise not to mention his name.

I take the album with me to the bar and, with rock music blasting away in my ears, open it up. The very first picture is the one by Nick Ut of the naked girl burned by napalm, running down the road screaming. It's as horrifying as ever. After that, there are a couple of pictures of soldiers shooting guns and of mutilated bodies that mean very little to me since I haven't seen them before. I feel a shock of recognition at the next one: a thin Vietnamese with his hands tied behind his back, being shot through the head at point-blank range by a South Vietnamese general. The man who pulled the trigger became a symbol of evil. These days, I read in an American magazine, he owns a gas station in the American South.

One of the girls looks over my shoulder. "War, always war," she says and makes a face.

The next part of the album is a chronological record of the fall of South Vietnam. To begin with, the city of Hue, near the 17th Parallel, is being captured by the North Vietnamese Army. A column of cars is winding its way over the mountain road to Danang. A steady stream of cars and buses, filled to overflowing, is taking the beautiful route that Mark, the American GI, remembers with such fondness. In Danang, the myriad refugees are trying to board American naval vessels. Hordes of them are crowding the decks, while motor scooters and motorbikes dangle from ropes thrown over the railings. Then Saigon falls, and the pictures show the dramatic images of the storming of the American Embassy: people trying to climb over the gates and being beaten back by the Marine guards. A heavily laden helicopter is ready to take off, except that the door won't shut because yet another Vietnamese is trying to squeeze himself inside. An American fist slugs the man full in the face.

Mr. Vuong has come to stand beside me. "The war," I sigh. "It still isn't really over."

He nods. "We Vietnamese are always suffering. That is our fate."

"But why?" I ask.

He mulls over his reply: "We're being punished, for driving the Chams from their land, for trying to wipe them out. Their spirits will continue to haunt us."

A noisy group of men I've seen before enter the bar: U.N. soldiers stationed in Cambodia. Mr. Vuong excuses himself to attend to his new customers.

I buy a few cans of Heineken and walk to the antique store.

"Cyclo, Madam, cyclo," shouts a shabby-looking man pedaling alongside me. When I take no notice of him, he hurls an epithet at me: *"Lien Xo,"* Russian, the greatest insult a foreigner can have in Saigon.

Mr. Trang is dining on roast quail as I enter the store. "They take good care of me," he says by way of apology. Business has been good today: a Korean bought three porcelain vases. "Asians don't even take the trouble to bargain with you. That's how rich they are."

His daughters are upstairs, and his wife is puttering around in the back, in the kitchen. As she speaks a little French and doesn't want her husband to talk too much about the past, I ask him in English: "What about the fall of Saigon, Mr. Trang. What happened after that?"

"Well," he begins, weighing his words carefully, "the South Vietnamese government had already officially resigned. Naturally we knew that the North Vietnamese Army was on its way. It was said that they would reach Saigon at a certain time, I think at twelve o'clock. At eleven thirty, the Vietnamese journalist I usually worked with plunked his Viet Cong membership card down on the table. I didn't have the slightest idea that he'd been playing a double game all those years."

"What did you say?" I ask shocked.

Mr. Trang laughs. "I congratulated him and said that I hoped we'd become even better friends in the future. What else could I do?"

It wasn't a solution I had thought of. "Didn't you want to escape to the U.S.?"

Mr. Trang glances apprehensively in the direction of the kitchen. "I had all the papers ready. American visas for the entire family. But . . ." he pauses for a moment and then bends closer to my ear. "My wife didn't want to go there without any money. 'How can we live without money?' she kept asking."

Hardly a superfluous question, of course. In the midst of all the chaos, Mr. Trang sold their house, the two stores they owned and their car. All these transactions took time. "And then it was too late," says Mr. Trang with his hands raised in a dramatic gesture. "The borders were closed, and the last planes had already taken off."

"Then you were left with nothing," I sympathize. "No job and no house."

Mr. Trang whispers: "But I was wearing a money belt with three hundred taels of gold in it." While I'm still trying to figure out how much money that is, Mr. Trang explains helpfully,

"These days one tael is worth four hundred and fifty dollars." That works out to a hundred and thirty-five thousand dollars!

"A fortune!" I acknowledge in amazement. "How on earth did you dare walk around with so much money on you?"

Mr. Trang laughs. "I had to be very careful."

The family moved into a hotel, the hotel I'm currently staying at, and bided their time. As soon as they could, they bought another house, the building that would later become the antique store. For years, Mr. Trang was without work. The family lived off their hoard, as did many in the South after the war. Since staying inside for long periods of time made him restless, he spent his days strolling around the city and observing the upheaval. A lot of people had left, and everyone was trying to sell their possessions so they could have some cash. "Besides," Mr. Trang explains, "they thought that owning foreign goods might get them into trouble."

Mr. Trang bought the most unusual assortment of goods at bargain prices. Every day, he came home with his arms loaded. His wife and children tucked away his finds until they ran out of space. They worried about his insatiable need to collect more and more, but he didn't let that stop him. "It was just something I liked doing," he explains. If he were living in the West, he'd probably say: "It was good therapy."

Mr. Trang's strange behavior was not lost on the new authorities. "A secret agent tailed me all day long." But Mr. Trang wasn't perturbed. On the contrary, he asked the guy to carry his purchases. "'As long as you're here,' I told him, 'make yourself useful.'"

The police came to his house to interrogate him. "'I'm not doing anything illegal,' I explained. 'In fact, I'm cleaning up the city.'" Even the Viet Cong had no reply to that.

"Weren't you ever sent to a re-education camp?"

"No," replies Mr. Trang, casting a glance at the crucifix. "Someone has been watching over me my entire life."

Since he had moved right after the fall of Saigon, there were no neighbors who could heap accusations on him. Here, he was unknown. Besides, the district he moved to, District 1, was one of the most tolerant. But he only discovered that later, after years of uncertainty, with the threat of punishment hanging over his head. "If I'd known in advance that I wouldn't have had to go to jail, I wouldn't have made plans to leave. I love Saigon. I didn't want to go to the U.S."

Things are different for his children. "They might have had a better life there. But we didn't make it. We were too late."

His wife sweeps demonstratively under our table. There's been enough talk, she thinks. Tomorrow the store has to open early, as it does every day. But Mr. Trang ignores her.

"For years after the war we hardly had any contact with anyone else. Nowadays I talk to foreigners from time to time, since they don't live here. They'll be leaving. The situation has gotten better since 1990, that's true. But still, the neighbor you're having such a nice chat with might have been ordered to spy on you. You never know what kind of pressure people are under. Outside of my family, there isn't one Vietnamese I trust, not one."

Mr. Trang and I have known each other for about a month when I decide to call in his help. I have a problem I'd rather not discuss with a man, but I dare to take Mr. Trang into my confidence.

It's still early in the morning and one of the daughters is sweeping the store when I pose my question: "Mr. Trang, I'm having trouble with a strange kind of pain in my stomach. Can your wife or one of your daughters recommend a gynecologist I can go to?"

Startled, he consults with Lan, the middle daughter. She'll take me to a gynecologist on her motor scooter, he promises. But we have to wait until four-thirty, since that's when the doctor finishes her job in the hospital and begins her private practice.

The waiting room is full when we arrive. The women look either pale or jaundiced. One of them asks faintly where I come from and then returns to contemplating her own problems. A girl and a young man are sitting in the corner. Racked with pain, she lays her head on his shoulder.

I shudder. When it comes to illness, I'm no hero. The moment I feel something the slightest bit out of the ordinary, I imagine the worst. Once I was hospitalized for an ulcer that never materialized. Not long after that some poor cardiologist had to be disturbed on a weekend because I had all the symptoms of a heart attack. More than once I've been convinced that viruses were ravaging my body, and yet time and again I turned out to be in perfect health. All I had was a bad case of nerves.

When it's my turn to be put in the examining room, I note that there are already two women ahead of me. While the secretary writes down my name, the second patient is waiting on a chair and the third is lying on a table behind a curtain. It looks like a factory, and yet Lan had assured me that the treatment here was better than anywhere else.

The gynecologist speaks a little French. As she removes her latex gloves, she says: "There may be a small tumor. It would be better to have an ultra-sound scan made at the hospital."

She writes out a referral, and the secretary hurries us out the door. Benumbed with fear, I climb on the motor scooter behind Lan.

The next morning she drives me with great caution to the hospital. There are more than a hundred women in the waiting room, and they look even worse than the women waiting yesterday at the doctor's office. Most of them are in the last months of pregnancy. Even so, they're thin, with sunken cheeks. Sitting upright on the hard benches takes all the effort they can muster. Still, they don't complain. They sit in silence, though one or two summon enough energy to give me a friendly smile.

"You need to drink a lot of liquids," Lan says to encourage me, "since otherwise the scan doesn't work properly." As there are women sitting here every day waiting for the same test, a lot of liquids are being drunk in this room. Vendors have therefore installed themselves outside the hospital. They pour some watery lemonade into a plastic bag, add a straw and pass it through the barred window.

Entering the examining room, I see that there are already ten patients lined up in a row ahead of me. Like them, we take a seat against the wall and watch the others being examined. Everyone talks softly. It looks like some kind of magic act is being performed. A woman's stomach is modestly laid bare and then smeared with a gel. Next, a woman in a surgical mask moves a piece of equipment back and forth over the patient's stomach. It emits inaudible sounds, and the results can be read out on a monitor.

When it's my turn, Lan and the other women murmur encouragement. This doctor also seems to speak some French. Intently watching the screen above her white mask, she remarks: "There's nothing unusual, nothing at all."

But then what's the matter with me? That evening I decide to call the insurance company in Holland that handles my medical insurance and promises to be on call 24 hours a day to deal with emergencies occurring abroad. "Do you know what time it is here?" inquires a disembodied voice on the other end of the crackling line. After hearing my story, the voice hands down a decision: "I can't okay anything until I've discussed this with one of the doctors who's treating you."

I hadn't thought to get phone numbers. The gynecologist didn't have a phone, I was sure of that. I did see a phone in the hospital, on a table in some office, but how could I be sure the doctor from the ultra-sound department could be reached via that phone?

"In that case, the best thing for you to do is to go to a five-star hotel," the insurance lady resolutely advises. "They're sure to have an English-speaking doctor we can talk to."

Saigon's only five-star hotel floats on the Saigon River —it's actually a boat. Until a few years ago, this ship plied Australia's Great Barrier Reef. The vessel was towed to Vietnam when it appeared that Saigon was in dire need of first-class accommodations.

Dr. Kiet's office is on the quarterdeck. As I explain the situation, he frowns in concentration. He's prepared to examine me, it seems, but does not have the authority to confer with anyone overseas. "After all, you're not a guest in this hotel," he points out.

He's right. But neither am I planning to become one, since a room costs two hundred and seventy-five dollars a day. It doesn't really make sense to me. What does one little phone call matter? Or is there another reason for his reluctance? I agree to his proposition in the hope that he'll answer anyway if my insurance company does call.

His diagnosis is swift: "You have an infection. Fortunately the best French medicines are available here." And he proceeds to fill a syringe with antibiotics.

An hour later, sitting in my hotel room, I have the feeling the walls might come crashing in on me. I need space, I conclude. And fresh air. Since the top floor of the Rex Hotel has a pleasant roof garden with a magnificent view, I decide to walk over there. On the way, I notice that my legs don't seem to be moving the way they should be and that the huge crown above the hotel entrance keeps floating further and further away. After what seems an eternity, the elevator brings me to the top floor. I realize right away that coming here wasn't a good idea. Even though my chair isn't anywhere near the edge, I'm seized with fear at the terrifying height.

What should I do? Maybe I really do have cancer, like a friend of mine who got sick in a faraway, destitute country. I decide to go visit the Trang family and walk back to Dong Khoi Street, worrying the whole way.

In the antique store everyone is, as usual, quietly going about their business. Lan inquires kindly how I'm feeling and gives me a cup of tea. "No worry," she says softly. She shows me a letter with an American stamp. It's from her brother, who lives in Dallas. From the pictures he's sent I can see that he looks like Mr. Trang.

"Four years ago," Lan explains, in halting English. "In a boat." After being shuffled from place to place, he finally arrived in the U.S. Not long afterwards, he married a beautiful Vietnamese who had lived in Texas for a long time. Soon his wife gave birth to twins, which accounted for most of the snapshots. In that short amount of time, he had also managed to get a degree in accounting and to find a job.

"Well," I say, impressed. "Your brother is certainly a man who can move mountains."

"He's lucky," she replies modestly. "Just lucky."

The next day I go to the floating hotel for another shot, but decide to forego the call to Holland. I can't bring myself to saddle the unsuspecting Dr. Kiet with the steely insurance lady.

The day after the third injection, I wake up and look around me in surprise. The nagging pain has disappeared! Was there nothing the matter with me in the first place, or did the infection clear up thanks to Dr. Kiet's diagnostic skills? A little while later, while I'm making my way down Don Khoi Street, a horrible thought enters my head: maybe it'll come back. No, I decide. It's over. I quicken my step and resolve to go on a trip. To the mountains. To Dalat.

"Cyclo, Madam, cyclo," rasps a voice beside me. I rummage in my bag until I find the address of the travel agency where Tuyet had had my visa extended. Since I can't leave Saigon without a travel permit, the first item on my agenda is to get a permit.

The cyclo driver drops me off near the Notre Dame Cathedral, tilting the cyclo to make it easier for me to clamber out. The owner of the travel agency sighs as she examines my papers; she remembers me and my case. Her hair is done up in a traditional hairstyle and she has a kindly face.

Clacking her tongue, she studies the wretched note appended by the Immigration Police. She promises to call one of her contacts and reaches for the phone. Just then, two men with a tool chest come in, and she jumps up in alarm. The men waste no time but start measuring all the doors and windows in the office.

"They're Chinese carpenters," she explains. "They have a very special knowledge of these matters." She whispers: "There's something wrong with this office. Business is good, and yet I can't seem to save any money. I spend every penny I earn."

The men bend over a mysterious-looking piece of paper and then point excitedly to the doorway between the office and the living room. It seems the proportions are wrong, and that's the source of the trouble. According to the piece of paper, the door's present width leads to waste and financial loss. That means the door will have to be changed. Nodding her approval, the travel agent watches as the men go at the door with sledgehammers. In between blows, she promises to arrange a travel permit for me, but points out that in ten days, when my visa expires, there'll be nothing more she can do for me.

"You can clearly read the word *sortie*," she says with furrowed brow. "And that *exit* is an order. There's no way we can get around it."

She watches me expectantly. She doesn't like being the bearer of bad tidings. According to Tuyet, her agency is very successful, and yet her eyes are so sad. Her son and daughter live in the U.S. Might that be the reason?

"Are your children overseas doing all right?" I ask.

She nods. "They're doing very well. They've graduated and have already found jobs."

"Were they boat refugees?"

The woman shakes her head: "No, they left in a plane, one of the last."

"In '75?" I ask, surprised. "They must have been very young." She's in her early forties.

She nods. So that's her sorrow. "They went with one of my aunts. They were six and seven years old at the time. My husband and I were going to follow two days later, since we still had a couple of things to arrange. And then it was too late." She sighs, and her normally busy hands are lying idly on the table. "I saw them for the first time last year. My children are all grown up." Tears slide down her cheeks. "It wouldn't have been so bad if my aunt had taken good care of them," she explains between sniffles, as if she feels the need to defend herself. But that wasn't the case.

"My aunt. Well, that's a long story." Her children were passed around from one person to another. They had a very difficult time. "I knew about it," she says, and the memory torments her still, "but I couldn't go to them. I sat here like a prisoner, with no way out."

In the meantime, the carpenters haven't noticed a thing; they haven't looked up from their work even once, but have kept on ripping out the unlucky door and chucking the debris outside.

"Still, they've turned out all right," I remark, taking her hand in mine to comfort her. She smiles — she's got herself under control again.

"If only they marry soon," she concludes. A Vietnamese mother continues to bear responsibility for her unmarried children, regardless of their age.

"And the outside door?" I ask in an attempt to change the subject. "Is it also going to be torn out?"

"No, no," she exclaims, startled. "That door brings good luck."

As I walk into my hotel, the desk clerk and the doorman look at me and then whisper something to each other. "Are you really a tourist?" asks the desk clerk. She's already asked me that a dozen times. Has she been ordered to report on my activities? She's certainly in a position to know exactly what I'm up to, provided the cyclo drivers outside the hotel who drive me around keep her informed of my movements.

Walking to the antique store, I decide not to trouble Mr. Trang with either my visa problems or my suspicions that I'm being followed. He's already done enough for me, and I don't want him to be sorry he ever met me.

As usual, the family is going about its business. Lan informs me that her father is taking a bath and gives me a cup of tea. The letter from the U.S. is still lying on the table. I ask her if I can take another look at the snapshots. I'm fascinated by the son in the New World. I'm surprised at the abstract decors in which he poses himself, his wife and their two little children. There's one of them on a bench in a brand-new shopping mall. There's not a soul in sight. Just plastic palm trees and a fake horse that jiggles up and down when you throw in a coin. The next one shows their newly built tract home. The streets are deserted and none of the lawns have been planted yet. In another snapshot, he's sitting in his car with a grave expression on his face. The last one shows him in front of a tall office building, totally devoid of people. It's as if he's created the world in which he lives with his own two hands. Having landed in a barren wasteland, far from Vietnam, he scooped up a handful of clay and molded it by the sweat of his own brow into a house, an office, a shopping mall and a car.

Mr. Trang makes his appearance. His hair is wet, and he's clad simply in his white underwear. He looks at the pictures over my shoulder. "He made thirteen escape attempts," he chortles, as if it's a joking matter. "He made it on the fourteenth try." He falls silent for a moment. "He's the only one of my children who wanted to leave, the only one who's got any ambition. There was no stopping him, so I didn't even try. Besides, who's to say what the right decision is in this case?"

Mr. Trang paid for all the escape attempts. Sometimes they cost a thousand dollars, but they usually cost more. "I gave him a total of twenty-five thousand dollars." Mr. Trang laughs. It's only money, is his philosophy.

"In those years he was constantly in and out of jail. He was sent to Vung Tau, in the Mekong Delta. Every time we received notice, his mother went and brought him food." But the moment he was released, he went out looking for another chance. "Like most people, we agreed on a sign. For example, if he sent a picture of a woman we didn't know, it meant someone had double-crossed him. When we got a snapshot of our youngest daughter, we knew he'd made it."

It was not a journey blessed with good fortune. They ran into pirates from Thailand, who stripped everyone on board of their money, gold and jewelry. They searched every nook and cranny. Then they led all the women away, raped them and brought them back to the men. After they left, the ship drifted around aimlessly with a broken engine and no fuel.

The next morning, they saw another ship approaching. "More pirates," says Mr. Trang, shaking his head. "Once again, the pirates searched through the entire boat, and were furious when they couldn't find anything. Fortunately, they were finally willing to believe that others had beat them to it. Then they too raped all the women." A few days later, Thailand's Coast Guard found the ship and towed it to a harbor.

"What a nightmare!" I exclaim.

Mr. Trang sweeps a piece of fuzz from the table with his hand. "*C'est la vie*," he says matter-of-factly.

On Sunday morning I report to the store. The steel shutter is still closed, but Mr. Trang has invited me to accompany him to the tennis court today. "I'll introduce you to all my friends," he promises, speeding along on his motor scooter. Mr. Trang only sees his friends during their weekly tennis match. "It's better that way," he explains. They prefer to attract as little attention as possible.

We follow the banks of the river and then make a turn. Mr. Trang drives onto the grounds of an old-fashioned schoolhouse. Someone has strewn a flamboyant carpet of red flowers in the middle of the playground. Behind that is a mottled grass court, consisting mostly of bare patches. Mr. Trang doesn't notice; he's ready for a game of tennis. Rubbing his hands in impatient glee, he waits for the other players to arrive.

"There's Chinh," he calls as a young man comes walking over

the playground. Chinh is Vietnamese but grew up in the States. Currently living in Saigon, Chinh is in the business of exporting frozen fish.

A cyclo deposits an older woman by the gate. "Madame Lan," announces Mr. Trang in a tone of respect. Once upon a time she studied chemistry at the Sorbonne, and she now runs a little embroidery shop. She draws a pink dragon fruit from her bag and presents everyone with a piece.

The next to arrive is Mr. Du, who starts shouting greetings at everyone from a long way off. "Hello, hello. Have we got company today?" Mr. Du walks with a strange gait and talks in an incredibly loud voice.

"Mr. Du used to be one of the richest men in Saigon," Mr. Trang says by way of introduction. "He used to own a couple of factories, twenty stores and god knows how many apartment houses. How much money did they confiscate, Du?"

"Oh," Mr. Du says with a nonchalant wave of his hand. "What does it matter? Fifty million dollars? A hundred million?"

Mr. Du was arrested in 1975 and spent fourteen years in jail. "I had everything arranged. I had a visa for the U.S. But my mother didn't want to go." So Du stayed.

"Every day I was in prison it was work, work, work. There was very little food and I kept having to confess everything all over again. I must have written the same confessions hundreds of times."

Mr. Trang and the fish exporter hit a ball back and forth over the net, which is drooping between the posts.

"Let me show you something," says Mr. Du and awkwardly rolls down his socks. "These scars around my ankles are from the leg irons they chained me up with. They used to tie your feet crosswise in back of you. That stops the blood circulation, and you faint."

He must have gone a little deaf, since he talks so loudly. "I've got a passport again," he trumpets. "I can start traveling again if I want to." He reaches into his breast pocket and pulls out the document. Born in 1941, I read. That's funny. The man from the Musicians' Union had predicted I'd meet someone born in that year. I look at Mr. Du in surprise.

"Are they still making problems for you?" I ask. "Are you still being kept under surveillance?"

Mr. Du shakes his head decidedly from side to side. "No, Charlie hasn't got time for that anymore. These days, Charlie's out chasing after the dollar." He laughs loudly.

The last player approaches the tennis court. Thomas, as he's called, isn't Vietnamese, but German. "From *East* Germany," Mr. Du adds by way of clarification. Mr. Trang trots up to say hello. It seems that Thomas used to work for the East German government. He was their Vietnam expert, as he speaks the language fluently. After the German reunification, he found himself without a job. But before long, a British company wanting to do business in Saigon hired him because they needed someone who knew the language.

Mr. Trang translates the conversation for me, since they've switched to Vietnamese. "Thomas has discovered a Russian radio station that broadcasts in Vietnamese. They keep talking about glasnost and democracy." Everyone laughs, including Chinh, the American.

But it's Mr. Du who savors the irony the most. Calling out over the court in his rasping voice, he concludes: "Our friends the Russians are knifing Charlie in the back."

THE CENTRAL HIGHLANDS

In Search of the Montagnards

One of the waiters from Restaurant Thirteen promised to bring me to the bus station at the crack of dawn. While I'd like to spend the rest of my life visiting Mr. Trang and whiling away the hours in cafés, these activities aren't my sole reason for being in Vietnam. I'm anxious to see the Central Highlands. To see the Montagnards. After all, three-fourths of Vietnam is not inhabited by Vietnamese but by more than fifty-three different ethnic minorities. The mountain tribes were referred to collectively as "Montagnards" by the French, and the Americans later adopted the term as well.

I leave the hotel carrying a shoulder bag. A cyclo driver pedals along slowly just in back of me. He can see from my bag that I'm headed somewhere, but I'd rather have the waiter bring me to the station since he speaks English. Finding the right bus to Dalat and dealing with the ticket sellers is no easy matter.

The waiter just woke up and is standing on the sidewalk combing his hair. He points to the motorbike he's borrowed for the occasion. First, he tells me, he has to put some gas in the tank, and since he doesn't have enough money he asks me for an advance. I give him ten thousand dong and wait. The cyclo driver has posted himself outside the restaurant, where he hurls a few vindictive comments at the staff.

The waiter returns with the motorbike, and I hop on back. The cyclo driver leaps from his saddle, races towards us swearing at the top of his lungs and blocks our path. Then he hauls off and smacks the waiter right in the jaw. The entire staff pours out of the restaurant, and the other waiters, the cooks and the cashier hasten to restrain the cyclo driver. They won't be in the majority for long, I fear, since cyclos come rushing up from all sides. I realize it's up to me to take some action, as otherwise the entire staff of Restaurant Thirteen will be wiped out.

Across the street an old cyclo driver is observing the fight from afar. Extricating myself from the free-for-all, I sprint over to him and explain that I want to go to the bus station, that I have to catch the bus to Dalat. He nods in understanding. I jump in the cyclo, and he pedals down the street as fast as his legs allow. When I turn around, it looks as if the entire mob is getting ready to set off in hot pursuit. But something makes them change their minds. Dejected, the belligerents lower their arms until they come to rest limply alongside their thin bodies.

Panting with exertion, the old man brings me to a parking lot on the outskirts of Saigon where a bunch of buses are waiting. "Dalat! Dalat!" shouts a man and grabs the cyclo. There are two seats left on the Dalat bus, and if I'm prepared to pay for two tickets, they tell me, we can leave right away. Not the best seats, mind you. I have to clamber inside a microbus through the rear. They shut the door, and we're jammed in so tight I feel like I'm in a submarine. One thing is sure: in an emergency, no one is going to leave this bus alive.

Our journey takes us north, over Vietnam's only four-lane highway, through the rubber plantations abandoned by the French. We turn towards the coast and head into the mountains, where we can look down at the emerald-green valleys below us. From time to time we pass a wooden house by the side of the road.

I let my eyes wander over the slopes: are there any Montagnards to be seen? In Vietnamese the Montagnards are referred to as *Moi*, savages. The two groups have never really hit

In Search of the Montagnards

it off, which is why the Montagnards, hoping for independence, took up arms against the Vietnamese, siding first with the French and then with the Americans.

In a 1968 *National Geographic* I saw some photographs of Jehs and Bahnars: short, tawny tribal peoples eking out an existence from hunting and primitive agriculture. In the evenings they gather around a fire, wrapped in handwoven cloth, while the flames glisten on their silver necklaces and jangling earrings. When they smile, they reveal teeth filed into sharp points.

In the sixties, the American Special Forces training the Montagnards in the Central Highlands had to be mindful of the fact that their native recruits believed their lives were ruled by spirits. I remember seeing a picture of a tall blond American in a loincloth, taking part in a Montagnard ceremony. After the war the Central Highlands were off-limits to all but Vietnamese nationals. Since then, little has been heard of the courageous Montagnards.

The bus is climbing higher and higher, and it's getting cooler. As far as I can see, the bus contains only Vietnamese passengers; apparently the lowlanders have taken to the hills. We're now so high up in the mountains that it's downright cold. Shivering, I put on the sweater Mr. Trang loaned me. The hills around us are covered with pine trees. The scenery makes you forget the tropics, which is why Dalat is so popular with Vietnamese tourists. It looks a lot like Switzerland up here.

The bus turns into a marketplace and comes to a stop. Dalat is the only city in Vietnam that doesn't have any cyclos. The streets are just too steep. Instead, the bus is greeted by a fleet of chauffeur-driven motorbikes. One of the drivers, a man in a beret, addresses me in halting French. I hop on the back of his motorbike, and we set off through the market, passing baskets of artichokes, carrots and strawberries. The French not only founded Dalat, they also taught its residents how to grow the ingredients indispensable to French cuisine.

We drive along the shore of the reservoir forming the heart of the city. The hillside is dotted with villas. The French used to come here to escape the heat of Saigon and the murderous malaria-infested Delta. While the stately homes are still nestled among the trees, these days the threadbare laundry of poverty-stricken extended families flaps from the balconies. During the war Vietnamese military leaders from both sides came here to relax. They breathed in the fresh air and took no notice of each other, only to resume their life and death struggle once they returned to the sweltering lowlands.

"Are there any Montagnards still living in the vicinity of Dalat?" I ask the driver. He nods and points to the distant hills. "Can you take me there?"

He shakes his head. "It's not allowed."

This was the answer I expected to hear. I asked various people in Saigon if they could arrange a visit to the Montagnards. Even those who would have jumped at the chance to perform some service turned me down cold.

We pass a French-style church with a narrow steeple. Further on, we pull up beside the largest building in Dalat, currently encased in construction scaffolding. "The Palace Hotel," says the driver with a flourish. According to a signboard a foreign company is restoring the complex to its former grandeur, turning it into a five-star hotel.

Next to the Palace is another hotel with a French-style stucco exterior. This is where I'll be staying. The desk clerk informs me that once they've finished with the Palace, this hotel is slated for renovation. This may account for the fact that the hotel is not entirely up to snuff. Her voice trails into silence as she reads the note on my visa, and her eyes fill with suspicion. I inwardly curse the head of the Immigration Police in Saigon for stigmatizing me in this way.

The door to the first room assigned to me won't open, and the second one is filled with a nauseating stench. The third one doesn't seem to have anything spectacularly wrong with it. The window overlooks a valley composed of fields and scattered houses. The hillsides resound with the sounds of people heading home from work and the shouts of schoolchildren with their bookbags on their backs. Seated in the window, I listen to the final chords of the day.

The next morning I present myself to the official Tourist Office and hesitantly state my wishes. "If it's possible I'd like to visit some Montagnards."

In Search of the Montagnards

"No problem," briskly retorts the man behind the counter. "We'll take care of all the necessary permits provided you rent a car, a driver and a guide from us."

That's funny. Apparently an ordinary citizen isn't allowed to make money off the Montagnards; the Dalat Tourist Office has the monopoly. Could that be the reason for all the secrecy?

Promptly at one o'clock a Russian jeep pulls up at my hotel. The guide, a young man who speaks fluent English and French, shakes my hand. He strikes me as the shy type, and when I compliment him on his pronunciation he replies modestly: "I used to be a student at Lycée Yersin." Prior to 1975 the school had an outstanding reputation, or so I've heard.

We quickly reach the outskirts of Dalat. As we wind through the fields I ask: "Was Lycée Yersin a Catholic school?"

"Yes it was," the guide answers. "I'm a Catholic. In fact, I almost became a priest."

"But you changed your mind just in the nick of time," I joke.

My remark makes him blush to the roots of his hair, as if I'd made an indecent proposal. He vehemently shakes his head in denial, wanting me to know he was sincere in his vocation. "In 1975 I was a seminary student," he sighs. He wasn't arrested when the North Vietnamese troops captured Dalat, but of course the new regime closed the seminary. "My French name is Anthony," he solemnly concludes his story. "I'm named after the patron saint of lost objects."

We drive through a gate and come to a halt in what appears to be a military post. Our papers have to be checked. Anthony steps out of the car and disappears into a building, along with a man in uniform. The driver and I sit in silence. Why is there such a large military post here, I wonder? Are the rumors of guerrillas in the mountains true? When I was in Saigon, people told me in a furtive whisper that a Montagnard army has been hiding in the jungle since 1975.

Anthony returns with a broad smile across his face. "Everything's okay," he reports cheerfully and gives directions to the driver.

Before long the jeep arrives in a muddy village. "This village is inhabited by people of the Lat tribe," Anthony explains. I look around me in surprise. The houses and the people don't look any different than the ones we just passed, except they're a little poorer. "This village is close to Dalat," Anthony explains. "The people have adopted many Vietnamese customs." He points out some differences. A woman walking along a path has wrapped her child in a cloth which is strapped to her back. "That's not something Vietnamese women do," he assures me. We see a man carrying a basket load of goods on his back, and Anthony informs me that this too is a typical Montagnard custom. According to Anthony, their hair is also different. Since the women all seem to wear their hair in a ponytail, I haven't the faintest idea what he means. But then a man walks by and I see what he's driving at: unlike any Vietnamese I've ever laid eyes on, the man has kinky hair.

The jeep pulls over and parks. Anthony and I continue on foot over a dike with fields on either side. We reach a large wooden building with a corrugated roof: a church.

"A *Catholic* church," emphasizes Anthony.

On the other side of the church we hear the sounds of hammering and sawing. Five frizzy-haired Montagnards are tackling some pine boards.

"They're building a house for the priest," explains Anthony. He asks them a question, and the men mumble in response. It seems the priest has gone shopping in Dalat. "He's a friend of mine," Anthony says. "We went to seminary together."

By the time the seminary was reopened a few years ago Anthony was married and had a daughter. His friend had more patience and was able to graduate and be ordained. "He lived with a Montagnard family for two years," recounts Anthony with a certain awe, as if he considers that to be quite a feat. "And now the government has finally granted the parishioners permission to build a home for the priest."

The men calmly go about their work. They're strong and powerfully built, and their faces are much broader than the average Vietnamese. According to anthropologists the Montagnards originally came from Indonesia or Polynesia. Their ancestors must have sailed across the ocean in simple boats centuries ago.

"*Bonjour,*" one of the men shyly whispers.

"Oh, you speak French?" I ask in delight.

In Search of the Montagnards

He looks at the ground. "I'm just a simple Montagnard," he explains. "I only speak a little French." Like Anthony, he was sent to a Catholic French school in Dalat when he was a child.

Our conversation quickly flags and Anthony comes to the rescue: "He isn't being paid for this work," he comments. The man nods. "He's doing it *pour le Bon Dieu*, for the Good Lord." The man picks up his saw again, and we continue on our way past wooden houses surrounded by gardens.

"Still, it's unusual," I say to Anthony, "that they've hired you, an ex-seminary student, to work at the Tourist Office. All the official guides I met in Saigon were sons of high-ranking cadre members."

Anthony blinks nervously. "After '75 a lot of people left Dalat. The newcomers, the Northerners, only spoke Russian," he explains.

The first Western tourists descended on Dalat in the late 1980s. Anthony was assigned the task of guiding them around, but the authorities didn't think he was 100-percent trustworthy. "I can't tell you how many self-criticisms I had to write," he sighs. A few years ago he brought two French people to this village. "They were upset by the poverty. And they were Catholics, like me." Trusting a fellow Catholic, they gave him money and medicine to distribute to needy Montagnards as he saw fit. The word of this donation got around, and he was summoned to his boss. "I told him it was for the poor, but he didn't believe me. He figured they only gave me money in exchange for some service." This nearly marked the end of his career: he was suspended for a year. His punishment consisted of trudging all over the mountains showing propaganda movies to the Montagnards.

"Are they all Catholics?" I ask.

"No, some of the villages are Protestant," he replies. "But the further inland you go, the fewer converts you find." He pauses to collect his thoughts and then explains that the Montagnards in the vicinity of Dalat celebrate Christmas because they believe in Jesus Christ. But they also celebrate Tet, the Vietnamese New Year, which is a custom they adopted from the townspeople. Deep in the mountains they don't celebrate either Christmas or Tet, since they have their own animist rites: "They sacrifice buffaloes or chickens to the spirits." I don't detect even a hint of censure in Anthony's voice. There's no doubt about it, he would have been a broad-minded priest.

"Do the Montagnards still remember the Americans?" I inquire.

Anthony casts a mournful look at the village while a couple of kids with unwashed faces and tattered clothes stare at us in curiosity. "The Americans," he says with a sigh. "That's a problem." Because the Montagnards sided with the Americans, the government still doesn't trust them. Hanoi is afraid the hill tribes are going to be rearmed by foreign powers. Anthony claims he's never heard of any guerrillas. But he adds, blushing in confusion, that it's better not to talk about things like that.

"The Montagnards are disappointed with the Americans," declares Anthony with a note of accusation creeping into his voice. He can empathize with the Montagnards. Since the war they've heard nothing more from their American friends. The clergymen and priests all went home, leaving them behind. "They were abandoned by the Americans," he adds angrily. It's a strange situation: the Montagnards, some of whom still roam the mountains in loincloths and have no tradition of a written language, have fickle friends on the other side of the ocean.

After the war the new government in Hanoi sharply restricted the rights of the Montagnards. In the schools the lessons may only be conducted in the Vietnamese language. The independence the Montagnards had hoped for was further from their grasp than ever.

Bluish hills rise up in back of the village. Behind them lies the vast jungle that on my map is filled in with tigers, elephants and rhinoceroses.

"Are the Vietnamese jealous of the Montagnards?" I ask, thinking of the many displays of smoldering jealousy I've been witness to since I arrived in this country.

Anthony nods. "Foreigners who meet Montagnards always like them better than they do Vietnamese," he admits.

A sturdy young woman standing in front of a house greets us shyly and asks if we want to see inside. "But it isn't built on poles," objects Anthony. "It's not a typical example of a Montagnard house."

In Search of the Montagnards

"That doesn't matter," I say, not wanting to refuse someone's hospitality because I suspect there's a nicer house down the road.

I follow the woman inside while her little boy clings to his mother's leg for dear life. The house has an earthen floor. In the middle of the room there's a table and two benches. On the wall is a picture of the Virgin Mary. The woman draws aside a curtain to reveal a broad bed.

"A large house, but little furniture," notes Anthony drily.

The woman has just returned from a trip to the hills. A basket that fits over your back is lying on the floor, full of green herbs. An old woman with a wrinkled face and elongated earlobes peers inside the window from the garden. "Her mother," translates Anthony. The young woman is twenty-five years old and a recent widow. One day her husband and her father went into the jungle for wood, and the tree they were chopping fell down and crushed them to death. She was left with her mother and three children. "She gave away two of the children," Anthony says.

"Gave away?" I exclaim in horror.

"It's better that way," he assures me. "They're living in a children's home in Dalat. They can go to school there." Without her husband she can barely eke out a living. She gathers firewood in the mountains and sells it in the market. She grows vegetables in her garden, but that doesn't bring in enough money. Only her youngest son is still living with her. She brought him to the children's home along with the other two, but had to take him home again because he couldn't stop crying.

Our attention is caught by the entrance of a young man wearing a white shirt and pleated trousers. He looks very different from the other people I've seen in the village. "Good afternoon," he says breezily in English. "Where are you from?" He smiles, revealing two rows of shining white teeth. He explains that he lives a few doors down. "You are welcome to come see my home." Only then does it dawn on me that he's a Montagnard. He does have curly hair, and his shirt is stretched over a very muscular torso.

Anthony looks him up and down without saying a word and then begins talking to him in Vietnamese. "This young man is going to work at the Palace Hotel after it reopens," he explains.

"Right now he's taking a course, training to be a waiter and learning to speak English."

"Yes, indeed," the young man assents with a grin. "Follow me."

"That doesn't seem like a good idea to me," Anthony sternly retorts. "It's late, and we have to be getting back to Dalat."

Undaunted, the young man turns to me: "I'd like to talk to you about the culture of my people," he says. "Can I meet you at your hotel?"

His offer leaves me speechless. Am I to understand that a good-looking, eighteen-year-old Montagnard would like to get to know me better? "I'm staying in Hotel Dalat," I hesitantly reply, "in room number..."

Anthony interrupts me. "I don't think it would be wise to make an appointment," he rudely interjects. He goes outside and calls the driver, who immediately brings the jeep around to the house and guns the engine. "We're leaving," he says and takes me by the arm. Throwing one last look at the muscular Montagnard, I let myself be escorted to the jeep.

We drive back towards Dalat in silence. The sun casts long shadows over the road. Anthony looks sad and I feel guilty, though I don't know what for. "I'm sorry," I say, "if I created a problem for you."

Anthony shakes his head. That's not what's bothering him. "The Montagnards are strictly forbidden to have any contacts with foreigners. If he were to come to your hotel and were to get caught, he'd be kicked out of his course. He'd be throwing away the one opportunity to do something with his life." He pauses for a moment. "You're going to leave, but he has to stay here," he concludes. I can hear the implied rebuke in his voice.

Our little outing is threatening to turn into a real drama. "I didn't know that," I say in my own defense. "He just seemed like a nice guy." Anthony stares straight ahead without saying a word. Is he jealous? After all, wasn't he the one who told me foreigners always like Montagnards better? Or is he a government spy whose job it is to alienate the tourists and the hill tribes? He must have noticed the suspicion in my eyes because he says, carefully articulating his words: "I've told you the truth. I only want to help the boy. Believe me. I know what it means to be in trouble with the authorities."

In Search of the Montagnards

When we reach the hotel, he holds the door open for me. Fixing his melancholy eyes on me, he says: "It's true. I'm not a Communist. I'm a Catholic."

My visa is due to expire in three days, and so I decide to spend what time I have left on the beach. Early in the morning I catch a microbus in Dalat that hurtles me down the mountainside to the coast. At a sweltering junction I switch to an overfull bus bound for Nha Trang, where a room overlooking the sea is awaiting me.

Stretched out in the sand, I see coming toward me a woman with two baskets balanced on the end of a bamboo pole. She removes the straw lid from one of the baskets to reveal steamed crabs. She also offers to prepare shrimp, the biggest I've ever seen, over a brazier which she also carries around in her portable restaurant. I decide to sample all her wares.

"And tonight?" asks the woman.

"Then I'll order some more," I promise.

"And tomorrow?"

"Tomorrow too, and the day after tomorrow. But then I'm going to Saigon."

From there I'm booked on a direct flight to Bangkok, where I hope to get a new visa, preferably one without the Immigration Police's damaging note. Then I plan to come back to Vietnam so I can see the rest of the country.

I close my eyes and only wake up at the sound of a female voice imploring me: "Madam, Madam. Time for crabs? Time for shrimps?"

HANOI

A French Wedding

The plane from Bangkok to Hanoi is virtually empty, an ominous sign. Below me green fields come and go between the clouds. In days gone by American pilots rained down bombs through clouds like these. When I was a teenager I used to watch the evening news. Little black dots would be ejected from a B-52, and while the cameras kept rolling the dots were sucked closer and closer to the earth.

The next broadcast would show the havoc on the ground, where people were stoically carrying out the necessary rescue work amid the heaps of rubble. We comforted ourselves with the thought that we too were helping the victims: my father donated money to the Dutch Committee for Medical Aid to North Vietnam, an organization whose slogan was "We help where the bombs fall."

I'm startled out of my reverie by the voice of the captain, who has a Scandinavian accent, as does the blonde stewardess who welcomed us aboard. Dressed in a Vietnamese *ao dai*, she looked big-boned and chunky. Only a few days ago a Russian Ilyushin was plying this route, and now we're in a spanking-new Boeing.

I'm reminded of an evening, more than twenty years ago,

when I couldn't sleep. The entire house was enveloped in darkness. Downstairs, I found my father watching a news program, with the bluish glow of the TV shining in his face. On the screen was an American pilot whose plane had been downed near Hanoi. Instead of his dashing uniform he was dressed in drab prison garb. He was sorry, he said. Until now he hadn't realized the suffering he'd caused. But now he knew that his bombs had landed on innocent women and children.

We were reassured by his act of repentance. We assumed that the U.S. would be forced to recognize the injustice of the war and that an enduring peace would follow.

At that time I had a very clear picture of North Vietnam. The North Vietnamese were hard-working people dressed in simple black cotton pants and tops. When the American bombers were headed their way, a siren was sounded and they quickly sought refuge in air-raid shelters. The North Vietnamese all fought for a clear objective, sacrificing everything for their ideal. They were poor, but what little they had was divided equally among them. I don't remember hearing a single report to the contrary.

To evoke the mood of the sixties, shortly before my departure I bought Susan Sontag's *Trip to Hanoi* at a secondhand bookstore. The name of a Third World Shop in Holland was stamped on the cover. The book practically reeked of incense and Afghan coats.

While the near-empty plane whizzes through the late afternoon I get caught up in the adventures of this American writer, who journeyed to North Vietnam in May 1968. After several chapters she's still said very little about Hanoi. Many of her sentences begin with "I," "I feel" or "my consciousness." It was indeed a time in which everyone was busy getting in touch with their own inner feelings.

Still, Hanoi does make its appearance from time to time. It's not what Sontag expected. As she describes it: "The first experience of being there absurdly resembled meeting a favorite movie star, one who for years has played a role in one's fantasy life, and finding the actual person so much smaller, less vivid, less erotically charged, and mainly different." Why Hanoi isn't the hero of her dreams she doesn't say.

Another one of her disappointments is that the Vietnamese

are much more polite and formal than the Cubans. "It fits with the impression Vietnam gives of being an almost sexless culture," she concludes in discouragement, which does "discomfort a Western neo-radical like myself." I gaze out the window in astonishment. Was the slogan "Make love, not war" interpreted so literally back then?

At some point Susan Sontag talks to her official guides about the fact that the Communist Party is virtually the only party in North Vietnam. They assure her that she needn't worry since the Party "had proved it deserves to hold power by being responsive to the concrete local demands of the people." Sontag is convinced. "For the Vietnamese 'the Party' simply means the effective leadership of the country," she concurs.

The thousands of Vietnamese boat refugees who fled the country in later years are proof to the contrary. I tuck the book away in surprise. Why did Sontag allow herself to be fobbed off with such simple answers? Didn't she want to know what was really going on?

Mary McCarthy visited Hanoi two months before Susan Sontag. Like Sontag, she stayed in the Thong Nhat or "Reunification" Hotel. She too wrote a book about her experiences. I had been given a copy of McCarthy's *Hanoi* by a friend of mine in Amsterdam who is seven years older than I am. It had been ages since she'd read it, she told me. It reminded her of the mass demonstration she went to in 1972 to protest the Christmas bombing of Hanoi.

McCarthy is more lavish with details than Sontag, telling us, for example, that the "keys at the [reception] desk were laid out in a fan pattern." Her book gave me a clearer idea of what Hanoi looked like. Yet McCarthy also subjected her thoughts to strict censorship. "What has happened to the landowners?" she asked the government official who escorted her. "If they agree to work with us, we accept them," was the reply. "We do not hold their past against them." McCarthy did not pursue the matter. "The subject did not seem to be of much interest," she concluded.

She has nothing but praise for the North Vietnamese authorities: "Not only were there no signs of disaffection; the announcement, on 21 March, of a decree against 'counter-revolutionary crimes' took even long-resident foreign journalists by surprise. Nobody could understand what or whom was aimed at. The list of fifteen counter-revolutionary crimes punishable by jail or death comprised treason, espionage, plotting, armed rebellion, sabotage, defecting to the enemy, disrupting public order, making propaganda, intruding into the territory of the DRVN."

It never occurred to McCarthy that laws are usually only made after violations or crimes have been committed. On the contrary, she assumes the government was mistaken. "But who *were* those future collaborators, unheard and unseen until this moment . . . ?" She reassures herself that "they were a mere apprehension in the mind of Hanoi."

The plane has been making a gradual descent. In the vicinity of the runway dozens of ponds are shimmering in the setting sun. Might they be bomb craters? Lurching over the bumpy asphalt, the plane taxies past a hangar on which the peace sign is visible in peeling white paint. I remember seeing a photograph of an American soldier in the middle of the jungle wearing the same symbol on a chain around his neck. It was just like the one my oldest brother wore back then. The peace sign went together with long hair and marijuana. Who on earth had painted that symbol on the hangar? Perhaps some delegate from a peace group from god knows where?

Even though the war is over, a hint of danger seems to be hovering over our little group as a bus transports us to the terminal. I flash the Immigration Officer a friendly smile as I hand over my passport. When he comes to the page containing my visa, he looks upset. Does he have a computer connecting him to the Immigration Police in Saigon? He calls out something to another Immigration Officer and hands him my passport. The second man indicates with a nod of his head that I should follow him.

The uniformed Immigration Officer is joined by a young man in civilian clothes who speaks excellent English. "You are in violation of the law," he translates in a stern voice. "You have not booked a package tour." According to official regulations, every tourist who comes to Vietnam is required to pay for hotels, transportation and a guide in advance. Here in the North they don't

A French Wedding

seem interested in hearing how their counterparts in the South usually take these regulations with a grain of salt.

"There is a solution," says the English-speaking youth, suddenly changing into dulcet tones. "You can book a trip with me. We can offer you transportation to Hanoi and assist you in finding a hotel. The price will be thirty dollars."

The Immigration Officer is holding my passport in his hand, which he keeps behind his back. "Yes?" he asks in a menacing tone.

"Yes, yes," I hastily reply. I hadn't expected to get off so easily.

They net two more victims: a well-dressed British father and his son, a man in his mid-forties dressed in black from head to toe. He probably used to be a hippie. No doubt he cut his hair so they won't think he's a junkie. You don't suppose he's making a pilgrimage to the Promised Land?

"Didn't book a trip!" the father snorts. "We've come to visit a friend of my son's who teaches English at the university here. What on earth do you mean?"

The son intervenes. "Shut up, Jim," he snaps at his father. "They've got to get some money somehow. The Americans destroyed their country."

"Why can't they earn their money like other people?" the father suggests.

"This is the last time I'm going to explain it to you," the son snarls. "This is Vietnam, not Mallorca."

Suddenly a strange figure pops up on the other side of a window: a blond man in a black cotton shirt and trousers, like the Vietnamese wore during the war. It seems he's the friend of the British son. He quickly maneuvers the two men outside.

Today's catch now consists only of me. The guide shrugs his shoulders. He obligingly carries my bag to a new Japanese van whose driver is patiently awaiting our arrival. The van slowly negotiates a narrow road between rice paddies.

"I saw a lot of ponds near the airport," I remark to the guide. "Are they all bomb craters?"

He mulls the question over in his mind for a minute. "Some of them are ponds and some of them are craters, but what difference does it make?"

My thoughts keep drifting back to the strange events in the arrival hall. "That guy in the black shirt and trousers," I say. "Wasn't he wearing the uniform of the National Liberation Front?"

The guide bursts into laughter. "No, that's the traditional clothing of one of our ethnic minorities, the Muongs." His answer only serves to pique my curiosity even more. What's an Englishman doing gallivanting around Hanoi in a Muong outfit?

I try to imagine what Hanoi is like but have little success. All I can come up with is an image of Susan Sontag handing out anti-war buttons to Vietnamese workers. What also comes to mind is a story I heard, in which Hanoi residents were said to greet each other on the street with a number: the number of downed American planes.

Our van clatters over an old-fashioned iron bridge spanning the Red River. When we reach the other side, we're finally in Hanoi. We pass numerous old French-style buildings. Everything is run-down and in need of repair. Well, not quite everything. A distinguished-looking doorman is standing at the entrance to a freshly painted white edifice. "The Thong Nhat Hotel!" I exclaim in delight. Susan Sontag and Mary McCarthy were not the only foreigners to stay there. Over the years all the other Western journalists invited by the North Vietnamese authorities were housed there too.

"It's been remodeled and is now known as the Metropole, the way it used to be," the guide dampens my enthusiasm. "It's also very, very expensive," he concludes matter-of-factly.

The road leads us past colonial houses which have clearly seen better days. Still, I'd expected downtown Hanoi to be in a worse state. Apparently relatively little was destroyed here during the war, so that no concrete monstrosities have had to arise from the ashes.

Hanoi appears to be a beautiful city. There's even something romantic about it. We're driving down a street lined with overhanging trees, so tall they tower above us. So Hanoi's characteristic trees weren't chopped down during the war and used for firewood!

In the meantime it's gotten dark, and the traffic is amazingly quiet. Only an occasional jingle is heard, as droves of bicyclists

A French Wedding

and an occasional motorbike weave their way home. The cyclos are bigger and ganglier here than in Saigon; we drive past one transporting two women and four children atop a bulky load.

We slow down at an intersection to make way for an ox cart brimming with long bamboo poles. The driver has fallen asleep at his post, and the ox obediently plods on through the darkness.

At a movie theater a bright light illuminates a hand-painted poster of the current attraction: a war movie. A Vietnamese soldier is embracing a woman with flowing hair while a helicopter hovers menacingly in the background.

"This is Hoan Kiem Lake, the Little Lake," says the guide, pointing to a black pool, "the heart of Hanoi." We turn the corner and pull up in front of a small hotel. "You have everything you need right here," he reports cheerfully. "There's an ice-cream parlor on the first floor, a restaurant on the second floor and hotel rooms on the third floor." I nod enthusiastically. In many a city that wouldn't sound like much of a recommendation, but it does here. Thank goodness he isn't planning to leave me behind in one of those dark, silent streets. Hanoi isn't exactly a beehive of activity at night.

The guide is in a hurry. He propels me past miniature tables where young families are eating sherbet and up two flights of winding stairs to the reception desk. "Yes, we do have a room," the desk clerk smiles.

"Then it's time for me to be off," the guide declares and makes a comical bow. "This is the end of your package tour."

The desk clerk apologizes for her poor pronunciation of English. "I only started learning the language three months ago." Her friendly tone is reassuring. I'd expected the personnel in Hanoi to be rigid and forbidding, as they are in many hotels in China, where a guest is thought of as a nuisance that has to be gotten rid of as quickly as possible. But this woman is ready for a nice chat.

"I used to study Russian," she tells me. "I lived in Moscow for five years." She has happy memories of that time. Physically she even looks a little Russian. She's fairly tall and sturdily built for a Vietnamese. "I'll probably never see the friends I made in Moscow again," she remarks with a note of regret. But almost immediately she shakes off the thought. "Shall I show you to your room?"

Everything smells new; the walls have recently been plastered white. The room's showpiece is a shiny formica wall unit. The window looks out on a dark courtyard which is briefly illuminated by a streak of light when someone opens a door to hang some washing out to dry. I catch a glimpse of wicker baskets and a broom made out of twigs, implements from another era than my wall unit.

Hanoi has been conducting a mad scramble to get its accommodations ready to receive foreign visitors, business people who have come to check out the investment climate. No one is waiting anymore for delegations from the peace movement.

I have a list of the telephone numbers of various ministries and official agencies. Yet I feel little need to view the city at the level of officialdom, to hear the bureaucrats utter their predictable phrases. I know what they'll say: Vietnam is heading towards a golden future . . . look at all the international contracts and joint ventures flooding in. But I'm more interested in daily life in Hanoi. Finding out what that's like won't be easy. How do you go about winning the trust of people who have been shut off from the rest of the world for so many years?

I decide not to call in the help of the press attaché at the Ministry of Foreign Affairs. I'm curious to know who will cross my path if I go about things the same way I did in Saigon.

Downstairs in the ice-cream parlor, I run into a fellow hotel guest. Patrick is English, the sales representative of a tea company. He looks like he's about twenty-seven, or maybe a little younger. Companies always send either their youngest or their oldest employees to outposts like these. While Patrick eats his chocolate ice cream, I imagine him as he might have been in days gone by: a British colonial at an Indian tea plantation, sipping his gin and tonic while lounging in a wicker chair.

"Life isn't too bad here," he mutters, "though this place could sure use a pizzeria."

Later on that evening, in the restaurant on the second floor, I share a table with another hotel guest, Andrew, who represents another breed of foreigner. Andrew is from Chicago, and — so

A French Wedding

his business card says — he's in Vietnam on behalf of a family-planning agency. "Condoms," he announces with the air of a magician pulling a rabbit out of a hat. The idea is for Vietnam to start manufacturing condoms, but he doesn't see that happening anytime soon. The Vietnamese are currently using Chinese condoms. "But," he snorts contemptuously, "they're made of poor-quality rubber, and they're too thick."

His face lights up with an expression of old-fashioned idealism, even though he's in his mid-thirties. "*Baukasu*," he says, "that's the word for 'condom' in Vietnamese. They also refer to them as 'raincoats.'" Ideally, he ponders aloud, they need to find a movie star willing to promote the use of condoms. In his fantasy he imagines Vietnam inundated with condoms: rubbers on every street corner, boxes of the things being sold by every cigarette hawker for miles around. "Otherwise the population of Vietnam will double in thirty years," he predicts despondently.

"Hardly a delightful prospect for an American," I joke. A shadow of gloom crosses his face. When he was a child his parents used to take him along to anti-war demonstrations. Until he came to Hanoi he believed the U.S. should never have gotten involved in Vietnam.

"And now I'm not so sure. I don't know what's right and wrong any more."

A Vietnamese doctor he'd met through his work had once griped about the government. To smooth matters over Andrew had said to her: "Well, in any case, it's your own government."

The doctor had flown into a rage: "It's not my government," she'd shouted. "This is a Communist police state."

That gave him something to think about. Had there really been an enemy back then who needed to be defeated? Were there Vietnamese people who had set great store by the American presence in their country? He gives his head a shake to get his thoughts back where they belong. "What the hell," he says, more to himself than to me, "I'm here to promote condoms."

After coffee, he hands me a small square package. With the face of a true believer, he urges me to "tell the world."

The next morning I wake up while it's still dark outside. It takes a minute before I realize what woke me: a rooster downstairs in the courtyard.

The steel shutter of a store selling Japanese consumer electronics is just being slid open as I step out the door. The hotel's nightwatchman is drinking a cup of tea on the sidewalk with his friends. An elderly peddlar with a basket of pomelos installs herself beside a woman selling hairpins and ear scratchers. An old, wrinkled beggar in baggy clothes comes over and jams a tattered straw hat into my stomach. I lay a grimy bill in it.

A crowd has flocked towards the French Opera House at the end of the street to watch a couple of men drape an enormous red flag across the front of the building. Under a yellow star are the numerals: "9-2-45," the date Ho Chi Minh declared Vietnam to be independent. The event is scheduled to be celebrated a few days from now.

The cyclo drivers take little notice of me. They're apparently not accustomed to hustling their fares. It's already hot, and besides the people here don't have the feeling they're liable to miss a fortune at any moment, as they do in Saigon.

I stroll past Hoan Kiem Lake, heading north towards the old part of the city. Three boys balancing on a bicycle pedal along beside me, filled with curiosity. In Saigon they'd have shouted "whereyoufrom?" or "whatzyourname?" Here the cat seems to have got their tongues. We eventually come to the end of the lake. They continue to follow the curve of the shoreline while I walk straight ahead onto Hang Dao Street. The stores are crammed with colorful clothes; a couple of Russian men lugging enormous bags are haggling over the price of a shirt. They're the first Russians I've seen in Hanoi. There're a lot more of them in Saigon. Café Givral in Saigon, which played an important role in Graham Greene's novel about Vietnam, has a virtually all-Russian clientele these days.

It suddenly occurs to me that what's missing in Hanoi are the *Viet Kieus*, the Vietnamese from overseas who have returned for a visit. In Saigon they own lots of restaurants, bars and stores, which they purchase under the names of relatives. Their linguistic skills enable them to bridge the gap between the foreigners and the locals. They spend lavishly and throw a lot of parties.

A French Wedding

They come to Vietnam bearing gifts and sporting the latest fashions. They don't dare go to Hanoi, they told me in Saigon. After all, they used to work for the French or the Americans, and many of them were boat refugees. They're still afraid of being punished.

But Hanoi isn't the gray Communist city of their fears. During the war almost all the shopkeepers had to close their doors, but now they're back in full force. The display windows along Silk Street are filled with silk blouses and fine embroidery, and hundreds of buckets are dangling outside the stores on Tin Street. In this district all the streets are named after the commodities and crafts established there centuries ago, and most of them are still in existence today. In former times the craftsmen in China also had their own streets, but that custom went by the wayside after the Communists came to power.

I stroll down an alley filled with Buddhist religious articles. The shopkeepers are more aloof than in Saigon; they don't push their wares. A lot of the time they look right past me. Almost none of them speaks a foreign language.

Thirsty, I buy a coconut in a tiny store. The proprietor adroitly chops it open with a machete so that I can drink the milk through a straw. As he doesn't speak any English or French, we watch the traffic go by in silence. There aren't any aging French cars here as there are in Saigon. No crank-up Citroëns, no dilapidated European buses. The trucks that rumble by are of Russian or Chinese manufacture, and the occasional new car that you see comes from Japan.

Down the street, two women are busily setting up a table and some stools on the sidewalk to form a makeshift lunchtime restaurant. Even though it's only ten-thirty, the first customers grab a seat, making their selection out of various kinds of meats and vegetables which the women serve over a mountain of rice. As I haven't worked up an appetite yet, I walk on.

Not far away I hear church bells chime. Looking around me in surprise, I head in the direction of the bells. I round the corner and find myself face to face with an enormous cathedral which at one time must have been painted white, but which is now a mottled brown with a few white patches. Still, a cross is nestled in between its twin steeples, which point confidently towards heaven.

Several foreigners are clambering out of a couple of brand-new microbuses parked in the cathedral square. A flock of Vietnamese children form an inquisitive circle around them. I too am curious to know what's going to happen next.

Excited voices speaking French resound over the square. Women in tight silk dresses and hats mount the steps in high heels and enter the cathedral. Suddenly it dawns on me: it's a wedding. I follow the guests inside, with in my wake a group of Vietnamese women in plastic sandals who barely come to my waist. I'm overwhelmed by the size of the cathedral. The organ rumbles, and a shrill-voiced Vietnamese girls' choir launches into a French melody.

I stride to the front at the head of a procession, with the Vietnamese women in their conical hats shielding themselves behind me. At a certain point they no longer dare to take another step. As inconspicuously as possible, I join the brightly dressed wedding party, seating myself at the end of a bench. A moment later a stern-looking French woman taps me on the shoulder. "Only men can sit on the left," she informs me. "They still do things the old-fashioned way here." I smile and move timorously to the other side of the aisle.

Next to me is a blonde woman in purple shantung with pearl earrings and a broad-brimmed blue hat flopping over her face. She's the bride's cousin, she tells me, adding that she arrived yesterday from Lille. The entire family has come from Northern France. "And then of course all their friends and co-workers at the bank have come from Singapore." So the bride and groom live in Singapore.

"Why on earth have they chosen to get married in Hanoi Cathedral?" I inquire.

"*Alors*," retorts the woman, clearly regarding it as a stupid question. "Because of the setting of course. It's just like France, only much more romantic. It's like a fairy tale."

I nod.

"Are you a friend of Jean-François or Stephanie?" she whispers, her suspicions alerted.

"Neither. I'm from the press," I hear myself say to my great surprise. The woman nods, reassured. Fortunately she doesn't ask

A French Wedding

"What newspaper?" since I haven't the faintest idea what foreign paper might be interested in this event. For a moment I pretend to be back in Vietnam's colonial past, casting myself in the role of a reporter for the *Hanoi Matin*. "Mr. and Mrs. Lefèbre are delighted to announce the marriage of their daughter to the successful son of the renowned surgeon Dr. Leplat. A wedding out of a fairy-tale book. We wish the charming couple great happiness."

There's a rustle and a shuffling of feet: the bridal pair enters the church, she in radiant white at her father's side and he in subdued black beside his mother. A Vietnamese priest addresses them in fluent French. His words sound like a swearing-in ceremony in this hot high-ceilinged expanse. *"Through the same Jesus Christ, Your Son, our Lord, who lives and reigns with You in the unity of the Holy Spirit, one God, for ever and ever."* The temperature seems to rise with every word. The heat is making my eyelids heavy, and I'm having more and more trouble keeping my mind on the service.

I take a peek at the men on the other side of the aisle. They're even hotter. Huge sweat rings have formed under their armpits, and the back of the man operating the video camera is soaking wet. He fiddles with his tightly knotted tie.

The two Asian women in front of me are attempting to waft a little cool air their way with inlaid mother-of-pearl fans. As I know from eavesdropping, they work with the bridal couple at the bank.

One of the French women steps to the front and sings *Ave Maria*, her voice filling every nook and cranny in the cathedral. The little old Vietnamese ladies in their shabby clothes listen expressionlessly.

By the time Holy Communion rolls around it feels like an entire day has gone by. The guests in their shimmering clothes form a line in front of the priest. The little old ladies can't control themselves any longer, and they quickly join the line, devoutly opening their mouths when their turn comes.

While the gathering inches towards the exit, I walk beside the cousin in the purple dress. She informs me that the guests are being transported to Halong Bay, a famous tourist attraction in Vietnam because of the splendid rock formations dotting the coastline. "We're going to sail around Halong Bay in a junk. And then comes the wedding banquet. The bride and groom had the wine flown in from France."

"A dream come true," I concur, and while the buses open up a swath in the crowd, I rejoin the little old ladies, who are talking a mile a minute, lisping through their almost toothless gums. I'm now the only foreigner in the square. A Vietnamese woman comes up to me and tentatively touches my arm, as if she thinks I've just descended from heaven.

Exhausted, I meander on my way. Although it doesn't seem possible that it could get any hotter, the temperature keeps rising. I feel like there's a heavy suitcase pressing down on top of my head. Sitting in the shade of a tree, near the statue of the Russian hero Lé Nin, as the inscription reads, I await the end of this sweltering day.

Hanoi Hannah

Darkness has descended, and it's cooled off a little by the time I decide that my next step will be to visit Mr. Thuy, a man whose address was given to me by a mutual friend in Holland who used to be active in the Dutch Committee for Medical Aid to North Vietnam. After one day in Hanoi, I'm grateful for his reference. It's not easy to get a conversation going with the people here.

Mr. Thuy must be about forty-five. According to my friend he's worked at the Voice of Vietnam radio station for the last twenty-five years and speaks excellent English. I'm curious to meet a Northerner with impeccable credentials who has been committed to Vietnam's struggle for independence since he was a child. I have no desire to call on him at work, since I'll just be given the official Party line. Fortunately, I have his home address as well.

Looking at my map, I can see that he lives on one of the city's broad boulevards. "One dollar," says a cyclo driver with a poor accent but a clear head for business. He soundlessly pedals me beneath the tall trees to Mr. Thuy's front door.

Two elderly women are sitting on the sidewalk in mini bamboo chairs enjoying the cool of the evening. Startled at the fact that I seem to be heading for their building, they put their heads together and whisper to each other. "I've come for Mr. Thuy," I explain. They shout a name, and a little girl appears. She leads me up a dark staircase and into a brightly lit and spacious apartment, unexpectedly modern after my encounter with the little old ladies downstairs. A Japanese TV is blasting away at full volume.

Mr. Thuy reacts with pleased surprise. He's thin and modest; his wife strikes me as being the more dynamic of the two. At first the conversation revolves around our mutual acquaintance, the Dutch man known to all three of us. He's fine, I tell them. They ask about some other members of the Committee they once met in Hanoi, and I have to admit that, to my regret, I've never even spoken to them. The conversation definitely begins to flag. I get the impression they're trying to figure out my relationship to the Committee, which they refer to as "an old friend of Vietnam."

"I don't know anyone except the man who gave me your name," I say, hoping to avoid further questions. Outside, beyond the thick foliage of the trees, I hear the jingle of bicycle bells and the sigh of rubber tires on asphalt.

After an oppressive silence, I ask what life at the Voice of Vietnam is like. Mr. Thuy confesses in a soft voice that he doesn't work there anymore, that he's now employed by a British company.

"Oh," is the extent of my surprised reaction.

"For financial reasons," he hastens to add, as if I were accusing him of treason.

"Yes," I say, "everyone tells me how hard it is to make ends meet. I've been told that some people even have three different jobs."

Mr. Thuy nods and seems to relax now that it's clear he won't be called upon to defend himself. "At the radio I earned ten dollars a month. Now I'm getting twenty times that amount." He pauses for a moment and then adds: "There's a brain drain going on in this country. Our ministries, our hospitals, our universities and our schools are being emptied. Everyone is grabbing the chance to work for foreigners."

Mr. Thuy is surprised at some of the other developments taking place in Vietnam. "It used to be that someone who was poor was automatically assumed to be better than someone who was rich. These days people think you're poor because you're lazy," he concludes.

I had assumed that Mr. Thuy was a hard-line Communist who would defend the Party's latest political course. But apparently it's not that simple. Once he might have believed in the Socialist paradise, but those days are over. Now he's a seeker.

I ask him what it was like to work for a radio station at the height of the battle. "The broadcasts always went on," Mr. Thuy replies, "no matter what happened." Sometimes the transmitter was moved to a cave, and for one whole year they broadcast from China. "The colleague I respected the most was Mrs. Ngo. Like me, she was born in a bourgeois family, which means we had to work harder than the others. The Americans used to call her Hanoi Hannah."

Hanoi Hannah! I'd heard so much about her. Of course American GIs weren't supposed to listen to enemy broadcasts. But a lonely soldier might conceivably tune his transistor radio to the Voice of Vietnam. "How many kids have you killed today?" a bewitching female voice would ask him. That was Hanoi Hannah, trying to persuade GIs to give up the fight or defect to the other camp. Her silky voice sent chills up and down the spine of men all over Vietnam. She was like a siren luring ships onto the rocks.

"What's she doing now?" I ask, unable to contain my curiosity.

"She's living in Saigon," Mr. Thuy answers succinctly. Hanoi Hannah in Saigon! What would an ex-GI think of that?

Mr. Thuy continues his story, becoming more and more serious; he has few happy memories of his radio days. "There was always a lot of tension at the station," he recounts glumly. "We had to maintain iron discipline, just like in the army. Any kind of criticism was out of the question. For example, I didn't think it was fair that people from better families were discriminated against, but I didn't dare say that." He shifts uncomfortably on his imitation leather couch, as if he's done something he's ashamed of.

"We were kept completely in the dark about a lot of things. We broadcast only the number of civilian casualties and never the number of military casualties. I listened on my headphones to the BBC World Service and heard totally different figures. I felt torn. I simply didn't know who was telling the truth."

Mr. Thuy seems to be taking stock of his life. "There was so much I didn't understand," he muses. "During the Watergate affair, for example, everyone kept talking about a bug. For the longest time I thought they were talking about an insect."

Still, life in those days wasn't all sad. Mr. Thuy enjoyed listening to the music of Pete Seeger and Joan Baez which the station used to broadcast. He still knows every word to *Where Have All the Flowers Gone?* by heart. He also cherishes his meeting with Jane Fonda. "She brought along her son Troy, named after the Vietnamese man [Nguyen Van Troi] who attempted to assassinate the American Secretary of Defense, Robert McNamara." He sighs. "She was very nice, very pretty too. And she had a beautiful radio voice."

"Did you also meet any captured American pilots?" I ask. It came out sounding like an accusation, though that wasn't my intention. I try to make amends: "I mean they were often encouraged to make certain confessions over the radio, weren't they?"

Mr. Thuy looks past me. "No," his answer is brief. "I was too young. My superiors recorded those interviews."

I remain silent, having no wish to delve into the painful subject any further. I now have a better idea of why Susan Sontag couldn't bring herself to keep on cranking out the questions and why Mary McCarthy sometimes deliberately turned the conversation to neutral subjects like plants and animals.

Mr. Thuy breaks the silence. "Wars, like paintings, are best when looked at from a distance," he sadly intones.

It's ten o'clock, late for Hanoi. The street sounds have died away. Mr. Thuy offers to drive me to my hotel on his motorbike. We descend the dark staircase. All around us are the rustles and sighs of unseen people who are silent witnesses to the fact that their neighbor is leaving with a foreigner at this late hour.

Mr. Thuy is nervous and can't get his motorbike started. I step off, and at last he gets the engine going. The houses along the street are shut for the night. There's only an occasional light glowing in a window. Because of the overhanging trees, it's pitch dark outside. It's like driving through a cave.

Mr. Thuy hesitates in front of the hotel, unsure whether to say something. After a moment he seems to make up his mind. "The next time you come," he says in a low voice, "I'll tell you a story about my father. Actually it's also about the father of my best friend. A story about two fathers. It'll help you understand me and my country. Why don't you come to my house again on the evening of September 2nd? That's our Independence Day."

I agree, and he roars down the silent street on his motorbike.

A Tale of Two Fathers

Today every building along my street is decorated with fluttering red flags, and the ice-cream parlor downstairs is filled to overflowing. There's such a large crowd standing around outside eating popsicles that the traffic has practically ground to a halt. Thousands, no tens of thousands of people, are out on the streets tonight. Exactly forty-seven years ago, Ho Chi Minh declared Vietnam to be independent.

I've heard there's going to be fireworks later on tonight by the lake. It's so congested along the shoreline that we're forced to inch along, slower than molasses. It's a wonder there's any movement at all. One entire family is seated on a bike, father at the pedals, mother behind him with the younger child on her lap and the older one perched on the handlebars, watching the teeming masses with a colored balloon in his hand. The sidewalks are lined with street vendors selling various kinds of fruit, tall bottles of Chinese beer and some green-colored beverage. One woman has a display case full of cakes and a sign reading *ga tô*. Not everyone has such impressive merchandise. An old man with a wispy beard has nothing more to offer than a bicycle pump which you can rent for a few cents to pump up your tires.

I wait by the lake for an hour in hopes of seeing an array of red and purple stars fill the sky, but there's not a single firework to be seen. A gigantic flag has been installed on an island in the middle of the lake. Thousands of red lights flash on and off, ingeniously giving the impression that the flag is rippling in the wind.

Seven o'clock has come and gone, and I wasn't planning on going to Mr. Thuy's much later than that. I thread my way through the sea of bicycles until I arrive, out of breath, on his doorstep. Mr. Thuy is home alone; his wife and daughter are down below in the swarm of people.

"I missed the fireworks," I say, "and I couldn't find the parade."

Mr. Thuy shakes his head. "They didn't organize anything this year," he replies.

"Why not?" I ask in surprise.

"Well, perhaps the government is afraid things might get out of hand. They aren't exactly reassured by events in Eastern Europe. By the way," he adds, "that's another reason people aren't anxious to occupy top government positions these days. If things do change, they're in a pretty vulnerable position. You know the old saying: the higher they are, the harder they fall."

Suddenly I see the festivities outside in a new light.

Mr. Thuy produces a stack of papers. He clearly isn't inclined to pursue the subject further. "The story of the two fathers," I say and scrutinize the photograph he places on the table before me. A large family is posed in front of a painted backdrop, a landscape with pillars in the foreground. The father, in a three-piece suit, comes across as a man who knows what he wants. The mother, looking pretty and demure, is holding the youngest, the little Thuy, in her arms. The six older children are arranged between their parents.

"In those days," begins Mr. Thuy, "my father had a delicatessen near the marketplace. Business was good, and everyone was happy. A few years later, in 1954, Ho Chi Minh officially came to power in North Vietnam. My father and the father of my best friend, who also owned a small shop, realized that a storekeeper could only expect to occupy a very humble position in a Communist society. So the two of them presented themselves to the government, asking, 'How can we be of service to you?'"

A Tale of Two Fathers

The two fathers accepted a secret assignment and set off for the South. The purpose of their journey was ostensibly to purchase some merchandise. In actuality they were ordered to infiltrate South Vietnam's business community. Mr. Thuy sighs. "Somebody informed on them and they were slapped into a prison in Saigon. They didn't stay in jail very long since they managed to bribe the guards." An expression of distaste crosses over Mr. Thuy's face.

After that the two men parted ways. His father's friend returned to his family in Hanoi. Thuy's father didn't dare come home, as he was afraid of falling prey to a power struggle within the Communist Party. So he fled across the border to Vientiane, the capital of Laos.

Mr. Thuy lays another photo on the table, one of a neatly dressed gentlemen in an office. The sign on his desk clearly indicates his position: operation manager. Something in his bearing makes you think that playing the role of an ordinary, inconspicuous office employee doesn't come easily to him.

"He did send us money," says Mr. Thuy in his father's defense. "And he sent us postcards to say that he was okay and that he would come back as soon as it was possible."

His father's anxious forebodings were not without foundation; his friend, who went back to Hanoi, was arrested and accused of being a double agent. "Later we found out that his neighbors had been keeping him under 24-hour surveillance," Mr. Thuy says, his voice breaking with emotion.

His father's friend died in prison a year later. "His sons didn't dare wear a mourning band." Since one of the sons was his best friend, Mr. Thuy vividly remembers their sorrow. He adds, with a note of accusation creeping into his voice, "In those years there were no lawyers and no laws."

His friend was the best student in his graduating class. "But he wasn't allowed to go to college because of this blot on his record. He was the son of a bourgeois capitalist, and his father had been a flunky of the French imperialists."

For nine years he worked in a cooperatively owned plastics factory. "I have a picture of him during that period," Mr. Thuy says. The photograph shows five shabbily dressed young men sitting side by side exuberantly celebrating a birthday. Mr. Thuy points to the one wearing a large pair of black glasses. "That's him." I see what Mr. Thuy means. There's no genuine merriment in his eyes. His smile is forced.

"In 1980 he became a boat refugee," recounts Mr. Thuy, pouring tea into our cups. He gestures broadly: "Now he's a computer expert in New York earning four thousand dollars a month. He's become a man. If he'd stayed in Hanoi, he'd have become a beggar." He quickly leafs through a stack of photos and pulls out one of them. "Here, this is what he looks like now." I see a distinguished man in his forties sitting in a modern American restaurant. Mr. Thuy doesn't want even the slightest detail to escape my attention: "See, his face has filled out, and he's wearing contact lenses. He's become self-confident." But I'm more struck by the dark bags under his eyes, which seem to imply that his high-paying job wasn't handed to him on a silver platter. His face has lost its air of naivety. His mouth is compressed into a tight line. Something seems to have died inside him. But I don't say this to Mr. Thuy, since I don't want to contradict him in the middle of his story.

"Back then, we were also looked upon as children of a traitor," Mr. Thuy resumes. His oldest brother was denied permission to go to college, and the same fate was about to befall his next oldest brother. "My mother was galvanized into action. She started knocking on every government door she could find." A miracle occurred. "It seems the Ministry of Foreign Affairs was keeping tabs on the Vietnamese living abroad. Each country had its own room in the Ministry. At a certain moment my mother wound up in the room in charge of spying on our fellow countrymen in Laos. They knew exactly who my father was, and my mother was welcomed as the wife of a hero."

It seems that Mr. Thuy's father was one of North Vietnam's foremost spies in Vientiane. He was the one who provided the people in the Laos room with all the information they desired. "He knew it wasn't easy for us," Mr. Thuy remarks, adding with gratitude in his voice, "but he also knew he could help us by becoming a spy." Unfortunately, no one in the Laos room had found it necessary to inform other departments of this fact. "So

A Tale of Two Fathers

no one knew that my father wasn't a traitor or an anti-Communist, but a loyal patriot devoted to his fatherland."

Luckily this oversight could be corrected, and the children were all allowed to go to college. After that a contact person appeared on their doorstep at regular intervals bearing messages and gifts from their father in Vientiane. At the time, Mr. Thuy was learning English from a Russian instructor who came from Irkutsk, and his father sent him an English dictionary. "Dictionaries were so expensive and so few and far between in those days that I used to take it to bed with me."

Outside, the traffic is beginning to die down. The bicyclists are apparently tired of their revels. I think back to the time when Mr. Thuy met Jane Fonda and the delegates of various European peace groups. He would have addressed them with a polite smile, not breathing a word of the drama of these two fathers. Foreign guests liked to think the North Vietnamese were united in their struggle. Little did they guess that it was fear that kept the masses in line.

Despite his rehabilitation, Mr. Thuy's father didn't dare return to Hanoi. The contact person divulged the fact that the father had a new family in Laos; Mr. Thuy now had two half-sisters. In 1976, one year after the war ended, his father came to visit Hanoi. "He checked around, listened to the complaints of all his old friends and concluded that there was still no place for a former entrepreneur," Mr. Thuy recalls with sorrow.

His father paid a high price for his double life. He became an alcoholic. Back in Laos, he developed a serious liver problem and was sent to France in hopes that a famous French surgeon could save his life. "He died on the operating table. His second wife and two daughters had him buried him in Lyon," Mr. Thuy says quietly. "He was a patriot. He loved Vietnam," he insists.

"And your mother?" I inquire.

"She died ten years ago."

"Was she sad that your father had another wife?"

"No," says Mr. Thuy with a smile. "All seven of her children turned out all right. We were considerate and polite to her. That's what makes an Asian woman happy."

Outside, the streets are not deserted as they usually are at this hour. Young people are cruising around on their bicycles, looking for some action, but everything is closed. Or not quite. A light is still burning in the store next to my hotel. Dozens of people are crowded around the sidewalk; there are still some popsicles for sale.

The Battle of
the Embargo

The evenings are long in Hanoi. I'm glad when someone tells me there's going to be a party tonight around the swimming pool at the Australian Embassy. Almost all the foreigners living in Hanoi will be there, I'm told.

It's still stiflingly hot when I join the animated assembly. Over at a corner table I recognize the British father and son who arrived on the same plane I did. They're accompanied by their friend, once again dressed in his black Muong outfit. "I loathe the embassy crowd," he booms, "but unfortunately there's nowhere else we can drink a beer."

Andrew, the condom expert, is regaling someone at the bar with all the expressions for condom which he knows in Pidgin English. He apparently picked them up when he was peddling his wares in Papua New Guinea.

An Australian with an ad for glass-fiber cables emblazoned across his T-shirt presses a blue can of Foster's beer in my hand. His job is to install phone lines in Vietnam. At the moment he's moaning to his supervisor because the satellite TV dish he's been longing for hasn't yet materialized: "I'm bored out of my gourd every night."

His supervisor grimaces. "We have to get permission from the Ministry of the Interior," he explains. "Of course that means we have to grease a few palms. That's not the problem. The problem is that the dish can only be purchased through the Ministry of Telecommunications. They're charging five thousand bucks, even though we could buy the damn thing for a thousand in Singapore. But okay, I don't want to harp on that. Anyway, the guys in the Foreign Affairs Ministry are blocking the deal because they want their cut. They think we're trying to bypass them."

"Just hand them a bag full of money," the bored technician implores him, "and send the bill to the main office."

The supervisor sighs. "There are limits, Jim. Bribing three ministries for one satellite dish is a bit much."

I decide to add my voice to the conversation: "Who pays for those high-tech cables you're installing here?"

"You do," the two men exclaim triumphantly. "Have you ever called anywhere outside the country?"

I nod. "But," I add, unable to suppress my astonishment, "it wasn't cheap."

"That's exactly what we mean," laughs the supervisor. "They charge you twenty bucks for a three-minute phone call or fax, and forget trying to make a collect call. You figure out the profit they make! That's what they're using to pay us."

"And what we're going to use to pay for our satellite dish," the glass-fiber guy concludes hopefully.

"Cheers," says a young man who has come to stand next to us. He has an exceptionally fine face, as if someone designed it after giving the matter a great deal of thought.

One of the men introduces him: "This is John, our Hungarian."

I look at him in surprise. "My mother was Vietnamese," he explains. John was born and raised in Hanoi, where his father was a diplomat.

The glass-fiber guys, who have heard this story before, resume their noisy conversation.

John turns to me. "When I was in Hungary," he says, "I was homesick for Vietnam. So I came back here to study. The secret police kept me under constant surveillance. Every week I had

The Battle of the Embargo

to fill out a form with lots of questions. I must have an enormous file."

He traveled back and forth between Budapest and Hanoi on a regular basis. The flights were invariably filled with party officials, bleached-blonde Russians, and Vietnamese guest workers off to work in Eastern Europe.

"Do you think of yourself as Hungarian or Vietnamese?" I ask out of curiosity.

"I'm Hungarian," he retorts unequivocally. His answer surprises me; he could easily have lost his identity somewhere in the middle of all those visas, stamps, authorities and misunderstandings.

While threading my way to the bar for another round of drinks I run into a Dutch aid worker I'd met earlier in Saigon. He spent years working in the Vietnamese refugee camps in Hong Kong. Since no countries have offered to take in the remainder of the refugees, all of them are going to be repatriated to Vietnam. He's here to prepare for their return. "How can they stand it?" I ask. "They've spent years on a bare rock in Hong Kong without any hopes for the future."

The Dutchman shrugs his shoulders. "They've got a roof over their heads, three meals a day, free medical care and schooling for their children."

A Brit interrupts us with an arresting conversational opener: "I'm in deep shit," he begins. "You know we invested forty thousand dollars to modernize that factory?"

"Yes," the aid worker nods.

"Well, now it seems that the product we're manufacturing is endangering the health of the workers."

"And you only just found that out?"

"We took over the project from the Hungarians, who pulled out after their version of the Velvet Revolution."

"Didn't the Hungarians know about the health risks?"

"That's just it. I finally got the former manager on the line. He's gone back to Hungary. So I ask the guy: 'You must have factories like this in Budapest?' And you know what he said? 'Yes, we used to have some, but we only let convicts work in them.'"

"Why don't you just submit a new proposal?" advises the aid worker.

There's a shout of laughter from the other side of the pool, where a group of elegantly clad French women and charming French men seem to be having a good time. They form a separate group and aren't mixing with the other guests. "The French don't have anything to do with us, and we don't have anything to do with them," the Brit succinctly summarizes the situation.

A man of about twenty-five joins our group. Bob is his name, and he's an economics student from Germany who's doing some research into Vietnam's investment climate. "We were talking about the French," remarks the Brit.

"They don't finish anything they start here," Bob states categorically. "They think they have a head start because they colonized this country, but they're lagging way behind. They've blown their one chance to amount to anything in Asia." He unblinkingly observes the group on the other side of the pool without a shred of mercy.

"And who's in the lead?" I ask.

Bob doesn't hesitate a second. "The Japanese. They've researched the entire country and have detailed plans ready. As soon as the American embargo is lifted, they're ready to go."

The embargo is a subject dear to everyone's heart. A group of Americans who have taken refuge inside where it's air-conditioned is conducting a heated debate on the subject. A blonde business consultant with a Southern accent says: "If Bill Clinton ends the embargo, investors are just going to pour into Vietnam. The hotels won't be able to handle the flow, and the bureaucracy will grind to a complete halt."

"If you ask me," another American adviser interrupts her, "there will be many more investments in the South than in the North. The South is bound to develop at a rapid pace. It won't take them long to start complaining about having to foot the bill for the North as well." He continues to argue his case with great fervor: "We shouldn't underestimate the power of the separatist movement. What I envision happening is that the economic development will create a time bomb in Vietnam. When it goes off, the country will split into North and South again."

"Well," responds the blonde business consultant, "I don't know if the South is so attractive to investors. In Saigon they're liable to rip the sunglasses right off your face, and the power supply leaves a lot to be desired."

An older American, a copper-mining specialist, adds his two cents' worth: "But that's going to change once the new power line has been installed from the North to the South. From what I heard, it's almost finished."

His remark is greeted with a salvo of jeers. "They're never going to pull that off!" someone exclaims.

"Transporting electricity over nearly two thousand miles! They must be out of their minds," declares a young lawyer from New York.

"They'll have to install a guard at every pylon," sniffs a woman from New Orleans. "The locals will steal everything, including the nuts and bolts."

The blonde business consultant nods. "An insane waste of everybody's time and money," she sadly agrees. After a pause in which nobody says anything she sighs: "I've got a problem with my visa again." She talks about it as if it's a recurring illness.

"Is it bad?" commiserates a dazzlingly dressed Californian.

The blonde nods. "I've been issued a business visa so I can gather information for my *Vietnam Newsletter*. I asked for an extension so I could get ready for the arrival of an American trade delegation. No way, they tell me. If I want to escort a trade delegation I need another kind of visa. I'll have to leave the country and request a new visa."

"That's going to cost you a bundle," concludes the Californian.

A man with a mustache exclaims cynically: "Help with visa problems? That might be the best business in all of Hanoi."

I walk over to the swimming pool and test the water with my hand. The temperature is perfect. But, they tell me, no swimming is allowed during these parties, since the Embassy wants to maintain a certain decorum. Anyone falling accidentally into the water will not be allowed to come back, and there's no one in Hanoi willing to incur that punishment.

I'm reminded of another social highlight for foreigners in this town: the weekly gatherings of the Hash Harriers, an organization of expatriates from a variety of countries. I'd been to one of their meetings a few days ago. We met on the shore of Ho Tay Lake, the West Lake: a bunch of Australians, Brits, Americans, Dutch, Swedes, a Frenchman and a Japanese. They'd organized a trail hunt. After an hour we were all back at the start, with the sweat pouring off our bodies. But the fun had only just begun. Every newcomer was required to drink a bucket of beer by way of initiation. Anyone who had fallen or lost anything along the trail was obliged to accept the punishment: you either had to guzzle the beer or else pour it over your head. Soaked with sweat and beer, we headed for a nearby restaurant. Before long the Hash Harriers launched into their club songs, which tradition demanded be accompanied by suggestive gestures. The waitresses ensconced themselves behind the bar and gaped at the spectacle, their eyes as big as saucers. They eventually ran into the kitchen, screaming all the way. It's no wonder, I muse, that the Australian Embassy likes to keep a lid on things.

While sipping my Foster's I let my eye rove over the guests. The foreign-aid experts, the UNICEF and UNIDO representatives, are clumped together on one side of the pool. They're all hoping the World Bank will come across with big bucks so they can build roads and start improving Vietnam's infrastructure. They're raring to go. Once the World Bank gives its fiat, they can finance hundreds of medical and educational projects. The buildings needed to house these organizations are already under construction in Hanoi. Since there are lots of top-salaried jobs up for grabs, they're attracting a great deal of attention. Vietnam will soon be overrun by well-meaning advisers.

On the other side of the swimming pool are the financial experts, the representatives of the numerous Western banks who have recently opened their doors to business. "We can't guarantee any investments made in this country," one of them explained to me earlier. They're waiting for investors who are willing to take risks.

The legion of advisers and business consultants can be found inside. I can hear one of them saying: "Vietnam's development doesn't interest me in the least. I'm here to sell the sizzle, not the steak."

The foreigners rent Hanoi's huge French villas, install satel-

The Battle of the Embargo

lite dishes on the roofs and have swimming pools dug in the back yards. They love Hanoi, they say. It's beautiful, quiet and inexpensive. They swear that Hanoi is the real Vietnam; Saigon is merely a degenerate copy. More than one person has told me there are no beggars in Hanoi. Still, everywhere I go I'm pursued by hollow-cheeked old ladies with beseeching eyes and little boys with signs in English saying they're orphans. I've heard many a foreign woman claim there is no prostitution in Hanoi. Yet I know that when their husbands walk down the streets alone, they are approached by cyclo drivers with the magic words "Madam Vietnam?" It's true that everything is cheaper in Hanoi than in Saigon. But the people of Hanoi are also a lot poorer than those in the South.

It suddenly occurs to me that I haven't seen even one shop in Hanoi where you can buy gold. All over Saigon you can find jewelers selling gold bars, since their value is more stable than the dong. Some Saigonese families have been hoarding hundreds of grams of gold since the war. One reason Hanoi's civil servants are so anxious to be transferred to the South is that they expect to cash in on the action.

The Americans seated around a table are continuing their discussion of The Embargo. Or if you prefer, the reason why it hasn't been lifted: the more than two thousand American MIAs who still haven't been accounted for. "A waste of money," according to Andrew, the condom expert. "Besides, why aren't they looking for the hundred thousand Vietnamese who vanished without a trace?"

The blonde business consultant replies: "Nobody objects to looking for the MIAs. But the MIA issue should be kept separate from the trade issue." She's in her mid-thirties, too young to clearly remember the war. Apparently various Vietnamese in high positions have asked her if she's in line to become the new American Ambassador. "I doubt it," she told them. "But the location for our new embassy has already been determined. I just had it confirmed today from a reliable source."

Reproachful glances are cast in the direction of a table in a dark corner occupied by a group of burly military men in civilian clothes whose job it is to track down any and all leads on MIAs.

In the eyes of the business people and the aid workers these men are the source of all their problems, since they're making it impossible for Vietnam to resume normal relations with other nations. As they see it, if these men weren't so hell-bent on achieving their objective, the rest of the world could get down to investing its money and conducting its trade. The war could finally become a thing of the past.

I met one of the men, Lieutenant Flannigan, a few days ago when I visited the vast U.S. Army complex on the outskirts of Hanoi, which serves as the coordination center for their search. I walk over to say hello, and Lieutenant Flannigan politely rises to his feet. "Good evening, ma'am," he says, immediately offering me his chair. The Western advisers I'd been chatting with a moment before chuckle in amusement. In their eyes these military guys are old-fashioned and macho.

"What would you like to drink?" asks Lieutenant Flannigan with a Texas accent. He brings a beer for me and a Coke for himself. He might be a redneck in the eyes of the foreign advisers, but he does speak fluent Vietnamese, which is more than most of them can say. He's spent twenty years perfecting his knowledge of the Vietnamese language.

"I started learning Vietnamese back in '72," he says in his Southern drawl, "and we began withdrawing troops in '73." So there was no call for his services while the war was still in full swing. In the intervening years, Lieutenant Flannigan listened to Vietnamese radio stations and read the newspapers of his former enemy to keep his linguistic skills up to date.

He came to Hanoi a year and a half ago. "I'm doing this job out of a sense of loyalty to my fellow servicemen and their families." When I remark that there's been quite a lot of criticism about the amount of money spent on the search for MIAs, he responds with wholehearted sincerity: "Anyone who doesn't know for sure what happened to their husband or their brother is most grateful to us for going to all this trouble."

"The foreigners in Hanoi are clearly divided into two camps," I note.

"Well," Lieutenant Flannigan replies, "seventy percent of the American population is convinced that there are still living

The Battle of the Embargo

Americans in Vietnam. And as long as the majority is of that opinion, we'll keep on doing our job." Lieutenant Flannigan estimates they'll need another ten or fifteen years to wind up their work. "We're trying to reconstruct what happened to the MIAs to the best of our ability. We follow every lead. We give serious consideration to every tip that comes in. And even if we find only one tooth, we have enough technical expertise here to be able to identify the victim," he concludes solemnly.

As Lieutenant Flannigan informed me earlier, there have been sixteen hundred reported "sightings" of living Americans since 1975. Unfortunately, two-thirds of the sightings involved the same man: Bob Garwood. His jaw hardened at the mention of Garwood's name.

"Garwood was a collaborator," he explains now. "He hung around after the war, doing odd jobs and looking after his pet monkey." The authorities in Washington were inundated with reports of an American in Hanoi with a monkey. They only ended in 1979 when Garwood decided to go back to the States. "It seems he's working as a gas-station attendant these days," says Lieutenant Flannigan, his voice betraying his outrage.

When Lieutenant Flannigan came to live in Hanoi, he heard various stories of some caves where several hundred Americans were supposed to be living. "Our research showed that there wasn't a grain of truth in those stories," he explains.

"What makes people say such things?" I ask.

He throws his hands in the air. "Maybe someone paid them to say it. Maybe there's someone who doesn't want the embargo lifted."

The other men at the table, who have been silent up to now, decide it's time to join the conversation. Flannigan shouldn't be so serious, they grumble. Tonight it's party time.

One of them is about thirty, quite a bit younger than the others. He's a big muscular bodybuilder type. Lieutenant Flannigan introduces him: "John is part of the team that's been spending the last couple of weeks investigating the town of Hoa Binh."

"How's life in the country?" I ask.

John takes a deep breath, expanding his chest to even more imposing proportions. "It's a weird place," he says in a deep voice. "There's nothing in Hoa Binh, not even a Kentucky Fried

Chicken." He allows a moment of silence to pass, as if he wishes to let this pearl of wisdom sink in. The others continue their conversation, using the kind of military jargon that prefers to call a car a "vehicle."

"We're not allowed to fraternize with Vietnamese women," Lieutenant Flannigan says out of the blue.

"Really?" I ask in great amusement. "By the Vietnamese government?"

"Of course not," says Lieutenant Flannigan, unable to disguise his disgust at the stupidity of my question. "By the Americans. After all, the embargo is still in force. You could easily make yourself a target for blackmail."

"Oh right," I nod sympathetically, thinking back to all those stories about the war, when the Americans saw Vietnam as not only a symbol of anguish but also a sexual paradise.

I cast a glance around the table, at the obdurate faces of men who identify totally with their work. Why were they unable to beat the Vietnamese?

The war correspondents of those days haven't stopped mulling over that question. In his book *A Bright Shining Lie* Neil Sheehan writes that the Viet Cong weren't necessarily invincible. Time and again, he is forced to conclude that the Americans were often ignorant. "Over the years [the guerrillas] configured the decks of their sampans to utilize the available space to best advantage . . . Once one learned the arrangement it was not difficult to tell that these sampans did not belong to farmers," he writes. "When [the Viet Cong] assembled in a hamlet . . . they usually restricted the movements of the population. If anyone on the Saigon side was alert, the fall-off in the number of peasants coming to market was a tip of the Viet Cong's presence."

According the Sheehan, there was nothing magical about the strength of the VC. The Americans simply did a poor job of observing what was happening right under their noses.

After I finished reading his book, I wondered what might have happened if the U.S. had managed to conquer Vietnam. As Sheehan was critical of government policy during his stint as a war correspondent, I assume that's not the ending he would have chosen. The men seated at the table around me presumably would have.

THE BATTLE OF THE EMBARGO

Their conversation has veered into the more grisly aspect of their work: the collection of bones. "A Vietnamese national reported to us with what he claimed was the skeleton of an American," Lieutenant Flannigan sighs, "but they turned out to be the bones of a sixty-seven-year-old woman." After the war Vietnamese farmers and mountain dwellers went searching for the remains of American soldiers. They were sure somebody would be willing to pay good money for them some day. They dug up graves and hid the skeletons in their homes. Under pressure from the Americans the Vietnamese government took measures to check the spread of this practice. Specially appointed officials traveled all over the mountains to let it be known that possession of anything other than the remains of close relatives was strictly forbidden. Repentant peasants turned over thousands of skeletons. These were transported to the vast complex in Hanoi where Lieutenant Flannigan and his crew subjected them to investigation. Virtually all of the bones appeared to be those of Vietnamese. "We were able to establish that one bone was that of a French man," grumbles the disappointed lieutenant at my side.

Still, thanks to the advances in DNA research, their work occasionally results in something useful. "We recently held an official ceremony at the airport for the remains of eight U.S. servicemen. After that the coffins were released to their next of kin in the States."

"An American ceremony at Hanoi Airport?" I ask incredulously. The very same airport surrounded by American bomb craters?

"Yes, ma'am," the military men say in chorus.

I return to the group of American advisers, business people and the lone condom expert. Andrew is busy imitating Lieutenant Flannigan's self-conscious bearing and gestures. Someone else is winding up a story whose beginning I missed: "In the North you've got real Communists. In the South they're just a bunch of amateurs."

It's gotten late. "Time to be on your way," one of the embassy staff reminds us. We walk through the gate, giggling like children on their way home from a birthday party, and head into Hanoi's deserted streets.

The Sorrow of War

Shortly before I left for Vietnam I went to visit Dr. Buoi, a psychiatrist from Hanoi who was spending some time in Holland. I went to see her at a dormitory in Leiden University where she was being housed while conducting her study of the Dutch mental-health-care system. She smiled when I asked her to give me her impressions.

"In Holland people are being treated for various kinds of stress that are considered part of everyday life in Vietnam," she said after a moment of reflection. According to her, Vietnamese people don't need this kind of psychiatric treatment. In the course of centuries they've had to steel themselves against many blows, which has given them great inner strength. "We survived a thousand years of Chinese occupation. Then French colonization began at the end of the last century. That was briefly interrupted by Japanese domination during World War II. And then came the war with the Americans. Besides that, our country is constantly threatened by typhoons. We've learned to cope with suffering."

"But haven't things been going better since the war?" I inquire.

"We're all having a hard time earning enough to survive," Dr. Buoi explained. "A lot of people have two or three jobs. That doesn't leave us any time for post-traumatic stress disorder."

The door to her room had been left open. From where I was sitting I could see into the communal kitchen across the hall. Students walking in and out to get a cup of coffee or a glass of milk cast us suspicious glances. Maybe they thought we two older women were keeping tabs on their activities. "Shall I close the door?" I asked.

Dr. Buoi stared at me in noncomprehension. "I can't help noticing," she said, "that you live behind closed doors here in Holland. Each person is alone with his own suffering. In my country relatives, friends and neighbors are constantly coming and going. That's another reason fewer of our people need a psychiatrist: our sorrow is shared sorrow."

It was an interesting thought. Has a long period of peace and affluence caused us to lose our psychic equilibrium? Do the Vietnamese really have more inner strength? Didn't the war leave behind the traces we thought it would?

In Hanoi I dial the number of the Bach Mai Hospital and ask to speak to Dr. Buoi. The line crackles for awhile and then I recognize her voice. "Just stay put, I'll come get you," she exclaims. "I'd like to show you my department."

Before long she knocks at the door of my hotel room, accompanied by two unassuming men. She's wearing a simple striped blouse over a pair of comfortable gray slacks. Her hair is short and boyish. She's brisk and efficient, just the way I remember her. "I don't own a motorbike," she apologizes, "so these gentlemen have come along as drivers."

Our two chauffeurs weave sedately through the traffic on one of the broad boulevards bisecting the city. We pass through a gate and enter the extensive hospital grounds. The two men disappear into a laboratory, and Dr. Buoi leads me into a hospital ward lined with simple beds, ten on each side. Men in plain hospital garb gaze at us in apathy. Their hair has been cut so short they look more like prisoners than patients. There are no bedside tables. None of the men are reading books or magazines. They have nothing to do all day but stare at the damp spots on the wall.

One man is not lying in bed, but is standing in the middle of the room. His eyes light up when he catches sight of me. He walks up and taps me on the arm. "Look, look," he says in English and athletically flips himself over backwards, landing effortlessly on two feet. He grins. "Look," he shouts and performs another backward flip. Two nurses lay a gentle but determined hand on his skinny shoulders, and Dr. Buoi suggests that we continue our tour. As we cross an empty courtyard, the young man is still shouting "look, look."

"Did those men fight in the war?" I ask.

"Some of them were in Cambodia," Dr. Buoi replies, "but most of them are too young to have fought in the American war. We don't know whether their illness was triggered by the war. They might have had these problems if their lives had taken a different course. They are either schizophrenic or psychotic. We make our diagnosis and then treat them accordingly."

"Can you do anything for them except prescribe pills?" I inquire. With the exception of the athletic young man, all the other patients in the ward seemed to be heavily sedated.

"We talk to them," says Dr. Buoi gently, "and we talk with their families. But we can't do anything that costs money, because we haven't got any."

Since the breakup of the Soviet empire, Vietnam can no longer obtain low-priced equipment and pharmaceuticals from Moscow. Dr. Buoi looks glum. For a moment she may have been seeing her hospital ward through the eyes of a Dutch person.

It's quiet in the other buildings. What everyone knows, though it's not publicly acknowledged, is that most doctors are not spending very much time at their work these days. The majority of them are moonlighting in some form or another, as otherwise they wouldn't make enough to feed their children.

I notice a group of people silently huddled around a coffin beside a blank wall. Dr. Buoi opens her mouth to say something, but changes her mind. I pretend not to see them since it's too painful. I can't imagine a worse form of advertisement for a hospital.

"I'll show you where the bomb landed during the Christmas bombing of 1972," says Dr. Buoi in a solemn voice. She'd told me about that when we were in Holland. We walk over a path connecting several departments. "Look," points Dr. Buoi. "Right here, under the ground, there's a tunnel. During the war we used it to get from one building to another." I can imagine her, twenty years younger, hurrying through the dark catacombs.

She comes to a standstill by the entrance. "This is where it landed." The spot is marked by a statue of a woman heroically raising her clenched fist in the air. In her lap she's holding a little girl with long flowing hair, as limp as a rag doll. Roughly forty names have been chiseled in the stone.

"Most of the patients were evacuated to the countryside," Dr. Buoi recalls. "Only the most serious cases were left behind in Bach Mai Hospital. When the siren sounded, we took cover in the various air-raid shelters. One of them received a direct hit. I raced over there, but it was covered with rubble. We could hear the people buried under the debris moaning and shouting." She pauses for a moment. "I heard the voice of my best friend. She was going to get married in two days. I knew her fiance too. But there was nothing we could do. The rubble was too heavy, and we had nothing but our bare hands. We heard them die, slowly."

She straightens her back. "And yet I don't suffer from post-traumatic stress disorder," she concludes valiantly. "A terrible thing happened, but I continued to function normally. The war left me with only one problem: a lack of energy. Sometimes I'm absolutely exhausted."

We say goodbye to each other. One of her colleagues drives me back to my hotel. Like her, he's in his forties. But he doesn't speak a word of English or French. We ride through the city in silence. He placidly steers the motorbike through the disorderly traffic and waves amicably to an acquaintance he chances to see.

If someone were to ask me for my impression of him, I'd have to say he strikes me as a man who's satisfied with his life. Before I hopped on the back of his motorbike, Dr. Buoi laughingly patted him on the shoulder and said: "During the war my esteemed colleague marched three thousand miles through the jungle. And he doesn't suffer from post-traumatic stress disorder either."

Back in my air-conditioned room, I spend a long time mulling over my visit. Can people really be so strong? Have Vietnamese veterans really become decent husbands and fathers while American veterans are marked for life?

I remember meeting a Swedish Vietnam expert in Saigon who told me about an author in Hanoi, a veteran who wrote a novel based on his memories of the war. He said it was a haunting book, written in a style you rarely find in Vietnam. No heroics, no rhetoric. Just a simple portrayal of the cruelty of war.

The author could presumably tell me a lot about the aftermath of war, but how can I get in touch with him? I decide to call Mr. Thuc in Saigon, the creative hand behind the romantic movie scripts. I'm sure he'll be able to help me.

"I know who you mean," he says over an unexpectedly clear line. "His name is Bao Ninh. He's not exactly a favorite of the regime. But why don't you contact Mr. Nham, a literary critic in Hanoi who's a good friend of mine. You can reach him through the Writers' Union."

The desk clerk lends me her bicycle, and I pedal along the shore of one of the city's many lakes in the fierce midday heat. It's quiet outside the Writers' Union. I step into a high-ceilinged room, where a secretary is seated under a sluggishly revolving overhead fan, typing something on an old manual typewriter. The keys land with a thud against the paper. She gestures that Mr. Nham isn't in and calls to a man in the next room who's clearing off his desk. He does speak English. "He'll probably be in tomorrow," he explains.

"Maybe you can help me," I say. "You're also employed by the Writers' Union, aren't you?"

"Not anymore. As of tomorrow I'm working for the Swedish Embassy."

"Do you know the writer Bao Ninh?" I inquire. He nods. "Do you think you could help me get in touch with him?"

He smiles. "Bao Ninh isn't a member of the Writers' Union." Thinking aloud, he hesitantly adds: "I could tell you something about the literary world in Hanoi." But he changes his mind. "It wouldn't be wise," he decides, without offering an explanation. He hands the secretary a bunch of keys and says to me, "You apparently know Mr. Nham. Why don't you ask him to introduce you to Bao Ninh?" Then he politely says goodbye and walks out the door, undoubtedly closing a very important chapter in his life and taking the story with him, since he doesn't dare tell it to me.

Mr. Nham is in his office the next day. He's apparently been informed that a foreigner is looking for him, for he jumps to his feet when I enter the room. He gestures for me to take a seat. He speaks Russian, but not English or French, which makes him blush in embarrassment. For a couple of minutes we sit across from each other like two deaf-mutes. Then inspiration strikes. He takes a piece of paper and writes tomorrow's date and a time: 9:00 A.M. Then he points to me. His plan is absolutely clear. He's going to find an interpreter, and the two of them will meet me at my hotel tomorrow morning.

At the appointed hour Mr. Nham presents himself at the reception desk with one of his colleagues, who's even shier than he is, if that's possible. Mr. Nham gives him a gentle shove in my direction as a hint that he should take the conversational lead. I invite the two gentlemen to my room, where they seat themselves uncomfortably on a plastic-covered couch. "We're not used to meeting foreigners," confesses Mr. Vinh, the interpreter, adding disconsolately: "We don't have any business cards either." It's customary in Vietnam to exchange business cards, but they don't have the money for such a luxury item. I offer them something to drink from the refrigerator which is whirring away in the corner of the room. After my repeated urging, they both order a Coke.

"How can we be of your service?" asks the interpreter at Mr. Nham's instructions.

It seems impolite to come right out and say I want to meet the writer Bao Ninh, as if I haven't the slightest interest in the two of them. So I say to Mr. Nham: "I'd like to hear your opinion as a literary critic. Do the books written in the North differ very much from those in the South?"

Mr. Nham ponders the question and formulates his answer carefully: "The North represents the old Vietnam. We refer to the South as the 'new' country, because large parts of the South were only inhabited by the Vietnamese a few hundred years ago."

The two men turn to each other and debate the matter before continuing. "The heart of Vietnam lies in the North. This is the source of new ideas. In the South people like listening to rock 'n' roll and making money. We're not very good at those things, but that gives us more time for reflection."

Mr. Nham takes a small sip of Coke. "To use a metaphor," he continues, "Hanoi is the house, and Saigon is the door. Or maybe a better way of putting it is that Saigon is the stage and Hanoi is the place where the play is written and directed. It gets produced in Saigon and then the story comes back to Hanoi, mixed with commentary and Western influences."

"So the most important writers are Northerners?" I ask, hoping to steer the conversation towards my objective. Mr. Nham nods emphatically. "Like Bao Ninh?" I add, trying to casually drop his name into the conversation.

"That's right," agrees Mr. Nham. "He was recently awarded a literary prize."

"I'd really like to meet him."

Mr. Nham's face darkens. "That'll be difficult," he replies. "He's probably not even in Hanoi. He travels a lot." He looks sorry he ever agreed to help me.

"Do you think you could find out for me?" I insist.

"I don't know where he lives," mumbles Mr. Nham evasively. He clearly doesn't wish to set up a meeting with Bao Ninh. Is he afraid it will get him into trouble?

"I understand that you're a very busy man," I say, changing tactics. "Maybe you could just make an appointment for me, and I could go to see him alone."

"Bao Ninh doesn't speak English." The two men stare impassively at me for a moment and then look down at their shoes. "There are lots of good writers in Hanoi," declares Mr. Nham, visibly upset. "We can make an appointment with someone else."

Their efforts to discourage me only make me more determined. "One of Bao Ninh's books is due to be published shortly in English, and that's why I'd like to meet him. I understand that you can't spare the time to go with me, so I'll get my own interpreter."

"Well, I know where Bao Ninh's father lives," Mr. Nham admits, suddenly more obliging. "I'll ask him," he says, adding hastily, "but I can't make you any promises."

Memories of the Wood of Crying Souls

At the reception desk an odd-looking man has been asking for me. He's thin, and his glasses are so thick that his eyes look like they're under a magnifying glass. "I've been sent by the gentlemen from the Writers' Union," he explains.

I invite him to my room. He immediately lights up a cigarette and plants it between his nicotine-stained fingers. He reaches into his bag and pulls out a piece of paper on which a map has been drawn. Underneath it is a message in curly handwriting: "You are expected at Bao Ninh's on Monday afternoon at three o'clock."

"I'll be glad to go with you if you wish," offers Mr. Duong Tuong amicably. He speaks both English and French fluently.

"I'd be delighted" is my astonished reply. I didn't expect the solution to my problem simply to come walking through the door.

"I know Bao Ninh," Mr. Duong continues. "He's got an excellent reputation. I also know his father, a famous scientist. They live next door to each other." He takes a contemplative drag on his cigarette.

I get the impression that arranging my meeting with Bao Ninh isn't the only reason for his visit. He takes a long look around the room and says circumspectly: "I understand you're interested in certain aspects of Vietnamese society which I can explain to you more easily than most people. I have a lot of contacts in the literary and artistic world." He doesn't say this boastfully, but rather with an air of apology. "I'm an independent journalist," he continues. "I'm free to do what I want." He snorts in amusement.

    I can follow every movement of his eyes through the thick lenses. It's as if you can see right into his soul. Mr. Duong only entered my life a few minutes ago, and I like him already.

    "I can show you a side of Hanoi that foreigners don't usually get to see," he says, extinguishing his cigarette in the ashtray on the table. It gradually dawns on me that Mr. Duong is offering to introduce me to the world of critical intellectuals, maybe even to some dissidents.

    "That would interest me a whole lot."

    A smile of satisfaction crosses over his deeply lined face. "I'll write down my address," he replies, immediately becoming practical. "You're welcome to come to my house on Wednesday. We can discuss our plans then. It's not too far away. It should be easy to find. Here, I'll draw you a map."

    Handing me his sketch, he gets to his feet. "But first we'll go see Bao Ninh. I'll come by for you at two-thirty." I promise to wait for him downstairs.

    On Monday afternoon the ice-cream parlor is teeming with youthful foreigners, world travelers busy exchanging information. Their bulging backpacks are propped against the wall. The men in particular look incredibly big and blond compared to the Vietnamese around them. Their long legs protrude from torn jeans and their sleeveless T-shirts reveal bare arms, tanned shoulders and hairy armpits. Their entire conversation revolves around money: where you can find a cheap place to stay in Saigon and how you can avoid taking expensive trains.

    A gleaming motor scooter pulls up to the sidewalk and stops. It takes a moment before I recognize Mr. Duong as the driver. I hadn't expected to see him on such a beautiful scooter. "Dream 100 11" is lettered across the gas tank; it's the most expensive model you can buy in all of Vietnam. We'd agreed to go by bicycle, and I'd arranged to borrow the desk clerk's Chinese bike for the occasion.

Mr. Duong laughs at the look of astonishment on my face. "It's too far," he explains. "I've borrowed this scooter from a successful young artist. The only problem is that I don't really know how it works." He revs the engine.

I seat myself cautiously on the back. With a loud grinding of the gears Mr. Duong shifts into first, and we're off. As we race through an intersection he keeps his eyes glued to the dashboard in fixed concentration. We pass through the district where bathroom fixtures and toilet bowls are sold and drive past the grounds of a former factory that is rumored to be the next site of the American Embassy. The traffic thins out, and the stores lining the street have fewer and fewer goods for sale.

We find ourselves in a suburb of Hanoi, which consists of long rows of housing projects. Once they were painted pale yellow, but the rain has left gray streaks in the paint.

After some hesitation Mr. Duong pulls up in front of Block B5. He doesn't dare leave this valuable scooter unattended. He takes a look around and pushes the scooter over to a lean-to where an old woman is displaying her wares: cigarettes, boxes of matches and a couple of bottles of beer. She nods, promising to keep an eye on the scooter.

We climb several flights of dismal concrete stairs to the fourth floor where a man is waiting for us on the walkway. "My name is Bao Ninh," he says, in one stroke exhausting his supply of English words. He's dressed in jeans, a white shirt and plastic slippers. A mournful mustache in the form of a half moon droops around the corners of his mouth. He moves with a ponderous gait. For some reason he seems to lack the physical grace that characterizes so many Vietnamese.

We enter a square living room and take a seat on straight-backed wooden armchairs. Mr. Duong and Bao Ninh chat for a moment in Vietnamese. I can't tell whether they know each other well or not. A coffee table is invitingly arrayed with grapes, shrimp crackers and teacups. Bao Ninh seems out of place in this charming stage set. He shifts uneasily in his chair and lights a cigarette. There's something menacing about him.

"What would you like to know?" translates Mr. Duong, and the two men fix their eyes on me. I sit up in surprise. They're expecting a serious answer to their question, but I haven't the faintest idea what the man sitting across from me is like. In the last few days, when it seemed I was never going to be able to arrange a meeting with him, the writer's elusiveness endowed him with the aura of a movie star. But of course he's not a movie star. In point of fact he was a Viet Cong soldier. He was "the enemy" who made Americans like Mark shake in their boots. Terrifying rustles in the jungle at night might have been Bao Ninh on patrol. I feel the polite smile disappear from my face. This is not going to be a cheerful conversation. Descending into the ravine of gruesome memories takes all the courage I've got.

I make a tentative start. "Why is your book called *The Sorrow of War?*"

"That's what they call it in the South. I wasn't allowed to call it that in the North," scoffs Bao Ninh. "The word 'war' is taboo here. You can talk about the 'struggle for liberation,' but there's no way you can use the word 'sorrow' in connection with the war. So here in the North the book is called *The Fate of Love*."

He falls silent. While Mr. Duong translates his words, his eyes rove around the room, as if he's bored. He's deadly serious; his mouth may be smiling but his eyes are not. In the corner of the room there's a small table that's entirely taken up by a portable typewriter. Mr. Duong had told me that Bao Ninh only bangs away at it during the night.

"The main character in your book . . . is that you?"

"I've changed a few minor details, but like my main character I knew from the time I was seven years old that my generation would have to fight the Americans. I went to school and led a seemingly normal life, though I knew duty was eventually going to call." In 1964, the day Bao Ninh finished high school, he reported to the army. "Together with all the boys in my class. There were thirty of us. Only four of us survived, including me."

He gets up and goes behind a curtain, reappearing with some bottles in his hand. "Would you like some beer?" he asks. "Chinese beer?" He starts pouring beer into our glasses.

"The second part of my book is about the years after the war,

Memories of the Wood of Crying Souls

after we had achieved the goal for which hundreds of thousands of young people sacrificed their lives." He carefully pours the beer so that it just reaches the rim and doesn't run over. "After all, we were independent, and Vietnam was finally reunited." His voice fills with reproach. "But we also fought for freedom, economic security, justice and democracy, none of which we have." He grinds out his cigarette in the ashtray. "That's why the main character in my book feels so lonely and disappointed after the war. He thinks back to all his friends and wonders if they died in vain."

His words strike a familiar chord. The war meaningless? And that from the mouth of an ex-corporal in the National Liberation Front? His face assumes an expression of stubborn resentfulness.

"The American veterans say almost the same thing," I murmur in surprise.

Bao Ninh laughs grimly. "It just took us longer to figure it out. We were so busy trying to eke out a living after the war that we didn't have time for contemplation."

Mr. Duong translates the bitter complaints without emotion. I keep getting the impression that Bao Ninh wants to say something, but I don't know what. It makes me nervous, because if I don't ask he won't tell.

"What bothered you the most after the war?"

Bao Ninh laughs sourly. "Being broke," he replies succinctly. "We still have to spend all our time making just enough to get by."

"You can't support yourself with your writing?"

He waves his hand in a gesture of contempt. "The money I earned from my book just about paid my beer tab. There was a second printing in Hanoi, but I haven't received even one dong from that. No, I earn my living doing something totally different. I'm in the import-export business."

"Oh," I say in surprise, "what do you import and export?"

"Oh, this and that. From China." He looks as if he's sorry he mentioned it. When I press him for details, he says: "It's not interesting. I just do it to survive."

Rumors of illegal trade across the borders are rife in Hanoi. The Vietnamese transport crabs, dogs, metal and timber to China in whatever mode of transportation they can afford: trucks, baskets or bamboo poles. They return laden with beer, clothes, pots and pans and other household items which can be seen for sale in stores all over the city.

"So you know China well?" I persist.

Bao Ninh nods. "Chinese women are terrible," he says in disgust. "No, Saigon is more fun. The people there are more easygoing, life is more exciting and the women are not as prudish as they are here." He sighs.

I have the impression he's too big for his body and is about to burst. The living room seems too small to hold him, and he talks about Hanoi as if he's outgrown it. Maybe being constantly on the go helps assuage his restlessness.

Bao Ninh looks surly when I ask him how the war changed him. "It left me with an ache in my head."

Mr. Duong gravely explains: "Bao Ninh means he suffers from some kind of brain damage. For example, he can't stand revolving ceiling fans. They remind him of American helicopters."

"There are a lot of war veterans in these projects," continues Bao Ninh. "Across the street the entire block consists of disabled veterans and their families. These apartments were assigned to us as a reward for our services. A lot of the men sit around the house all day drinking, mostly home brew made out of sugar cane. There used to be a lot of fights. The women and children were the ones who paid the price; the whole neighborhood could hear. The electricity used to go out a lot and every time there was another power failure everyone started swearing and bellyaching: 'Can't they even make the damn electricity work?'" Both he and Mr. Duong grin. I can imagine Bao Ninh screaming with rage along with the rest of them. "No one dared lay a hand on us. After all, we're the war heroes. In the meantime middle age has caught up with us, and things have settled down. The sons are stronger than the fathers. The next generation is keeping the veterans under control."

Bao Ninh married late; his daughter just turned ten. His wife, a tall stylishly dressed woman with her hair in a curly permanent, comes home from work. She's a teacher. In her presence the writer seems to relax a little. I ask her if Bao Ninh is difficult to live with. She laughs. "It's easier than it used to be," she replies loyally.

His parents live in the apartment next door. There's a connecting door, so that they can walk in and out of each other's apartments. Dr. Buoi was right in that respect: Bao Ninh's sorrow is shared sorrow. An American with the same background would probably be divorced and living a thousand miles away from his parents.

On April 30, 1975 Bao Ninh and his squad marched into Saigon. "I was flabbergasted," he recalls. "I never thought I'd survive the war, and I sure didn't think we'd win. I was in a daze."

"And happy?"

"No, there'd been too many losses. I felt sad."

His book is being translated into English. Who knows, I suggest, maybe it'll even become a best-seller in the U.S.

The author straightens his back. Any financial improvement in his situation would be more than welcome, he tells me. "The first thing I'd do would be to buy a house," he says. "This apartment reminds me of an army barrack." He looks around the living room in loathing. Though the walls have been painted a delicate blue, there's a definite military feel about the place. Maybe it's because the windows overlook a concrete walkway that resounds with hollow footsteps.

"Would you like to go to the U.S.?" I ask.

He shakes his head no. "Various fortune-tellers have predicted that I'd never cross the ocean. According to the cards, I've used up all my chances. They went up in smoke during the war."

We've now been talking for about three hours. Mr. Duong, pale from exertion, puts out his umpteenth cigarette in an overflowing ashtray. I'm limp with exhaustion. I feel like I've just run the marathon.

Bao Ninh refills our beer glasses, as if he doesn't think the conversation is at an end. Is there something else he wants to tell me? I wait and he says nothing. I hesitate to announce our departure. Mr. Duong keeps looking at me expectantly.

Another half an hour elapses before we finally take our leave. In the doorway Bao Ninh presses a few sheets of paper into my hand: some pages of his book which have been translated into English. "Oh," I exclaim in both surprise and disappointment, since I would have preferred to read them prior to our meeting. Now there's no way I can ask him specific questions about the book.

Voices and Visions

It's gotten dark outside. We look up at the fourth floor, but there's no one in sight. Weather-beaten and aged before its time, the apartment building stares implacably down on us.

I wake up in the middle of the night with my teeth chattering. The air-conditioning has turned the room into a refrigerator. I switch it off and open the window. Total silence reigns in the courtyard next door. A wave of hot air rushes in through the window.

I remember the sheets of paper Bao Ninh gave me that afternoon and fish them out of my bag. I still can't imagine exactly what he must have gone through.

"It had been late August," I read. "Along the stream, the dog roses blossomed in the rain, perfume filling the air. At night, the perfume condensed. It got into your sleep, turned into strange dreams, created a voluptuous, drunk obsession . . . It's also said it grows more abundantly where there have been many deaths. It's a blood-loving flower, which is hard to believe, it smells so sweet."

The main character, Kien, is in a reconnaissance platoon which comes up with the idea of drying the flowers, leaves and roots and mixing them with tobacco. "It tasted very good. After only a few puffs, you felt as if you were quietly floating . . . You could use the smoke to forget a soldier's life, forget hunger and suffering, forget death, forget tomorrow totally."

Soon Kien's entire regiment was enthusiastically smoking dog roses. But not for long: "There followed an order from the political commissar prohibiting its use. The flowers were searched for, and rooted out of the Wood of Crying Souls."

One day during the rainy season in 1974 Kien and his reconnaissance platoon are sent back to the Wood of Crying Souls, not far from a former leper colony. One of the soldiers, Tiny Thinh, shoots an orangutan. It's so big three men have to help him drag it back to camp. "But, oh god, when it was killed, shaved hairless, it appeared to be a fat woman with ulcerous skin, half white, half grey, eyes rolling."

I toss the sheets of paper on the table in revulsion. The breeze wafting in through the window seems to reek of burning hair. I open the refrigerator to get a drink of cold water and a sweetish, nauseating stench greets my nostrils. I head for the bathroom, where I turn on the faucet and let a stream of cold water run over my hands. After a while I calm down again. Only then do I remember that someone from Saigon had given me a durian. It may be a delicious fruit, but it stinks to high heaven.

Dreaming of a Vietnamese Village

Downstairs in the ice-cream parlor I drink a cup of coffee and read the English-language *Vietnam News* that I bought from a raggedy little boy. He's plopped himself down on the stool beside me in hopes of selling me some postcards, but I'm not in a buying mood. "Three hundred thousand pairs of shoes sold to Poland," I read, and "starting in September it's forbidden to import bicycles, electric fans and thermos bottles."

The *Vietnam News* is printed in Hanoi, but the hotels and restaurants advertised in it are all located more than a thousand miles to the south, in Saigon.

Hanoi, I read, has been host to one delegation after another: from France, Egypt, the U.S. and Russia. Here in the North the general populace seems to be paying scant attention to these delegations. They're too busy seeing to their daily survival. Myriads of them are digging in the bowels of the earth in search of tin: not far from Hanoi two hundred people have been killed by mud slides, illness and violently resolved disputes.

But there's also good news. A large, mysterious-looking goat, a hitherto unknown mammal, has been found in a remote forest. While sipping my second cup of coffee, I decide it's high time I explored the mountain regions outside Hanoi. After all, you can't discover what a country is really like without leaving the city limits. There must be more out there, on some misty hillside far away from these concrete pavements.

But what exactly am I looking for? Every time I go on a trip my head is filled with certain images. Sometimes they resemble the pictures favored by tourist brochures: a sunny coastline or an emerald-green jungle. But most of the time I imagine myself taking an active part in these scenes: galloping on a horse alongside Mongolian nomads, or sailing up a river on a Chinese junk with a Cantonese captain at the helm. What usually prompts me to pack my bags is a strong desire to feel at home somewhere else.

In my mind's eye I picture a small village wedged between craggy cliffs. Tiny figures in conical hats wind up the day's work in the rice paddies and head home over a path lined with flowers. In a simple peasant hut I meet a wise old man who proffers me a glass of rice wine and unveils the mystery of the Vietnamese soul to me. They're dreams.

Two familiar faces enter the ice-cream parlor: Matilda, the blonde American business consultant, and her husband, Drew. With a sigh the postcard peddlar relinquishes his stool and goes outside. We seem conspicuously large and noisy compared to the modest Vietnamese around us.

Matilda orders something in Vietnamese, which she pronounces with a strong U.S. Southern accent. One of the bevy of waitresses brings two chocolate ice-cream cones to our table.

I decide to let Drew and Matilda in on my secret longing. "I'd like to make a trip to the mountains," I announce. "After all, Vietnam was originally a land of peasants. Everyone belonged to a village. So that's where you have to go if you want to find out what Vietnam is really like."

Matilda sizes me up with the air of a professional. "Well," she says, "we're going to Bat Trang this afternoon. That's a village just outside Hanoi. We've rented a car and a driver, and you're welcome to come along if you want."

At the agreed-upon time the driver parks in front of the Army Guest House where Matilda and Drew are staying. He gets out of

Dreaming of a Vietnamese Village

the car and goes over to wait under a tree; as his gestures make clear, the car is a veritable oven. Matilda and Drew come outside with a middle-aged Vietnamese man in tow. Mr. Thi, Matilda explains, is an acquaintance of theirs. He designs company logos, an entirely new profession in Hanoi. Mr. Thi sits up front with the driver, and the three of us clamber into the back of a sweltering Russian-made Volga.

We proceed down Ly Thai To Boulevard and clatter over the bridge to the other side of the Red River. We make a right turn onto a dike and roughly follow the course of the river from a great distance. "Bat Trang is known for its ceramics," instructs Matilda.

"Every family has its own kiln," Mr. Thi adds. He was born in Bat Trang and is making use of this opportunity to pay homage to his ancestors. He's promised to act as our interpreter and guide since Matilda's scant knowledge of Vietnamese won't get us far. She's come to Hanoi for a few months to concentrate on learning the language and to gather information for her *Vietnam Newsletter*, which has subscribers all over the world.

"Who knows, maybe we can rustle up some business in Bat Trang," she muses. Her husband Drew owns a company in Hong Kong and has flown over for a few days to be with his wife. When the embargo is lifted, the two of them plan to open a consulting business in Saigon.

We drive past a lake dotted with lotus blossoms. A flat wicker boat is bobbing up and down on the water, and the woman inside it is busy harvesting the roots. On the other side of the road a paddleboat is slowly making its way over a canal. Leaning way back, an old man is pumping the pedals with all his might. They used to have these kinds of boats in China, but I've never seen one before.

Nestled in a curve in the dike is a small village, motionless in the midday sun. A neglected temple towers above the rooftops. A little boy dreamily clutches a rope slung around the neck of a buffalo grazing beside the road.

"Some things never change," philosophizes Mr. Thi, the logo designer. The countryside around us is flat. This region is part of the immense Red River Delta that stretches to the coast.

We turn onto a narrow road and stop before a barrier. "We

have to buy a ticket," explains Mr. Thi, who scurries off towards an office. A ticket to enter a village?

"Bat Trang is a very special village," he says upon his return. Since the road is no longer paved, the driver parks the car, and we walk the rest of the way to the village over a dusty street lined with squat houses. Some of them are decorated with glazed tiles. "Made in Bat Trang," Mr. Thi confirms. One house has been transformed into a shop. Basketfuls of blue and white vases and statues of various kinds are on display. A salesperson is nowhere to be seen. It's apparently too hot to do business.

Mr. Thi, in the role of guide, strides briskly ahead. It's clear from his attitude that he doesn't want us wasting our time in a bunch of shops. He promises to show us the one with the best selection.

"Just wait. It'll be owned by his cousin," the wary Drew mutters under his breath.

On the way Mr. Thi points to some brick-lined reservoirs where the white clay for the earthenware is stored. We soon find ourselves in a maze of narrow alleyways. "Every one of these houses is a ceramics factory," remarks Mr. Thi.

"How long have they been making ceramics in this village?" I ask.

"Oh, about six hundred years," Mr. Thi answers breezily.

A man comes over and greets him effusively. "That'll be the cousin," mutters Drew.

The man leads us to his house through a walled garden. In the courtyard a woman is removing tiles from a mold. Covered with coal dust, she shows us the hellish heat firing the kiln. Clumps of slack have been piled against the chimney to dry, so that they can be used again to stoke the fires.

Passing through a sweltering room in which two men and two women are painting covered serving dishes, we arrive in the showroom. The shelves are filled with vases, bowls and statues. Mr. Thi explains that he can't quote prices, as they depend on a variety of factors. We are served cans of lukewarm soft drinks.

Mr. Thi's cousin clears his throat. "As you can see, we manufacture attractive products which we'd like to export abroad. Perhaps you would be so kind as to give us your opinion."

Matilda inspects several vases which have been laid out on a table for her. "We're only here to make an inventory of the products manufactured in Bat Trang," she says noncommittally. "As long as the embargo's still on nothing can be exported to the United States."

A fan is produced to cool the room, but there appears to be a power failure. It's so hot we can barely breathe, much less talk. To put an end to this futile meeting Mr. Thi offers another suggestion: "If you wish, we can go see my parents' home." We trudge tiredly through the alleys and pass under a gateway. In the courtyard of his parents' house, the names of his ancestors have been chiseled into a memorial marker. Mr. Thi is visibly moved by it. Bowing several times, he prays before the stone marker while his relatives bring us some ceramic stools to sit on.

On the way home we sprawl wearily in the back seat. The sun is low in the sky. In the lake where the old woman had been harvesting the lotus, a couple of little boys are now bathing buffaloes. Further away, a man and a woman are watering their rice paddies, swinging a wicker scoop in a broad arc.

Suddenly the car screeches to a halt. A terrified man snatches his bicycle away from the wheels of the car just in the nick of time. Motorized traffic is still a rarity here. We proceed on our way and are soon clattering once more across the bridge.

Back in the ice-cream parlor I ask the waitress to bring me two glasses of cold lemonade. Discouraged, I'm forced to conclude that this little jaunt has not brought me any closer to The Vietnamese Village of my dreams. It looked more like an obligatory stop on a package tour. I console myself with the thought that Bat Trang is probably too close to Hanoi. If I want to see a real village, I'll have to head into the mountains.

I walk up the winding staircase to the third floor and knock on the door of the condom expert. "Andrew, do you feel like making a trip to the mountains tomorrow?" I ask. "I'd like to go inland to where the ethnic minorities live."

"Well, as luck would have it," replies Andrew, "I've got to do some research on the availability of condoms outside the city. This would be as good a time as any."

Around the corner from the hotel is a travel agency that issues the permits we need to venture outside Hanoi. Andrew and I are bowled over by our welcome. The minute we walk through the door three girls jockey for position, elbowing each other in a race to get to us first. They all speak English, and all three of them would like nothing better than to escort us to our destination. Andrew and I confer. Having a guide isn't a bad idea. After all, without an interpreter we can't converse with the people we meet. We opt for a long-haired girl named Lychee, because she was the first to get to the door. She promises to pick us up tomorrow morning at seven with a brand-new Japanese car and a driver.

The next morning Lychee is dressed even more elegantly than she was at our first encounter. She's wearing a long skirt, high heels and oodles of makeup. Andrew and I clamber into the back of the car and head west out of the city, which brings us to a rural road full of potholes. We're still in the Red River Delta; stretching as far as the eye can see is a plateau covered with rice fields. A peddlar is walking down a path with colorful plastic buckets balanced on the end of his bamboo pole. He's probably heading for the village down the road, where the houses are clustered in a tight knot, as if they're seeking mutual protection.

The mountains on the horizon rise up almost vertically from the ground, their contours softened by early-morning mist. Tall clumps of bamboo are growing along the side of the road. We stop for a moment to take a look. "It's beautiful," says Andrew.

"Yes," I agree, "it looks just like China." This is not intended as a slur on the natural beauty of Vietnam. It's simply the only thought that comes into my head. It does look like China.

The heat begins to take hold. Not far away we can see a stone farmhouse with a huge antenna on the roof. The nearby mountain is being excavated, and the villagers are no doubt carting the rocks here and using them as building materials. A rattling Chinese truck drives down the road.

"You know what," says Andrew, "it reminds me of Nepal."

"Oh," exclaims Lychee, "my last customer said Vietnam looked just like Cuba."

We climb back in the car. According to a white signpost on the side of the road we still have thirty miles to go before we reach our destination, Hoa Binh.

Dreaming of a Vietnamese Village

Lychee has apparently decided she's going to ply us with questions rather than point out the sights. She asks us how big are families are, how much we earn and what kind of work we do.

Andrew explains that he's in the family-planning business. Oddly enough, one minute Lychee's English seems perfectly fluent, and the next minute she doesn't understand a word. "Family planning," Andrew patiently repeats.

She stares at him intently. "For goose?" she asks.

Confused, Andrew shakes his head. "No, for people. There may be too many geese in the world, but at least you can eat them." She gazes at him in incomprehension.

"Condoms," he says, pulling out a package to illustrate his point.

Lychee's face lights up. She fishes in her bag and produces a box of Chinese condoms. She always carries them with her, she's happy to report.

"Great!" Andrew commends her.

"I'm going to have to change my tactics," he says to me. "Vietnamese women aren't as prudish as I'd been led to believe."

We pass a flood-control dam built by the Russians. There are still some Russian families living in Hoa Binh. Their job is to ensure that the dam is maintained properly. "They aren't in any hurry to go home," scoffs Lychee. "Back home they're even poorer than we are."

Hoa Binh's main street reminds me of the stage set of some Western movie: a row of nondescript storefronts along a dusty street. "Can we stop for a minute?" asks Andrew. He wants to conduct some market research. "Here's a list of several basic products like rice and soap," he says showing Lychee the list, "and it also includes condoms. I'd like to know what all the things on the list cost. That way I can figure out if people can afford to buy condoms."

Lychee giggles and shoves the paper towards the driver. He takes the list and returns a few minutes later with all the prices properly noted. "Thanks," says Andrew, and rewards him for his services by pressing a supply of condoms in his hand. The driver quickly tucks them in the glove compartment and steps on the gas.

Lychee directs him to an address just out of town where we

can find a local guide. We pull up at an office in which a slender woman, stylishly attired in beige pants and a spotless white blouse, is seated at a desk. According to Lychee the woman is not Vietnamese. "She's a member of the Muong minority." She knows the area well and speaks the Muong language, so she'll be going along to show us a typical Muong village.

She climbs in front next to Lychee and directs the driver to a dirt road. After a while the road becomes too muddy to navigate. Our decision-making troika goes into a huddle and rules that we should park the car and proceed on foot.

Wobbling on her high heels, Lychee practically twists her ankle every time she takes a step. The Muong guide carefully skirts the mud puddles to keep from splashing her clothes. Lychee sticks close to her and pumps her for information. "That's odd," she says turning towards us. "She's thirty-five and isn't married yet, even though the Muongs usually marry young."

Bluish-green mountains shimmer on the horizon and rice paddies taper off into a steaming green forest. The Muong woman points out edible plants along the way.

Three houses, framed by tall bamboo shoots, are visible against a hillside. "That's where we're going," the Muong guide says, pointing to the houses. It suddenly occurs to me that her facial expression is totally different than Lychee's. She radiates the characteristic serenity of mountain dwellers, and yet her eyes and mouth are extremely expressive. She looks more Asian than the Lat women I saw outside Dalat. That isn't surprising since the Muongs can trace their origins to China, while the Lats originated in the South Seas area.

The Muong woman tells us about her childhood. During the war she lived on the other side of Hoa Binh, in a traditional house built on poles, in a region similar to this one. Her family had dug an air-raid shelter, but one night the planes came in without warning. The family awoke with a start and ran outside towards the shelter. Her father and sister-in-law were killed instantly. Her face tightens. Andrew's shoulders droop.

As we approach the hamlet a group of children come to greet us shouting "*Lien Xo*, Russian." They're thin but healthy. They don't look any different than Vietnamese children. They skip

Dreaming of a Vietnamese Village

and shout ahead of us until we reach the pole houses: magnificent and beautifully proportioned structures made of wood. A buffalo is tethered underneath one of them. I rub his velvety ears.

The Muong guide points to a log cut in two lengthwise. "It's a coffin," she explains. "When they get older, Muongs like the idea of having their coffins ready," she adds. "And in that tree over there," she continues, "there's an American bomb which didn't explode. The casing is used as a bell to summon the villagers."

She walks resolutely over to the hamlet's largest and best-kept house. "Here we can visit a Muong family." She asks us to remove our shoes before climbing the narrow ladder to the house, showing us how to rinse our feet with the water in a small bamboo trough.

In the semidarkness a young woman is poking at a fire under a blackened cooking pot, with a bunch of children scampering at her feet. A wrinkled old woman, dressed in a black sarong and a repeatedly mended short blue jacket, is introduced as the head of the family. Her husband died some time ago. Standing at her side, her grown-up son towers above her. They invite us to sit down on a woven mat. One of the young women brings us a thermos bottle of hot tea, and the son pours it into tiny cups.

It's sweltering, and the old woman gives us each a straw fan so that we can waft a little air our way. When she smiles you can see her teeth, blackened by chewing betel nuts. When I remark that the son isn't wearing the black cotton shirt and pants typical of the Muongs, he laughs. "That's old-fashioned," he tells me. He's dressed in olive drab, like a soldier. The entire family, including the old woman, speaks Vietnamese. But from time to time they're overcome by shyness, and then they lapse into Muong. Then our Muong guide translates their words into Vietnamese so that Lychee can translate them into English for us.

The oldest son has five children, we're told. His wife is the woman sitting by the fire with a baby on her lap. I see Andrew take a deep breath and for a moment I'm afraid he's going to launch into a lecture on the virtues of family planning, but fortunately he's diverted by the daughter-in-law, who serves us small glasses of potent rice wine.

The old woman describes their daily life while Lychee translates. The family grows rice. They sell part of it and keep the rest for their own consumption. On holidays they slaughter a chicken. The children go to the school up the road, where the lessons are given in Vietnamese. They prefer not to talk about the war. The old woman brushes aside our questions, saying her husband was too old and her sons too young to fight. Her husband died a few years ago of some kind of pulmonary disease.

During the war the mountain dwellers in the North weren't faced with the difficult choice of the Montagnards in the South: either joining the Viet Cong or fighting on the side of the Americans. After all, there was only one party in the North.

The old woman has kindly answered our many questions, but now she decides it's time to move on to the next item on the program. She sets a pile of red pillows in front of us. They were made by hand, she informs us, and they are for sale. Every young Muong girl is obliged to make a large number of pillows for her dowry: flat oblong pillows for women and tall, square pillows for men. They're as hard as rock. I pinch one of them and hear the rustle of hay. "They're lovely," I say. "I'd like to buy one of them."

The son has lit a long bamboo pipe and filled the entire house with smoke. He offers us a puff. Someone else goes over to a cupboard and takes out a mousetrap, made entirely of bamboo. Laughing, the son demonstrates how the mouse triggers a spring which delivers the coup de grâce. In answer to my question as to whether they eat the mice, the son nods but Lychee categorically denies it.

Well, I think to myself, here I am sitting in a remote mountain dwelling in the middle of a Muong family. There's even a glass of rice wine in front of me. It's just that I haven't come any closer to understanding the Vietnamese soul. I might as well be in Thailand or Indonesia. Another Westerner meeting the natives in their primitive huts: the conversation is predictable; everyone is full of good will; you're offered something to eat, drink and smoke; there are souvenirs for sale; and at the end of the visit a small amount of money discreetly changes hands.

As we get ready to leave I notice Lychee slipping the old woman a few bills. We drive the Muong woman back to her office and head through the green countryside to Hanoi.

DREAMING OF A VIETNAMESE VILLAGE

After a while we come to an imposing cathedral that I'd also noticed on the way down. The tall steeples, surrounded by rice fields and a sprinkling of houses, rise majestically in the air.

Forty years ago Graham Greene was also fascinated by the sight of cathedrals in North Vietnam. Flying over the Red River Delta not far from here, he saw no less than twenty of these monumental structures. They reminded him of the windmills dotting the landscape in Holland.

"Can we stop and take a look?" I ask. At first my request falls on deaf ears. Lychee insists that we only agreed to visit a Muong village. Grumbling, the driver goes to take a look. "The church is way off the road," explains Lychee, "and the path leading up to it isn't in very good condition." The driver finally gives his grudging consent. He turns the car on to a narrow dike leading towards the colossal edifice, looking forlorn amid the fields.

Lychee makes one last attempt to discourage us: "Catholics aren't known for their hospitality." Undaunted, Andrew and I step out of the car and walk over a mossy and neglected square to a staircase. We find ourselves in a high-ceilinged expanse where a young priest is giving a lesson to dozens of children lined up in the pews. Just as we enter he boxes a little boy on the ear. He catches sight of us and hurries over, smiling and extending his hand in a shake. He welcomes us in exquisite French. He gestures towards the children, who broke into two brawling factions the minute he turned his back. "They're very poor," he says in a piteous tone of voice. "All the people around here are very poor. Perhaps you'd like to make a small contribution to their education."

As I pull a couple of bills out of my bag, Andrew cautions me: "It'd be better to put it in the collection box." But the priest has already stretched out his hand. The money quickly disappears under his cassock. "The government is making life difficult for us," he whines. "We Catholics are being persecuted." His parish consists of four thousand souls, out of the nearly half a million Catholics in the North. This cathedral was built in 1920 and is in dire need of repair. "But we lack the funds, Madame."

Lychee has remained outside. Not even wild horses could drag her inside the cathedral. The driver is waiting beside the car with his mouth pursed in a disapproving frown. Having abandoned their pews, the children traipse behind us, whooping and shouting. The priest calls them to order in a vain attempt to calm them down, but they continue to buzz around us like a swarm of bees. They surround the car, making it nearly impossible for the driver to open the door. Dozens of tiny fists bang against the windows while the taller children pound on the roof. The driver mumbles something to Lychee along the lines of "what did I tell you?"

With her face screwed into an expression of distaste she says: "I once saw a movie about a boy and a girl who were in love with each other. They were going to get married, but then he decided to become a priest because he could get rich. He jilted her and broke her heart." She twists around in her seat to ask: "Do you think it's a true story?" I don't answer. And Andrew, no doubt musing about the uneasy relationship between the Catholic Church and the condom, keeps his silence as well.

That evening, seated on the plastic-covered couch in my hotel room, I review the events of the day. I've learned how the Muongs catch mice, but precious little besides. In any other country I might not have minded so much, but this is Vietnam. Even if I live to be eighty, I'll never be able to look at the landscape or the inhabitants of this country without thinking about the enigma of the war.

Among Dissidents

I walk down a broad boulevard which opens onto a square and turn into an alley. The white walls on either side of me contrast sharply with the azure-blue sky. This part of Hanoi no longer exudes a French colonial atmosphere. It looks more like an Arabian medina. In a curve in the alleyway I find the address I'm looking for: a nondescript white house with wrought-iron grilles on the windows, through which I can hear snatches of Simon and Garfunkel's *Bridge over Troubled Water*.

The door is opened by a young woman, Mr. Duong's daughter. She comments on the heat in fluent English, as if I'm a frequent visitor to her house. She steps aside to let me in and shyly acknowledges my compliment on her pronunciation. As we pause in the hall, she explains that she just finished her training and is now an interpreter. Beside the door there's a table with a personal computer. It must be on the blink, because a young man is bent over it, fiddling with its insides. The young woman introduces him: "This is my brother."

She ushers me into the living room. Mr. Duong is sitting at a desk which has been squeezed into an alcove, reading a back copy of *Le Monde*. The walls are covered from floor to ceiling with paintings in various shapes and sizes: a few abstracts and several portraits of Mr. Duong, whose thick glasses are a dead giveaway. The largest canvas depicts a female nude.

In the meantime the son has switched from rock 'n' roll to a staid Chopin piano concerto. "I have the feeling we're in Paris," I remark.

The bookshelf above the desk contains a row of books. I can only make out the names "Voltaire" and "Zola" on the torn and stained bindings. Mr. Duong follows the direction of my eyes and chuckles mirthlessly. "During our struggle against the French I was a war correspondent. I joined the Viet Minh when I was very young. Whenever we captured a French post all I was really interested in was finding some books in all the chaos. I read everything I could get my hands on. Amid the rubble and corpses, I scavenged for literature."

We take a seat around the dining table, and the daughter brings us a pot of freshly brewed tea. Her brother lays down his tools and joins us. He also speaks excellent English. He explains that his mother is still at work. She's a historian and works at a museum.

"Your family is so internationally oriented," I say. "I never expected to see a house in Hanoi with a record of Simon and Garfunkel and a book on Chagall."

The son smiles politely. "That's because of my father," he says. "Even when I was little he used to invite foreign visitors to our house."

"Didn't that ever get you into trouble?" I ask.

The son sighs and looks from his father to his sister. "Oh yes," he says, uncomfortably. "After the visitors left the police always showed up on our doorstep, demanding to know exactly what was said. Fortunately they don't do that anymore these days." His eyes slide past my face in shyness.

Mr. Duong breaks the ensuing silence, cheerfully unfolding today's plans. He was clearly not the type to let himself be intimidated by police surveillance and suspicion.

"Late this afternoon we're expected at the home of Nguyen Huy Thiep," he tells me with a twinkle in his eyes.

"Really?" I exclaim. When Mr. Duong came to my hotel I

AMONG DISSIDENTS

asked him whether he knew the writer Nguyen Huy Thiep. Actually, I wrote the name on a piece of paper because I didn't dare say it aloud: whenever I'd mentioned his name before people had rolled their eyes in horror and informed me that Thiep was known to be critical of the government. They preferred not to have anything to do with someone like that, because they were afraid of getting into trouble.

"Can I really go see him?" I ask.

"He's expecting us," Mr. Duong replies. "My wife will be home from work around noon, so we can have lunch here. Until then we can go visit a good friend of mine, the famous musician Van Cao. He's also a controversial figure."

Only now do I realize the extent of the favor the two gentlemen from the Writers' Union did me by sending Mr. Duong my way: he has fantastic contacts and is not afraid of the authorities.

The daughter gets out her bicycle for me. Since she's tall for a Vietnamese, the saddle is at just the right height. "See you later," she calls as Mr. Duong and I set off. On the way we pass the Cultural Center of the former Soviet Union, an architectural monstrosity that looks like it's totally devoid of life. I follow Mr. Duong down the main boulevard and into a side street. He comes to a stop when we reach a marketplace. All around us women in conical hats are displaying their wares: bunches of onions, spices and juicy fruits.

"Shall we take something to your friend?" I suggest.

Mr. Duong lets his eyes rove over the merchandise. "He doesn't like fruit," he says, "but he does like whiskey."

That's clear enough. "But where can we buy whiskey?"

Mr. Duong frowns. "You mean where can we buy *real* whiskey?" he corrects me.

The problem is that even when the bottle is labeled *Red Label* and the cap doesn't appear to have been tampered with, the chances are it will contain some tasteless alcohol dyed the color of whiskey. Mr. Duong mulls over the problem and reaches a decision: "Let's buy beer instead," he says.

Carrying six cans of Heineken beer carefully tied together with a string, we climb a staircase and enter a simply furnished room. Various belongings and boxes have been piled against the wall.

Voices and Visions

An emaciated man with long white hair and a white goatee is sitting in an armchair near the door. His body is so transparent he looks like a ghost. After we've been introduced, Mr. Van Cao whispers to me in barely comprehensible French: "I'm looking for a treasure, but I haven't found it yet." He smiles woefully.

That's funny. As I was walking up the staircase this was the last thing I expected him to say. And yet it seems appropriate. I've spent months in this country on a quest of some sort, and now I've run into a man who's devoted his entire lifetime to the search.

I seat myself on a couch near the armchair containing Mr. Van Cao's wasted body. He looks at me benignly, with eyes that hide nothing. He might as well be sitting there without his clothes on.

"He's like Icarus," says Mr. Duong with undisguised respect. "I'm always afraid he'll get too close to the sun and that his wings will melt." The three of us laugh, and not just at the analogy. For one brief moment all human endeavor seems to strike me as absurdly comical.

Mr. Van Cao's wife serves tea. Unlike her husband, she's bursting with health and looks twenty years younger. She gives me a nod of sympathy. Maybe she thinks I feel awkward between these two old men. I smile at her and she disappears, reassured, behind a curtain where I can hear her rummaging through her pots and pans.

Assisted by Mr. Duong, Mr. Van Cao recounts the story of his life. He left his parents' house at the age of fourteen to join the Viet Minh. His job was to "liquidate" traitors, as he puts it. I stare at him in amazement, unable to believe he'd been a political assassin.

"It was a very difficult job," adds Mr. Duong unnecessarily. I can hardly imagine the frail Mr. Van Cao creeping stealthily through the back alleys of Hanoi with a gun in his hand, and yet he must have. Oddly enough he doesn't go into the matter any further. Instead, he gestures, as if to say that it was all so long ago, and what's done is done.

Politics wasn't the most important thing in his life, he continues. Though it may seem odd, his true love was art. He became

AMONG DISSIDENTS

a poet and a musician. In later years he composed Vietnam's national anthem.

A dusty and neglected piano has been shoved against a wall. I ask him if he still plays and composes. "No," he shakes his head, "the time for making music is over."

With trembling hands, he writes a poem in my notebook:

*As long as the tears flow
You can forget your sorrows.
As long as the tears flow
You can bemoan your lost loves.
But when your eyes are dry
The world is ruled by darkness.*

I'm not much of a poetry lover, and yet I'm touched by these lines. Doesn't it all come down to compassion? I'm surprised that someone who has taken part in the struggle and endured countless years of war still has a gentle side.

"Mr. Van Cao longs for paradise, and when he's in paradise he longs to be back in the world," Mr. Duong comments.

"I could not be bought," I understand Mr. Van Cao to say. "It was the same with my devotion to art and literature. I don't compromise. This attitude of mine has always gotten me into trouble."

His troubles began in 1955, when at the age of thirty he became involved in the humanist movement. North Vietnam had been officially independent for one year. Many intellectuals, including Mr. Van Cao, thought the time for more individual freedom had come. They published a magazine. But the authorities cracked down on the group. "I wasn't treated as badly as some of the others were," Mr. Van Cao says diffidently. "Several of them were sent to camps. They only harassed me and made it impossible for me to work. My music was no longer performed, I wasn't allowed to make public appearances and my poems couldn't be published. In those years I earned my living designing book jackets."

However, since the government could hardly keep the national anthem from being sung, they had to make an exception for that. For a while they tried switching to another melody.

"There was a wave of popular resistance. People wanted to keep my song." Even today, his *Song of an Advancing Army* is always sung on important occasions.

For twenty-five years, from 1955 to 1980, Mr. Van Cao, his wife and their five children lived in virtual isolation. Anyone who came to see him had to contend with the secret police. "Only my best friends braved the reign of terror," says Mr. Van Cao, exchanging a look of understanding with Mr. Duong.

The situation improved somewhat in 1980. Though he received invitations to visit France and the U.S., he had to refuse, as his health didn't permit him to travel. Slumped from exhaustion, he attempts to prop himself up in his chair. He's drinking not only beer, but also strong rice wine, refilling his glass from time to time from a bottle he keeps under his chair. Alcohol has taken its toll on Mr. Van Cao, succeeding where the government has failed.

A stillness falls on the room. Mr. Duong clears his throat. "Let me tell you a story," he says, "about a Vietnamese man living in the U.S. One summer evening he's driving through a city and gets stuck in a traffic jam. He gets out of his car to see what's going on. To his surprise he sees a bunch of elderly Vietnamese standing in the middle of the street and looking up at a window, listening to someone playing the piano. He recognizes the tune immediately: Van Cao's *Lost Paradise*. An unbearable wave of homesickness passes over him."

Mr. Van Cao smiles. I can't tell whether he's listened to the story. Maybe he's just smiling because he feels like it.

Two women enter the room. I knew from Mr. Duong that Mr. Van Cao receives friends, acquaintances and interested foreigners at his apartment every morning. Since he doesn't have a pension, his admirers are in the habit of giving him a donation so that he can provide for his family.

These two women are not strangers. One of them, explains Mr. Duong, is the wife of the legendary General Giap, who routed the French Army at Dien Bien Phu. Apparently many of Mr. Van Cao's visitors are the people whose names fill the pages of our history books. This is General Giap's second wife, as his first one suffered a horrible death in a French prison more than fifty years ago. Like Mr. Van Cao, General Giap has fallen out of grace with the regime. They've shared the same circle of friends for decades. They've continued to see each other, even at the height of the repression, when daily life was being subjected to increasingly more control. The war demanded superhuman sacrifices. As I understand from their stories, their existence got grimmer with every passing day. Yet even under these circumstances they discussed world literature, art and music. They continued to believe that in a truly free society people should be able to say what they think and read what they want.

"For a long time we were closed off from the rest of the world," says Mr. Van Cao. "What we learned from that experience is that no "ism" lasts forever. Unfortunately, our wars only brought us further from our goal. We now understand that the only way to achieve progress and prosperity is through hard work. We know that it's up to us, not up to God."

Taking a sip from his glass he adds: "You come from Holland. I'd like to ask your government just one thing. Let several of our young people come to study at your art academies and universities so that they can enrich our country with their knowledge."

"That's a modest request," I reply, "after a hundred years of warfare." And I promise to include his words in my book.

It's time to go, Mr. Duong cautions me. Mr. Van Cao tires easily when he has visitors.

We retrace our steps, going back down the stairs to the market. Dazed, I look around me at the vendors and their wares.

"Let's go have lunch," the practical Mr. Duong proposes, and I follow him through the busy traffic. We park our bikes in the courtyard beside his front door. Delightful aromas come to greet us. Mr. Duong's wife is busy setting the table. She shyly shakes my hand. She doesn't speak a foreign language and asks her husband to offer her apologies.

Soon afterward she sets a steaming bowl of noodles on the table. The daughter follows with a chicken dish, cooked in soy sauce. We sit down to eat. All four of them are constantly on the alert, making sure that my plate is heaped with food and that my teacup is never empty. Mr. Duong urges me to eat. Mrs. Duong nods and checks to see whether I can manage my chopsticks.

Their kindness and warmth remind me of the Trang family in Saigon. The Duongs are every bit as cordial and prepared to accept a foreigner in their midst.

Though Mr. Duong and Mr. Trang are of the same generation, they're totally different. Mr. Trang never concerned himself with politics. He takes life as it comes and tries to make the most of it. Mr. Duong, on the other hand, committed himself to a political cause at an early age and is still trying to change the system. The years of struggle and privation have made an ascetic of him. He absentmindedly picks at his food and finally lights a cigarette. Despite their differences, the two men have one thing in common: they're both firm believers in the value of education.

Once when I was in Saigon I remember asking Mr. Trang what he'd learned in the course of his seventy-odd years. He deliberated for a moment and then replied: "The most important thing is to develop whatever talent you were born with." Mr. Duong shares a similar conviction and has raised his children accordingly. His son is a gifted computer expert and his daughter is liable to land a job with a foreign company; women who can speak fluent English are a rarity in Hanoi. Unfortunately, to Mr. Trang's everlasting disappointment, his children were denied access to higher education, and he was unable to provide them with as much learning as he'd hoped.

We stare at each other in silence, stupefied by the food and the midday heat. "Why don't we take a nap," Mr. Duong suggests. His daughter directs me to her room, and I lie down on her bed, a cool straw mat on hard boards. A dreamy poster of Madonna adorns one wall, and her scanty wardrobe is hung on hooks on another wall. Actually, there's no room for more, since you couldn't even squeeze a chair into this tiny room.

I awake with a start at the sound of an engine being revved in the courtyard. I look out the window and see Mr. Duong's son giving his father pointers on how to handle the ancient motorbike he's borrowed for the occasion. Mr. Duong nods absently, paying little attention to the instructions. Perhaps his thoughts are taken up with the writer we're scheduled to visit late this afternoon.

The heat has slowed us down. Twilight is approaching by the

time we roar out of the alley with the muffler rattling. As we leave the suburbs of Hanoi behind us, Mr. Duong calls back over his shoulder: "We've still got a long way to go."

At first it feels as if the road has gotten bumpy, and then we realize that the back tire has gone soft. Mr. Duong spies an old man with a goatee sitting by the side of the road with a bicycle pump. For a few cents we can put some air in our tires. The old man hardly looks up from his book. "What's he reading?" I want to know.

Mr. Duong, pumping away at the tire, shouts something at the old man. "It's a book about the war which the Vietnamese waged against the Chinese more than a thousand years ago," he translates. Breathing heavily, he starts the engine, which seems noisier than ever.

By the time we turn off the main road it's nearly dark. We pass under a stone gateway and come to a narrow path. It cuts right through a lotus pond. I concentrate on keeping perfectly still since I have no desire to end up in the water. The path winds its way past a group of houses. We meet a farmer with a bamboo pole on his shoulders and he flings himself against the wall to give us room to pass. We've left the city and the traffic far behind; the roar of the engine resounds between the houses.

Mr. Duong slows down and drives into an unenclosed yard. We stop with a jerk beside the vegetable garden. Inside, the centuries-old farmhouse is lit by harsh fluorescent light. Two little boys race through the living room, dexterously skirting the bicycles parked there. Their father, the writer, hurries to greet us. Mr. Thiep is a thin man with a serious mien. He's dressed in simple cotton trousers and a white shirt. He nervously shakes our hands.

Mr. Duong translates while I tell Mr. Thiep that I'm pleased to meet him and that I've heard a lot about him. He mumbles a reply. Mr. Duong says nothing. The writer gestures for me to take a seat on the floor, since there aren't any chairs in the room. Once we're settled Mr. Thiep switches off the bright fluorescent light. He strikes a match and lights a hurricane lamp, which he sets down in front of us. He then lowers himself to the floor and assumes the lotus position. The lamp's flickering flame is reflected on the red and gold ancestral altar at my elbow.

Mr. Thiep gets up again in an agile movement. He walks away, illuminated by the shadowy light, and returns with some teacups. He sits down again and serves tea. All the while his eyes are continuously on the move.

"You used to live in the city, didn't you?" I hesitantly begin. "What made you decide to move to the country?"

His eyes fill with suspicion. "My family has been living in this house since the sixteenth century. I've returned to my roots."

I turn to Mr. Duong in surprise. According to the story I'd heard, Mr. Thiep left Hanoi because the security police were giving him a hard time. "Didn't you have some problems in Hanoi?" I ask cautiously.

He irritably shakes his head no. I don't get it. Mr. Thiep is supposed to be one of Vietnam's most controversial figures and yet his life is a bed of roses? "Still, you aren't exactly a favorite of the authorities," I say. "Just what do they object to?"

Mr. Thiep's angry face looks even more menacing as he formulates an answer to this question. "Gullit and Van Basten also get kicked a lot, both on and off the soccer field," he says curtly and stands up again. He disappears from view only to reappear shortly with a plate of attractively arranged pomelo segments. Mr. Duong offers him a cigarette, and he inhales deeply.

"Perhaps you would be so good as to tell me what themes interest you in your work?"

"I write about ordinary people," he says, leaving me with the distinct impression that he doesn't wish to pursue the subject.

Since I haven't traveled halfway around the world to be fobbed off with an answer like that, I make another stab at trying to find his conversational button. "What's the message you want to impart to your readers?"

"I don't have any message. I just want to describe ordinary people with ordinary human aspirations. Other than that, there's nothing special I want to say."

I feel the sweat trickling down my front and my blouse is sticking to my neck. It's all I can do to keep from giving him a good shake. Mr. Thiep is like an engine that sputters hopefully and yet refuses to start.

Does he dislike going into detail, or is he afraid of saying something the authorities might be able to use against him? It might be better to switch to a more neutral subject, one that will allow him to determine the direction of the conversation and give me a better idea of what's bothering him. I arrange my face into an expression of genuine interest so he can see I'm prepared to listen. I force myself to ask very calmly: "What do your characters wish for? What are their dreams?"

He snorts derisively. "Ordinary things. They want to have food on the table and clothes on their backs. They want to be able go where they want and say what they think." He stops and waits impatiently for Mr. Duong to translate his words. Again I get the impression he cut his answer short out of fear. What can I do to reassure him? Maybe the best course of action is to ask him what he's afraid of.

"Do you feel there are restrictions on your freedom?"

"Like everyone else in this country, I'm living like an animal" is his curt reply. Mr. Duong patiently translates his words, as if we're carrying on a normal, everyday conversation.

I don't understand whether he means that life in Vietnam is terrible or that human existence in general is awful. So I ask: "Are things any better in other countries?"

Mr. Thiep takes a deep breath. "I haven't the faintest idea," he says caustically. "I've never been outside Vietnam." Mr. Duong adds that he's received invitations to go abroad, but has never been granted an exit visa.

After all the furtive stories I heard about Mr. Thiep, I expected him to be an imposing figure, the kind of man who bangs his fist on the table and knows no fear. However, the man before me is more like a deer with a pack of hunters at its heels.

Like Mr. Van Cao, his demands are modest. Mr. Thiep is not calling his countrymen to arms or crying out for the blood of the leaders who have failed the nation. He's not swearing to get revenge. He only asks to be allowed to live freely among free people. But, as he keeps repeating, that's impossible.

"Which do you find worse? The oppression caused by hunger and privation, or the lack of freedom of speech?"

"Both," he replies. "Like all writers in this country, I suffer from both oppression and repression." He restlessly gets to his feet again and disappears into the darkness to refill the teapot.

Unmoved, Mr. Duong smokes his umpteenth cigarette. He carefully catches the ashes in a matchbox since there's no ashtray.

"If Mr. Thiep is so controversial, how can he get his work published?" I ask him.

"We have a rather unusual system in Vietnam," Mr. Duong explains. "Many institutes have their own publishing house. They also publish things outside their own field. The only deciding factor these days is whether or not it can make a profit. Every manuscript has to be submitted to the authorities first for their approval, but it's hard to predict what the censor will say. And as soon as a story has been published in some magazine or newspaper, it can also be published in book form without having to be resubmitted to the authorities. Mr. Thiep's next story is going to appear in a Hue literary magazine called *The Perfume River*. The magazine has been banned on many occasions. Not because of Mr. Thiep, I might add. The point is that you never know how the censors will react."

Mr. Thiep's rapid steps are coming closer. "Everyone respects Mr. Thiep," adds Mr. Duong, who undoubtedly senses my discomfort. "They may not like him, but they all respect him." So Mr. Thiep is known to be difficult. That reassures me. I was afraid I'd done something to incur his wrath. I'd like to think of him as a nice person, but his fierce outbursts don't make it easy.

"Do you often receive foreign guests?" I say, attempting to interject a light tone.

"Sometimes the Ministry of Foreign Affairs brings a visitor," he answers, quasi-nonchalant.

"Oh really?" I ask in surprise. "I thought you weren't exactly popular with the authorities."

Mr. Thiep shrugs his shoulders. He doesn't understand it either, he says. But from time to time a foreign visitor demands to see Mr. Thiep. First someone from the Ministry arrives on a motorbike to announce the visit. On the chosen day Mr. Thiep puts on a clean shirt and waits. His neighbors let him know when a car parks at the gate where the narrow path begins. Then he knows his company is on its way.

"But can you talk freely with an official government interpreter in the room?"

"Sometimes I can, sometimes I can't," says Mr. Thiep, his face neutral, as if it doesn't matter one way or another.

"Are there people keeping track of your unofficial visitors? Is your house kept under surveillance?"

"Not any more," says Mr. Thiep, shaking his head in fierce denial. I'm beginning to get used to his abruptness. Mr. Thiep strikes me as a classic example of a tormented soul. He may have chosen to lead the life of a dissident, but he clearly did so only because he felt he had no other choice.

"Do they sometimes search your house?"

"That's been known to happen," he says, without elaborating further. I get the feeling he's holding himself back because he doesn't wish to show his country in a poor light.

Outside, an almost full moon is suspended above the garden. In the shimmering moonlight I can make out a gigantic statue of a Buddha seated on a lotus blossom. He seems to be floating above the ground.

"It's hot in here. Let's go outside," Mr. Thiep suggests. As we follow him out to the extraordinary statue, several dogs start barking furiously.

Standing at the foot of the Buddha, I can clearly see that the statue towers a good 12 feet above us. Mr. Thiep pats it reassuringly on the knee.

"He had this built from the royalties he earned on the English translation of his book," explains Mr. Duong, as if this is a perfectly natural way to spend your foreign-earned income.

Mr. Thiep drags some chairs over to the statue so that we can enjoy the cool evening air. A vase of flowers and a bunch of burned-out joss sticks are lying at Buddha's feet. No, Mr. Thiep shakes his head in answer to my question, he's not particularly religious. He makes an offering to his ancestors two times a month, but that's nothing special. Most Vietnamese do that. So he's not a born-again Buddhist.

Mr. Thiep goes inside to get our teacups. Upon his return he swears he's just an ordinary Vietnamese citizen. "I feed my pigs, work in my garden, try to make ends meet. Sometimes the farmers around here ask me for advice. Life is hard. None of us can lead a normal life."

Is he a pessimist, I wonder, who sees Vietnam and the Vietnamese as eternal victims? I ask him if he compares his country to *The Tale of Kieu*, a book in which the main character, a beautiful and virtuous young lady, is plagued with bad luck. In the course of the story she's sold into prostitution and is sullied for the rest of her life.

"That book only shows part of the truth," Mr. Thiep replies, adding that it's "entirely inspired by Chinese novels." And that's not meant as a compliment. "The first truly Vietnamese novel was only printed in 1930. Before that everything in our country was either Chinese or Indian," he remarks, unable to keep the irritation out of his voice. "Little by little, we're making progress. We Vietnamese are slowly finding ourselves."

Mr. Thiep doesn't live in a Frenchified world like Mr. Van Cao does. He grew up after North Vietnam gained its independence. During the American war he lived in a remote mountain village and taught history to children. "I don't know much about the world," declares Mr. Thiep. "When I was young I didn't get much of an education. I had to go out and earn a living."

I also get the impression that he isn't really interested in what happens beyond Vietnam's borders. He's turned inward, entrenching himself in his ancestral home outside Hanoi. I can't imagine him anywhere else, for example at a sidewalk café in Montmartre, though Mr. Van Cao, provided his health would let him, could slip right into the ambiance of a Parisian boulevard. Mr. Thiep is not cosmopolitan, nor does he want to be. He's intrigued by the question of Vietnamese identity, wanting to know what it means to be Vietnamese. And yet his fatherland has disappointed him greatly. History took a wrong turn somewhere, and Mr. Thiep is unable to come to terms with present-day Vietnam.

"Are the Communists to blame for everything that's gone wrong?" I ask.

"To some extent," replies Mr. Thiep, hedging.

"Or did the war destroy everything?"

"The war is only part of the problem," avers Mr. Thiep. "Money is in scare supply in this world. And hope is even more scarce."

It's gotten late; the moon is high in the sky. We take our leave at the garden gate. Mr. Thiep seems relieved that our meeting is over. His wife comes towards us out of the darkness and takes my hand in hers. She too seems pleased that everything's turned out so well, as if she feared we were going to fight like cats and dogs.

Mr. Duong starts his motorbike with a roar. Guided by the headlight we zigzag between the houses and across the pond. For a long while the only sound is that of Mr. Thiep's howling dog.

HUE

A Poet and a Princess

The North is sometimes referred to as the "cradle of Vietnam" since the Vietnamese people originally settled only as far south as the Red River Delta. They didn't start annexing the South until the tenth century, when they had shaken off a thousand years of Chinese domination. Consequently, the oldest monuments in Vietnam — temples, pagodas and the remains of imperial palaces — are to be found in the vicinity of Hanoi.

Even so, not once during my stay in Hanoi have I felt that I've really gotten in touch with Vietnam's distant past. Like the writer Mr. Thiep, I too want to find out what's unique about the Vietnamese. Yet I keep coming face to face with reminders of the American war or French colonialism which make it impossible for me to see Vietnam as it used to be.

So I decide that my next stop will be Hue, Vietnam's former capital. The last emperors ruled the country from the Forbidden Purple City of Hue, located along the banks of the Perfume River. Surely I'll be able to find someone in Hue who can explain what Vietnam was like before the period of foreign domination.

A cyclo driver pedals me to Hanoi Ga, the city's main train station, modeled along French lines. A motherly woman in uniform immediately takes me under her wing. Yesterday when I bought a ticket from her, she made me promise not to be late.

"I take you to your seat," she says in halting English. A porter in a worn pith helmet picks up my bag and swings it onto his shoulder in one easy movement. Like three ducklings we walk to the platform in single file and board the waiting train.

So far, my compartment is empty. "Here is your bed," says the woman, pointing towards a berth. And then she disappears.

"One dollar," demands the porter.

I shake my head no and make it clear in sign language that the cyclo driver brought me all the way from my hotel to the station for half that amount.

His face twists into an angry frown. He signs back that it would cost me twice as much in Saigon.

It's not my fault, I think, that everything costs less in Hanoi. I give him four thousand dong, roughly half his asking price and twice as much as I had in mind. He indignantly shoves the money aside, only tucking it into his pocket with a sigh when I offer it a second time. Muttering what I assume to be curses, he leaves the train.

His flat helmet is typical everyday dress for many men in Hanoi. It was standard army issue in the North during the war. Ho Chi Minh liked to have himself photographed in a helmet; it added a touch of heroism. Now that the war has been over for years, these men in their olive-green Ho helmets remind me of Chicken Little. It's as if they're expecting bombs or bits of debris to fall out of the sky any minute, as if they can't quite believe that peace has really come. I don't recall seeing anyone in Saigon wearing these helmets, though I did notice one or two in a museum, on sale to Western souvenir hunters. I can't help but wonder how the men of Hue look at life: will they be wearing helmets or not?

Two other passengers enter the compartment, a modern-looking young couple in jeans: his are black and hers are blue. She's wearing a T-shirt with bright squares of color, and her flawless face is framed by long flowing hair. He seems to be slightly older.

I hope they'll talk to me. Of course the absence of a common language makes communication difficult. But even so, I've had a hard time striking up a conversation with people in Hanoi. They tend to be stricken with embarrassment about matters entirely beyond their control.

The man looks from me to his wife, takes a deep breath and says: "We're going to Hue for our honeymoon." His young bride blushes with embarrassment and bows her head. She doesn't speak English. What luck that I can at least talk to him! He tells me he spent a few years at a university in Czechoslovakia, where he learned to speak a little English in addition to fluent Czech.

"This may seem like an odd question," I say, "but why don't the men in the South wear helmets?"

He laughs. "Walking around Saigon in a helmet like that is asking for trouble. It reminds people of the Viet Cong."

The train's creaking wheels gradually set themselves in motion. We pass Hanoi's modern suburban districts, which are already going to rack and ruin, and cut through pale-green rice fields. The countryside in the Red River Delta is flat, like Holland. I can tell where the waterways are because they're lined with poplars. My eye automatically records every pumping station; as a Dutch person, I can't help but wonder how the people here keep their feet dry.

The train crosses a path where a tramp is waiting for the train to go by so he can continue his journey. His clothes are mere rags, and a metal bowl is dangling from a rope tied around his waist.

Only now does the fourth passenger present himself in our compartment. It turns out to be a guide in his early twenties who speaks fluent English. He's going home to Saigon, he reports jubilantly. Ah, a Southerner. I scrutinize his lively face, his flowing gestures. He stands out next to the sedate honeymooners, who seemed so stylish to me when they first boarded. He not only speaks English, but he's picked up some New York slang from the four Americans he's guiding around. Since they're in another compartment, he goes to sit with them so he can be on hand if any problems should arise.

We stop at a small station. In Hanoi the platforms were off limits to anyone but passengers. Here, in the middle of nowhere, men, women and children come trotting up from all sides with an assortment of goods: hard-boiled eggs, tall bottles of Chinese beer, longans and hot water for those who want to wash their hands. Not a bad idea, I decide. A skinny little girl hands me a basin of steaming water through the window and shouts something to a woman, presumably her mother, who's heating a kettle over a nearby fire. When the train begins to move, I awkwardly maneuver the sloshing water back through the window.

Menacing clouds gather above the green fields; the trees bend in the wind. Before long darkness descends. A woman with a food trolley comes down the corridor distributing bowls of rice with some kind of indistinguishable meat on top. Our train ticket includes meals. We take a few bites, unable to muster a great deal of enthusiasm. The young bride wrinkles her nose in disgust. Her husband laughs and obligingly sets our half-eaten bowls in the corridor. This is the moment a small grubby man has been waiting for: he collects the leftovers in a bucket, murmuring "*cam on*," thank you. When the conductress yells at him to stack the empty bowls, he obediently makes a neat pile. The odds are that he doesn't have a ticket, but she turns a blind eye and allows him to go about his business.

Since it's too dark to see anything outside, I talk to the honeymooners, sitting hand-in-hand across from me. He tells me there were about fifty guests at their wedding. That must have cost him a bundle. His narrative is constantly being interrupted by his wife, who keeps whispering sweet nothings into his ear. After an hour I crawl into bed and turn my back on the two turtledoves, leaving them to bill and coo undisturbed. They switch off the light and giggle in the dark. The guide from Saigon tiptoes in and climbs soundlessly into his berth.

When I wake up the newlyweds are already sitting, washed and combed, on the lower berth and the Saigonese guide has joined his clients. "Are we already in the South?" I ask as we clatter across a bridge. I regret the question the minute it's out of my mouth. After all, the country is officially reunited and maybe a Northerner doesn't like being reminded of the border, the site of so many bloody battles. But the bridegroom merely points knowledgeably out the window: "This is Ben Hai," he says. "We're crossing the border."

It's early in the morning when I look outside my room in Hue's Hotel Morin. The café across the street is playing an

A Poet and a Princess

upbeat rock 'n' roll number. Next door is a movie theater. A huge hand-painted poster is advertising the coming attraction: *The Lover*, the movie based on the Marguerite Duras novel of the same name.

Hotel Morin was once a French department store, I've been told. In any case it's as big as any château along the Loire. A couple of tables have been placed in the shade of a tall tree in the courtyard, and several backpacking tourists are sitting around eating fried eggs and drinking beer. A Finn I once met in the ice-cream parlor in Hanoi raises his bottle in greeting.

Despite the fierce heat, I decide to venture out in the noonday sun to see the former imperial palace. I rent a bicycle from the hotel and pedal past Hue's French villas until I come to the Perfume River, where scores of sampans are drifting downstream, though one or two are chugging upstream against the current. I cross the steep Phu Xuan Bridge to the old part of the city and bicycle along the city wall until I come to an elegant gateway. This can only be the Ngo Mon Gate. I remember seeing a picture of it once, with elephants kneeling before it as they waited for the emperor. On the back of the largest elephant was the emperor's ornate howdah.

The Ngo Mon Gate is being restored. Today the construction workers are putting shiny new yellow tiles on its roof. The woodwork has already been repaired, and the phoenixes on the watchtower have been given a fresh coat of paint.

I pass through the gate and cross over another bridge. This brings me to a huge square, at the end of which is the Thai Hoa Palace, the Palace of Supreme Peace, where the emperor used to receive distinguished visitors. The palace is roofed with the same shiny yellow tiles as the gate, and pots of red flowers beautifully offset the yellow. Inside, the imperial throne, with its vermilion and gold dragon motif, is flanked by a pair of highly decorative pillars.

I can't help but sigh. What's happened to all the emperor's robes? I seem to remember from photographs that they were almost more impressive than the throne or the palace. The emperor was usually garbed in yellow. As in China, he was the only person allowed to wear that color. His robes were embroidered with dragons and swirls of gold along the hem. His feet were encased in embroidered slippers.

Throughout its history, Vietnam was frequently divided into North-South warring factions. But in 1802 a Vietnamese nobleman, aided and abetted by the French, seized control of the entire country and installed himself in Hue as Emperor Gia Long, the first of a long dynasty destined to meet an inglorious end in 1945. The last emperor, Bao Dai, is still alive and living in Paris. According to a Frenchman I met in Saigon, Bao Dai is in the habit of throwing wild parties.

An old man has been keeping an eye on me from behind a table. "Madame," he says, holding out a book written by a local historian. The title on the cover is *Anything Novel in the Royal Palace of the Nguyen Dynasty?* Intrigued, I open the book.

"*Deux dollar,*" says the old man in a faint voice. I can't bring myself to bargain with him and hand him the two dollars.

"May I sit on the palace steps to read it?" I ask.

He nods. Since there's not another visitor in sight, no one minds whether I plop myself down on the imperial staircase.

"As a rule the emperor had three meals a day," I read. "The menu of each meal consisted of fifty different dishes made by different cooks." Along with their meals, the emperors "often drank alcohol soaked with medicinal herbs to strengthen their health. Emperor Dong Khanh . . . was the first emperor who used Bordeaux according to the advice of the French doctors." While they slept, the emperors were watched over by thirty imperial concubines, the daughters of high-ranking mandarins. The emperors had myriads of children by their many wives.

"In Spring," the book continues, "the Nguyen emperors often held the days of travelling for pleasure on the Perfume River. The imperial Dragon Boat, which was as impressive and majestic as a floating palace, was pulled by six or eight other boats — each of which had from fifty to sixty boat men."

I close the book. The old man beckons to me and obligingly shows me the rear entrance to the Thai Hoa Palace so that I don't have to walk all the way around to reach the imperial dining room, but can enter through a courtyard. Many a distinguished guest was treated to an elaborate banquet in this great hall.

A Poet and a Princess

According to my book, there should be another palace up ahead, the Can Chanh Palace. I amble under a weather-beaten gate and find myself, much to my surprise, in the middle of a vegetable garden. Two women in conical hats are busy weeding. Farther away I can see the crumbling remains of a once-majestic marble staircase, but the rest of the palace is gone.

All that's left of the Trinh Min Palace, where the concubines used to while away the hours under the watchful eyes of the eunuchs, and the Khon Thai Palace, where the empress used to reside among her splendid furniture and priceless trinkets, are moldering foundations amid an onion patch. I had also been looking forward to seeing the emperor's study in the East Wing, "a large airy room with a lot of glass windows and doors." But it too seems to have vanished from the face of the earth. Of course I knew that Hue was the site of ferocious fighting during the war, but I had no idea that the damage was so extensive. It pains me to think of the paintings, the porcelain, the robes and all the other imperial possessions that could have filled several museums, crushed under the boots of soldiers.

I stare at the weeding women as if that would help me understand it better. One of them looks up from her work and smiles shyly. I turn around and trudge disconsolately back to the entrance, where a small café has been set up under a tree. I take a seat on a beach chair. You'd think we were at the seaside instead of in the Forbidden Purple City. A loudspeaker is dangling from one of the branches, blaring rock music. I order a coconut from a young man nodding his head in time to the music. Why, I wonder, did they have to wage a battle in the palace, of all places?

The battle took place in 1968 — only months before the student protesters in Paris manned the barricades — as part of the notorious Tet Offensive. Even the word "Tet" is enough to send shivers down the spine of many ex-GIs.

On the last day of January everything seemed so quiet. The Americans had negotiated a truce with the North Vietnamese Army, so that the Vietnamese could celebrate their most important holiday: the New Year, Tet. Throughout the South the hotels overflowed with what everyone assumed were visiting relatives. If you'd told the Americans that the holiday crowd included more than eighty thousand Viet Cong soldiers, they would have laughed in your face.

In the weeks and days preceding the Tet festivities, the Viet Cong deposited weapons and ammunition in strategic places. In the early hours of the dawn they launched an attack in almost every major city in the South. To the Americans, it must have seemed as if Armageddon was at hand. Buildings exploded into thousands of pieces and shots rang out from all sides. Saigon was in the grip of sharpshooters who even managed to penetrate the American Embassy.

For a time it seemed as if the Americans were going to collapse under the eerie onslaught. In a certain sense, they did. "Instead of losing the war in little pieces over years we lost it fast in under a week," wrote Michael Herr, the American war correspondent and author of *Dispatches*. Even today, the U.S. hasn't recovered from the psychological blow of the Tet Offensive.

The bloodiest battle was fought in Hue. The old city, the Citadel with the Forbidden Purple City, ultimately fell into the hands of the Viet Cong. The flag of the North Vietnamese Army fluttered above the palace.

Michael Herr, reporting from the scene of the battle, wrote: "We were only meters away from the worst of the fighting, not more than a Vietnamese city block in distance, and yet civilians kept appearing, smiling, shrugging, trying to get back to their homes. The Marines would try to menace them away at rifle point, shouting, 'Di, di, *di*, you sorry-ass motherfuckers, go on, get the hell away from here!' and the refugees would smile, half bowing, and flit up one of the shattered streets."

Michael Herr figured that there was roughly one Marine casualty for every meter of city wall captured. In the Citadel the Marines came upon the corpses of countless Vietnamese. During the siege the ravenous Viet Cong soldiers had even skimmed the edible vegetation from the moat. A scandal arose when a mass grave containing the bodies of thousands of innocent civilians was discovered in the flatlands outside the city. It was later proved that they had been executed by the Viet Cong. The massacre in Hue has gone down in history as one of the war's worst atrocities.

There's nothing more depressing than people turning on

their own kind. Like the Chinese students who informed on their own parents and tortured their own teachers to death during the Cultural Revolution. Like the Cambodians who first murdered any intellectual they could lay their hands on and then, to be on the safe side, unleased their fury on anyone who wore glasses. While the Vietnam War had its share of atrocities, the Hue massacre is the only recorded cruelty of that magnitude.

I'd like to talk to someone who lived in Hue during the war, someone who could bring the story to life for me, since the remains of the Forbidden Purple City have more to say about the dead than the living. I remember someone in Hanoi giving me the name of an acquaintance in Hue. I check my notebook and find what I'm looking for: "Mr. Hoang Phu Ngoc Tuong. Poet in Hue. Ex-Viet Cong soldier." Back in my hotel, I dial his number.

The man who answers speaks French. "I'll come get you," he exclaims enthusiastically. "Let's go have a cup of coffee and enjoy the moon along the banks of the Perfume River."

Not long afterwards he drives into the courtyard of Hotel Morin with the engine of his motorbike backfiring. As he surveys the building his hand automatically moves to his heart. "This brings back so many memories," he muses. "The Philosophy Department used to be housed here. When I was a student I fell in love for the first time right here in this courtyard."

He shakes off thoughts of the past and concentrates on restarting his stalled motorbike. Mr. Tuong is considerably shorter and thinner than I am, so that when I hop on the back of the bike, the front wheel pops up in the air. It doesn't seem to faze him in the least. He takes off at full throttle, and we zigzag unsteadily through the gate.

Even though it's dark the heat is still relentless. The entire population of the city seems to be seeking the coolness of the river. We pass a group of girls on bicycles with their *ao dai* fluttering behind them in the sultry breeze. "Schoolgirls," sighs Mr. Tuong. He pulls up at a brightly lit bar blaring a Beatles tune: "Nothing's gonna change my world," croons John Lennon.

"Ugh, let's get away from that awful noise," grumbles Mr. Tuong and beckons me towards a couple of chairs in the park beside the gently flowing water and rustling reeds. A young girl brings us two *café filtre*. Mr. Tuong looks up at the sky. "Ah, the moon!" he exclaims. He's right, suspended above our heads is an enormous moon, looking like a glossy onion.

Mr. Tuong smokes one cigarette after another; his coffee remains untouched. Years ago, he tells me, when he first started teaching, he spied for the Viet Cong. His father was a large landowner and his grandfather a mandarin, but he believed the class system should be abolished. "I was young," the poet says in a gentle voice. "I thought the war would put an end to all wars." When someone informed on him, he was forced to flee to the jungle, where he joined the North Vietnamese Army. "I was in the mountains not far from here. I was half-starved. I could look down on the plains and see Hue," he recalls. "I could see the Trang Tien Bridge, so small it looked like a toy. And I imagined I saw my sweetheart walking down the street with another man. I was at my wit's end." He heaves a sigh.

"And," I say to tease him, "did she have another boyfriend or did she wait for you?"

Mr. Tuong looks into my eyes, hurt to the quick. "I was gone for ten years. I knew she wasn't going to wait for me. That only happens in sentimental songs. In reality the soldier dies, or she goes off with someone else." He shakes his long hair out of his face.

"I didn't expect to run into a romantic poet like you in Vietnam," I remark. "I guess I thought that years of warfare would have nipped any poetic notions in the bud."

Mr. Tuong throws his hands in the air. "I also wonder how I wound up in this ill-fated country," he says. "Why wasn't I born somewhere where it's nice and peaceful, like Paris?" Disgruntled, he tosses his cigarette butt into the flowing water. He must have been quite attractive in his younger years. His eyes still sparkle, his hair is fashionably long and he has an irresistible laugh.

"Madame," he solemnly intones, "I'd like to present you with a volume of my poetry." On the cover there's a painting of a woman in an *ao dai* hovering above green waves. I can't read the poems in Vietnamese, but it's clear that the majority of them are dedicated to women. Most of the women are denoted by their initials, although here and there I can spot a name. One of them sounds familiar: Irina Zisman.

A Poet and a Princess

"I met her at a writers' conference in Moscow," comments Mr. Tuong discretely. After the war he traveled all over the world as the representative of Vietnamese literature. He's been to Cuba, Romania and the Soviet Union. "The Russian women were beautiful," he says dreamily, "but they were obsessed by politics. All they wanted to do was talk." He lays his hand on mine. "You're different," he says to flatter me. "You're, how shall I put it, gentler."

I expect his next remark to be that you shouldn't talk to women about politics, but about love, since it seems an appropriate moment to produce that old line. But Mr. Tuong is silent. He gazes at the moon and lights a new cigarette.

I clear my throat and ask: "Mr. Tuong, how could something like the Hue massacre have taken place?" His eyes briefly meet mine. Then he turns away and shrugs his shoulders. "It was a misunderstanding. The peasants in the North Vietnamese Army came to Hue, convinced that the city people were traitors and spies. They took their revenge." He adds softly: "So many people died needlessly. In the West, I know, many young people are pondering the question: Why am I alive? In Vietnam my generation is racking its brains over another question: Why did so many die?"

He pulls a magazine, printed on cheap paper, out of his bag. The photograph on the cover depicts some girls in a garment factory industriously toiling away at their machines. Mr. Tuong leafs through the magazine until he finds the right page: "This is one of my articles," he points. In the middle of the text is a picture of two young men. The one on the right, in a check shirt, has his hair combed in a 1950s pompadour. He's smiling suavely, exposing a perfect row of pearly whites, like a movie star. I read the names in the caption.

"But that's you," I exclaim in surprise.

Mr. Tuong nods and gazes glumly at his own picture. "It's a story about my youth." He falls silent and makes a deprecating gesture. "But let's talk about you. About your visit to Hue and what you want to see while you're here."

I tell him that I've been to the palace, or at any rate what's left of it. Mr. Tuong has no use for sentimentality. "The tombs of the emperors are still almost all intact."

"A tomb isn't the same as a palace," I somberly reply.

"*Ooh la la*," he interrupts me. "In this case it is. These are the palaces of the dead emperors." Tomorrow morning, he decides, he'll come get me. No, there're no two ways about it. I'm not going to leave Hue without having seen the mausoleum of his favorite emperor, Tu Duc.

The magazine is still lying open in my lap. I glance at the picture and then at Mr. Tuong's face, which is grooved so deeply it resembles a wood carving; at his teeth, which are stained by nicotine; and at his chin, which sports a large hairy wart. In spite of it all he still bears a striking resemblance to the young man in the picture.

The palace of Hue has been transformed into a vegetable garden, and Mr. Tuong has become an old, disillusioned poet. I feel a bittersweet nostalgia for the past. If I'd met the young Mr. Tuong back in the old days, I probably wouldn't have hesitated a minute but would have followed him into the jungle to fight for a better world. Is it possible to fall in love with the shadow of the past? To fall in love in retrospect?

At breakfast early the next morning in my hotel I run into the four Americans who traveled to Hue on the same train as I did. Today, they tell me, they're renting a car and heading south. They excuse themselves to go pack. Their Saigonese guide laughs and points to his bag: he's all set. While he and I drink a cup of coffee, I show him the magazine article written by Mr. Tuong and ask him to tell me what it's about. The Saigonese begins to read, wrinkling his forehead in concentration. He looks up after a brief moment. "It's written by a Viet Cong," he says. I nod, yes Mr. Tuong did fight in the North Vietnamese Army, but how could he see that so quickly?

He laughs. "It's full of Viet Cong expressions. I know what they mean since I had to learn them in school. But people like my parents who graduated before 1975 wouldn't be able to understand a word."

The story, I gradually learn, is about Mr. Tuong's many friends who came to a sad end. He buried some of them with his own hands, and every single day he feels guilty for having survived.

A Poet and a Princess

Years ago he and one of his friends journeyed through the jungle to the South. The friend was accompanied by his young wife, who had recently given birth to a baby girl. She left the infant with her parents even though she was still nursing, so that she could be with her husband. She often fainted from exhaustion during the long trek, and yet she kept going until she literally dropped dead. Mr. Tuong occasionally receives a letter from the daughter who had to make do without her mother's milk. She's now the same age as her mother when she died.

Then there was his good friend Thuy, a fellow student and later comrade-in-arms. Thuy could go without food for long periods of time. He simply smoked whatever leaves he could get his hands on. Nowadays Thuy is a teacher. Emboldened by *doi moi*, Vietnam's version of perestroika, which has also reached the city where he lives, Thuy recently wrote a newspaper article. It was unacceptable to the authorities, and Thuy was fired.

Another one of his friends, Vinh, was at the top of his class. He was so poor that his tattered shirt was only held together with tape. Every time it rained, his shirt fell apart, so that Vinh made sure he sat at the back of the class. He could have gotten a scholarship to study abroad. Or in the imperial age he would have become a good mandarin and married a princess. But Vinh chose to become a revolutionary. He died in a "tiger cage," an underground cell with bars across the top, in a prison in the Con Dao Archipelago, the one the French referred to as Paulo Condore.

Mr. Tuong concluded his depressing litany with the names of his old friends who are now being punished for having worked for the former regime during the war. "It's as if my entire generation is standing before a judge," he laments. He ends with the admonition: "You can't blame autumn because the leaves fall."

Just as the Americans arrive with their suitcases, the poet himself roars into the courtyard on his motorbike.

Mr. Tuong follows the course of the Perfume River, and we soon find ourselves outside the city. He turns the motorbike towards the hills, passing fragrant jasmine on the way. The road is full of potholes, but Mr. Tuong doesn't seem to notice; I guess his eyesight isn't what it should be. We race towards the holes at full speed. Mr. Tuong hardly misses a one, as if he's enjoying himself. The motorbike disappears into a deep pit and climbs back out with the engine whining. There's something wrong with the clutch, which means we have to get off and push the motorbike up the steepest hills, only to sail down the other side at dizzying speeds.

"You sounded pretty disillusioned in your magazine article," I yell above the noise of the motor.

"Oh well," he shouts back, heading straight for a colossal pothole, "there are two kinds of people in this world: cheerful pessimists like me or else melancholy optimists."

I laugh. "You described the problems of your friends, but not your own problems," I remark, holding on to the seat for dear life to keep from being flung from the bike as we approach another gaping hole.

Mr. Tuong looks at me over his shoulder. As luck would have it, we miss the pothole. "I'm still a member of the Communist Party," he confides. "And yet they won't issue me an exit visa, even though I've been invited to France and Germany." He throws his hands in the air, so that for a moment we're racing down the road with no one at the controls.

I close my eyes in anticipation of disaster. "Are you sorry you can't go?" I ask.

"I'm sure something will turn up someday," Mr. Tuong benevolently philosophizes. "That's the way life is. All living organisms are made up of cells which are constantly in the process of dividing and multiplying. Nothing ever stays the same."

We wrestle our way uphill, past a simple farmhouse with a hibiscus blooming in the garden. Though the landscape around Hue looks tropical, it can be rainy and cold here in the winter.

At last we arrive at the mausoleum of Emperor Tu Duc. Various people gesture for us to park along the side of the road; the locals try to earn a little extra money by watching over the vehicles of the visitors. The thin woman chosen by Mr. Tuong smiles with delight.

At a table near the gate a young man is selling tickets. "Two dollars," he says. I pay, but the ticket he gives me is worth only one dollar. I start to protest, but Mr. Tuong brushes aside my objections.

A Poet and a Princess

"What difference does one dollar make in the eternal scheme of things?" he asks.

As I don't have a ready answer, I follow him without a murmur. The path takes us past a lotus pond. "Tu Duc is my favorite emperor," explains Mr. Tuong, "because he loved literature and drama." The mausoleum is an expression of the emperor's character. Birds, flowers and nature predominate in the design. There are no massive buildings or monuments. The paths are not set out in straight lines. If fact, there isn't even one sharp angle in the whole mausoleum.

We pause in the emperor's pavilion, overlooking a lake. Mr. Tuong gestures towards the park-like grounds. "As you can see, the paths are all crooked. There's no orderly arrangement. That's how we differ from the Chinese. A Chinese emperor would want to have everything in straight lines, with vast squares and towering stone markers, to make the people feel small. We Vietnamese are different. We're chaotic and irrational. We like to follow the dictates of our heart."

I nod in agreement. That's why I like being with Vietnamese so much. Chinese people are often rigid. They have official procedures for everything, which sometimes makes it difficult to come in contact with them.

I tell Mr. Tuong about my visit to Canton, in southern China, two years ago. I was staying in a beautiful hotel with a swimming pool. The chairs were arranged in neat rows around the pool. When I moved one of them to face the sun, a uniformed employee scurried over to inform me that the chairs had to be kept in an orderly row. Not even a chair is allowed to be out of line in China.

Mr. Tuong laughs. "That'd never happen in Vietnam," he declares. "Like the Chinese we've been influenced by Buddhism and Confucianism, and yet our characters are irreconcilably different."

We proceed down another path. A bunch of vendors armed with cold drinks have installed themselves at a strategic point. They press the cans against my arm to demonstrate how cold they are. "Let's have something to drink," I suggest since the heat is unbearable. It feels like someone is hitting me in the face with a red-hot sledgehammer every time I take a step. "Three dollars," says one of the vendors, curious as to my reaction. I give her the money without a murmur of protest.

"Many people died building this mausoleum," I reproach Mr. Tuong. "As a revolutionary, you must condemn that?"

Mr. Tuong shrugs his shoulders and sips his Coke. "That was another era, another dynasty. Those times are gone forever," he says and hails a man with a large camera. "He's going to record us for posterity," he explains. "He's actually a math teacher, but you can't live on a teacher's salary." The photographer promises to deliver two pictures to Hotel Morin tomorrow.

"Oh, it's hot," I sigh as we climb back on the motorbike.

"Well then," Mr. Tuong decides, "it's high time we took a boat ride on the Perfume River." The bike inches up a hill and Mr. Tuong pulls over at the top. I gaze breathlessly down at the meandering river, following its course to where it disappears on the horizon between two blue mountains. The banks are lined with tall bamboo, and sampans putt-putt gracefully across the water.

We walk down to a beach at the river's edge, where Mr. Tuong begins bargaining with a little gray-haired old lady who has moored her boat to a broken-down landing stage. "Climb aboard," he orders. The woman smiles, exposing a row of black teeth, and cranks the diesel motor. We cast off and head for the middle of the river, in the direction of the blue mountains.

"I was stationed in those mountains years ago," muses Mr. Tuong with a note of nostalgia in his voice. "I was living in a Montagnard village, and one of my comrades was a beautiful girl from that village. One night I declared her my undying love and promised to come back after the war to marry her."

"Why after the war, why not right away?" I want to know. Mr. Tuong doesn't strike me as the type to postpone happiness.

Mr. Tuong throws his hands in the air. "Our struggle for liberation came first," he says. He tosses a pebble in the water.

"You never went back," I reproach him.

"Oh yes I did," Mr. Tuong replies sadly. "But I was too late."

Five years after they parted Mr. Tuong hiked up the mountains in search of his former flame. On the mountain path he came across an old woman. "I'm looking for Comrade Hoai. Can you tell me the way?"

A Poet and a Princess

The old woman gave him a searching look and asked: "So you know Comrade Hoai?"

"I sure do," replied the young Mr. Tuong.

"Follow me," said the old woman. The two of them climbed for an hour over a steep path until they came to a hut. "This is where I live," said the old woman.

Mr. Tuong looked at her in incomprehension. Only then did he realize that *she* was Comrade Hoai. "The Montagnards have a hard life. She'd gotten old in five years," concludes Mr. Tuong regretfully.

"You must have had lots of girlfriends in the mountains," I hint. "After all, plenty of young women took part in the struggle, didn't they?"

Mr. Tuong clucks his tongue in disapproval. "Oh no," he says, "we swore not to have any physical contact with women."

I stare at him in disbelief. "But you must have had affairs in secret?"

Mr. Tuong shakes his head decidedly from side to side. "Absolutely not. You couldn't justify such behavior to yourself. We had to devote all our strength to the fight. I put those kinds of thoughts out of my head." Staring over the river, he adds: "I lived for death, not for love." He dramatically raises his hands in the air. "When I got out of the army I was a thirty-six-year-old virgin. I had sacrificed my youth."

"Ah," I heave a sigh of compassion. I feel like putting an arm around his skinny shoulders to comfort him for the loss of his youth, but I'm afraid it'll only startle him.

In the meantime, there's a refreshingly cool breeze coming off the river, and we're sitting in the shade of a woven mat serving as a roof. The old woman shouts something above the engine's din. "She says that the emperors used to sail here in the olden days," Mr. Tuong translates. Seeing the Dragon Boat pass by must have been a beautiful sight.

"Are there still any members of the imperial family in Hue?" I ask Mr. Tuong.

"*Ooh la la*," he says. "Some of the emperors had more than a hundred children, and all of those children also had children. Thousands of people in Hue bear the imperial name."

"Oh really?" I ask intrigued. "Do you happen to know anyone related to the emperors?"

Mr. Tuong nods. "One of my former students is married to a prince. At any rate, he used to be a prince, since of course titles have officially been abolished. But that makes her a princess, you might say."

"Can we go visit them?" I ask eagerly.

"If you insist," replies Mr. Tuong, a little miffed. If you ask me, he'd like it better if I spent my entire visit in Hue exclusively in his company.

At the end of the afternoon we drive back to the city. Mr. Tuong doesn't even remember the biggest potholes we got stuck in on the way here. He heads straight for them without batting an eyelash.

"Shall we go grab a bite to eat?" I suggest. "You must be hungry."

Mr. Tuong waves his hand in the air, as if to say that he's not interested in such worldly matters as food, and shouts above the roar of the motor: "I'm your obedient slave."

"In that case I'd like to go to the floating restaurant on the Perfume River," I laugh. "I've heard good things about the food."

Darkness has fallen by the time we reach our destination and park the motorbike on the embankment. We walk over the gangplank to the restaurant, where we're greeted by a cool breeze. We choose a table near the water. Mr. Tuong orders steamed crab, thin noodles and squid in a sweet sauce. He barely touches his dinner. "I'd rather drink," he says and studies the rising moon. "It's a perfect circle tonight," he notes with satisfaction.

In the distance I hear the sound of approaching drums. "Tonight we celebrate the Mid-Autumn Festival," explains Mr. Tuong. "What you hear are children venerating the moon."

After dinner we stroll along the Perfume River, where we catch sight of a procession. The head of the procession is formed by a cyclo containing at least nine wriggling children and a bass drum. The tallest child is deftly banging on the drum. Then comes a mighty dragon, menacingly swaying its head back and forth to the rhythm of the drum, while its hind legs also keep step to the drumbeat. Bringing up the rear is a child in a mask: a huge broadly grinning papier-mâché head. "It symbolizes the earth," explains Mr. Tuong.

A Poet and a Princess

The kiddie parade catches sight of us and the air is filled with shouts of "*Lien Xo! Lien Xo!* Russian!"

"No, no," Mr. Tuong corrects them. "This lady comes from *Helan*, Holland." Dragon roars fill the air. Everyone laughs, and the dragon comes closer and closer.

"*Ooh la la,*" laughs Mr. Tuong. "The dragon is hungry." The whole point of this procession, he explains, is for the dragon to be given candy or some other favor. Suddenly the monster is standing in front of me fiercely shaking its head from side to side. I take five thousand dong out of my pocket. Mr. Tuong stops me just as I'm about to hand it over. "No," he cautions me, "you shouldn't make it easy for the dragon. He has to do his best to get it."

Clutching the money in my hand, I clamber on top of a wall and wave the bill back and forth. The dragon flails in the air with its forelegs; the drumbeat accelerates. The two youngsters in the dragon costume climb gracefully on to the wall, as light as feathers, keeping time to the music. I stuff the bill in the dragon's gaping maw. Instead of the tongue I expected to see, a tiny hand comes out and snatches the money from my hand. Back with its four feet on the ground, the dragon removes its head, leaving me staring into the sweat-beaded face of a grinning ten-year-old. He's as thin as a rake. I can't imagine him wearing that heavy dragon head for the entire evening.

The procession moves on in search of more gifts. Fifty or so laughing and shouting children, the tallest one no higher than my waist, traipse along behind the dragon.

"*Alors,*" concludes Mr. Tuong. "Let's go see the prince. He's still living in the same house where he was born." We drive slowly through the dark city, past sweetly scented gardens, until we reach a branch of the Perfume River where dozens of sampans, lit by kerosene lanterns, are moored. Mr. Tuong switches off the motor. The conversations being carried out from one boat to another resound across the water. Since Vietnamese basically consists of one-syllable words, their talk sounds like the strumming of a guitar. Far away we can still hear the banging of various drums. The city is full of parading dragons.

Mr. Tuong goes inside to see if the princely pair is able to receive us. I wait in the darkness under a pair of enormous trees.

There must be jasmine blooming nearby. Mr. Tuong returns in the company of an elegant woman with long hair parted in the middle. "The princess, Madame Moon," says Mr. Tuong by way of introduction. She reminds me of Joan Baez in the heyday of the Vietnam protest. Madame Moon speaks both French and English. "I'm home alone," she apologizes. "My husband and our sons have gone to town to celebrate the Mid-Autumn Festival."

Madame Moon leads us to the porch of an old house with a vaulted roof and draws up some weather-beaten chairs for us to sit on. Mr. Tuong lights a cigarette. "Madame Moon was the most beautiful student I ever had," he confides.

"Ah," she counters sadly. "And now I'm old." I expect Mr. Tuong to offer a denial, but he heartlessly holds his tongue.

"Madame Carolijn is interested in stories about the imperial family," he tells her.

Madame Moon laughs. "My husband is the youngest son of his father's fifth wife. That means he was pretty far down on the ladder. As for his being a prince, well, it didn't amount to much," she laughs. "There are four other houses next to ours. That's where the other four wives lived. There was apparently a lot of hostility and jealousy among the wives. When there was a disagreement my mother-in-law, as the fifth wife, was always obliged to submit to the will of the others. So my husband had a very unhappy childhood."

"That's how things went back in the days of feudalism," concurs Mr. Tuong.

Madame Moon straightens her back and says: "Still, one of the five women got a divorce. So it's not true that they had to accept their fate. She went back to her village and led a normal life."

Mr. Tuong refrains from comment. He knows that Madame Moon doesn't see the old world in the same bad light as he does.

After a short silence Madame Moon abruptly announces: "We're leaving, probably next week."

Mr. Tuong is surprised. "So soon?"

She nods.

"Where are you going?" I ask.

"To Houston, Texas," she says softly. "I have no choice," she adds defensively, as if she assumes we disapprove of her plan. "I have to consider my children's future."

A Poet and a Princess

Her brother-in-law, a doctor, lives in Houston. He's been maintaining his brother and his brother's family since 1975, sending them a hundred dollars a month. That allows them to live comfortably. Many a Vietnamese family has to make do with a tenth of that amount. But that's not the problem. She's afraid that if they stay in Vietnam her children won't be able to get the education they want. What professions might be open to them? She can't expect her brother-in-law to support his nephews indefinitely. "My children are still young enough to make a new start over there. It's now or never," she concludes.

"Madame Moon," says Mr. Tuong softly. "Sing something for us. You have such a beautiful voice." She laughs, but moments later a melancholy aria is wafting its way across the dark garden. "*La Bohême, la Bohême. Ça voulait dire on était heureux.*" She takes a deep breath and continues singing as if the words are painful: "It was many years ago. We were happy, though we had nothing. La Bohême! La Bohême! We were young, we were foolish." As the last notes fade away, Madame Moon and I wipe the tears from our eyes.

Mr. Tuong clears his throat. "The story of how Madame Moon and the prince fell in love is really something. *Très romantique!* How long did you know each other before he asked you to marry him?"

I turn to her. "Seventeen hours," she confesses. They were both working at Hue's City Hall, for the "former government." She was an accountant and he was what you might call a mayor. When they met they both knew that South Vietnam was on the brink of collapse and that, given their positions, their heads would be the first to roll. He asked her to marry him, and six days later Saigon fell. "We were the first to be married under the new regime," she glumly recalls. "The new seals hadn't arrived yet, and that created a lot of problems for us later when we decided to emigrate to the U.S. Our marriage certificate didn't have an official seal."

They had four children and kept themselves aloof from the outside world. They had each other, and they worked hard in their garden. "I cultivated flowers and vegetables," she says. "I created my own paradise." She was busy from sunrise to sunset. "Only I never managed to breed a good rose," she says with a sigh of regret. "It just can't be done in this climate."

When her children started school and she had to fill in the forms, she wrote under "parent's occupation": gardener. As soon as he could her brother-in-law in Houston filed an application for family reunification. They were told they would have to wait about ten years. "I've waited and waited," she laments. "Those ten years are up, and now I'm old."

After a moment of silence she turns to Mr. Tuong: "You should know what the future has in store for Vietnam. After all, this is what you hoped for. You're still a member of the Party, aren't you?" she jokes. Yet I'm startled by the implied barb.

Mr. Tuong responds to her goading by taking a long drag on his cigarette. "I'm a romantic," he says in his defense. To change the subject he adds: "Madame Moon is a very famous cook. She knows the specialties of Hue better than anyone else. Her meals are always surrealistic."

"He means that at my house, you don't eat what you think you're eating," Madame Moon explains. All of her meals are vegetarian, although you wouldn't know it to taste it. She serves what looks like roast pork, paté and chicken in a sweet sauce, except that everything is made from soy beans. In the olden days the emperors observed the Buddhist tradition of eating two vegetarian meals a month. To compensate for the lack of meat and fish on those days, chefs were hired to prepare special dishes out of soy beans. Madame Moon has mastered this art, and she now serves her exquisite dishes to Hue's distinguished visitors. The French and British ambassadors can count themselves among the lucky guests at her table.

"A representative of the Communist Party came and begged me not to leave Vietnam," she remarks shyly. Her departure would mean the loss of one of Hue's special attractions. Madame Moon's eyes are filled with tears. "I told them: 'If you lend me twenty thousand dollars, I'll stay. Then I can turn this house into a real restaurant to support my family, and we won't be dependent on my brother-in-law.'"

Mr. Tuong chokes in his cigarette smoke when he hears how much she asked for and says he doesn't think there's that much money in all of Hue.

Madame Moon nods. "That's the problem. Hue is so poor.

A Poet and a Princess

Many people are predicting that the situation will change. But when?" she'd like to know. "If I decide to stay, how long will I have to wait?" No one answers.

"This may not be polite," I say, "but I'd really like to see the inside of your house. Will you show it to me?"

Madame Moon is startled by my request. "We're in the middle of moving and the house is so messy," she demurs. I brush aside her objections. "Okay, but only the living room," she decides. Mr. Tuong prefers to stay outside, he says, enjoying the moon and his cigarettes.

The princess leads the way. A yellow silk drape embroidered with dragons and Chinese characters is hanging in the hall. "A family heirloom," explains Madame Moon. The living room has a gleaming wood floor and an impressive beamed ceiling. In the middle of the room is a simple wood table that can seat about a dozen people. High on the wall are photographs of two people. "My husband's father and grandfather," she explains. They have long, gray goatees and hats which jut out on either side. The edge of the embroidered silk collars on their tunics is just visible. "My husband's great-great grandfather was Emperor Ming Manh," Madame Moon says with a smile, as if she can hardly believe it herself. "The oldest son of his first wife became emperor, and the rest of his numerous sons were princes who in turn beget many sons." She giggles. "My husband's father and grandfather were also mandarins, since they passed the Imperial Examinations. After that they spent their lives in high administrative positions. The stepped bonnets they're wearing in these photographs are special hats that only mandarins were allowed to wear."

She sighs and walks over to a glass display case containing her porcelain collection. She shows me dozens of blue and white bowls and platters. "I can't take anything with me," she laments. "It's strictly forbidden to take antiquities out of the country." For weeks she's been trying to sell her possessions to friends and acquaintances so that she'll have a little money when she arrives in Texas. "But what do people who barely have enough to eat want with imperial porcelain?" she wonders. "Maybe I can find a buyer in Saigon." She'll have to purchase a car when she gets to the U.S., since she knows you can't go anywhere in Texas on foot. In any case she'll have to drive her children to school.

She opens a drawer and pulls out an embroidered cloth, appliqued satin silk. I can vaguely make out a dragon head. Madame Moon glances outside, where we can see Mr. Tuong's cigarette glowing in the dark. A conspiratorial smile appears on her face. "All the girls in my class were in love with him, you know," she whispers, "including me. Like all the other girls I thought he only had eyes for me."

I burst into laughter. "He's a real ladies' man, that's for sure," I say.

"My husband can't stand him," she confesses. "Men always hate him."

The sounds outside reach us through the open windows and the wind rustles in a bamboo hedge. Far away in the city we can still hear the drums.

Madame Moon's face clouds over again. She never stops worrying about emigrating to the U.S., she explains. "I'm afraid of leaving my past. Maybe we're making the wrong decision. My husband has to obey his older brother, and I have to follow my husband."

For a moment I contemplate telling her: for goodness' sake, stay in Hue. You're going to miss your house, your neighbors, the magic of this night. This is the last time you'll ever hear the drums beating in the autumn. No garden in Texas is redolent with so many wonderful fragrances and, believe me, no two-door refrigerator is worth it.

But I hold my tongue. Because I too am afraid that the changes will come to Hue too late for her children.

I put an arm around her shoulder, and the two of us stand for a moment in the middle of the room without saying a word. "Maybe you can start a catering business in Houston," I suggest. "How about calling it 'Hue Imperial Catering?' Wouldn't that look great in gold lettering on a delivery truck?"

Madame Moon seriously weighs my proposition. "I don't have a driver's license," she objects. "And I'm too old," she concludes sadly.

"No, you're not," I say. "You don't look a day over forty."

She shakes her head and the corners of her mouth turn down in a frown. "I toss and turn in my bed at night, worrying about everything. I'm becoming obsessed with time. We've waited ten years for this opportunity. I'm fifty years old now, and I lie awake night after night, hearing every second tick away in my head."

FAREWELL TO SAIGON

New Memories

Mr. Tuong insists on taking me to the station. He crams me and my voluminous baggage into a cyclo and drives alongside, with the engine of his motorbike backfiring from time to time. He escorts me personally to the compartment where a berth has been reserved for me.

This time I seem to be out of luck when it comes to my fellow passengers. The berth across from me is occupied by an overbearing nonstop talker who keeps bragging about the fish-export company he works for and the important business that brought him to Hue. Then he fires a volley of questions at me: "Where do you come from? How much do you earn? Where's your husband?"

Since I don't feel like carrying on a conversation with him, I get up and stroll through the train. The diesel engine chugs its way up a mountain. The third-class car contains wooden benches, and some of the passengers have made themselves comfortable by slinging hammocks between them. A young man with ferocious tattoos on his arms is swaying contentedly above a lumpy heap of baggage. Several women in conical hats are squatting in the aisles, chatting with each other while keeping an eye on the baskets of fruit displayed at their side. A cooling sea breeze wafts in through the open windows. Outside I can see an enchanting sandy beach and blue waves lapping at a coastline. The train crawls through a gorge at a snail's pace. Not that it ever reaches dizzying speeds, mind you: trains in Vietnam move at an average of nineteen miles an hour. On the other side of the gorge the sunlit ocean pops back into view.

Back in my compartment the businessman continues to bombard me with questions. "Why aren't you home with your children?"

"Because I don't have any," I snap back at him.

"A woman who doesn't have any children is egotistical," he growls.

"So why aren't you at home with your two daughters," I retort angrily.

He flashes me a look of triumph. "Because I have important work to do. Besides, it's normal for a man to be egotistical. All men are."

I can't think of a quick reply to that one, and so I immerse myself in a book. A passenger from an adjoining compartment comes in for a chat. He's meticulously dressed in a striped shirt, and his hair is fashionably cut. He's clearly quite enamored of himself. "Where are you from?" he too wants to know. "How long have you been in Vietnam? How long are you going to stay?"

The businessman, stretched out on his berth with a magazine, begins to get that familiar look of jealousy in his eyes. He doesn't like it when another Vietnamese starts talking to "his" foreigner. He says something to the other man, who angrily exclaims in English: "Boy, has he got a lot of nerve!" and beats a hasty retreat.

Peace at last, I think. But then two young men appear in the doorway. "Can you give us a lesson in English?" they ask. "Can you tell us what the difference is between 'maybe' and 'perhaps'?"

"I haven't got the faintest idea. I'm not English," I say, hoping to discourage them.

"If you don't have time now, we'll come back later," they insist. "How about seven o'clock — is that okay?"

"I'll be asleep by that time," I reply irritably.

"Then we'll come back before then."

I shake my head no.

New Memories

Vietnamese can be extremely persistent, as I've discovered time and again. They don't give up. I can easily imagine why the Cambodians, whom the Vietnamese consider to be lazy barbarians, keep a watchful eye on their ambitious neighbors.

We stop in the seaport of Danang. Dozens of women and children storm the train, hoping to sell their wares. The platform is lined with shops where passengers can buy whatever they might need during a train journey. I sprint over the track and buy a washcloth and a couple of bottles of drinking water.

The train sets itself in motion again, this time following the main highway. The asphalt is covered with gigantic potholes. An ox cart with a broken wooden wheel is stranded alongside the road. Buses overflowing with passengers overtake the train. Even an ancient Citroën, the luggage on the roof weighing it down so much it's practically scraping the ground, passes us by. While the setting sun fills the sky with pinkish stripes, I watch a group of people threshing rice on the shoulder of the road. The man operating the thresher is wearing a blue cotton shirt, the back of which is soaked with sweat. His helpers spread the rice over the asphalt to dry. As soon as darkness falls, I clamber into my bed and let myself be rocked to sleep by the swaying train.

We stop with a jolt in Nha Trang at four in the morning. The businessman gathers his things together and leaves the train. I can hear his loud voice booming along the entire length of the platform. The darkness doesn't discourage the vendors. Dozens of children swarm aboard with rose-colored dragon fruit, the largest of which must weight at least a pound. It's become my favorite fruit. I buy four for a dollar and bite into the white flesh, dotted with thousands of black seeds.

At the first light of day I discover a desert-like landscape outside the train. Stretched out before me, as far as the eye can see, is a vast expanse of salt flats. A dry, relentless heat blows in through the windows.

The other passengers in my compartment have left the train, and I'm now its sole occupant. I go back to sleep, and the next time I wake up the train is in the middle of a tropical forest; the leaves brush the windows. It's raining, and a magnificent rainbow arches over the hills.

Voices and Visions

We crawl towards Saigon's outlying districts. The houses are built right next to the tracks. Some of the hovels are made out of little more than straw matting. The train cuts through the outskirts of Saigon like a scalpel through flesh, and I can see right into the wound. One woman is hanging tattered laundry on a clothesline, another is cooking over an open fire. One man is lugging a heavy cart load of goods, another stares mournfully out of a dirty window.

I mentally brace myself for my arrival at the station, where I know I'll have to fight my way through throngs of vendors and cyclo drivers. My baggage has grown to such proportions that I can't manage it on my own, which makes me an attractive prey to the sharks in their ranks. The train comes to a shrieking halt in the heart of Saigon.

Seated under the rotating ceiling fan in my hotel room I listen to the clatter of the noodle-soup vendor outside my window. Three mendicant monks with shaved heads and bedraggled saffron robes are slowly crossing the street, one step at a time. The traffic grinds to a halt to allow them to pass. The monk at the head of the procession is clutching a begging bowl in his hands.

Soon after checking into my hotel I went to see the Trang family. True to form, they were all in their dimly lit store. Mr. Trang was sitting in his bamboo chair, his wife was manning her post at the cash register and the daughters were waiting on customers.

An unfortunate incident occurred in my absence. Lan, my favorite Trang daughter, lost a huge amount of money in some business transaction. The story was too complicated to explain, apologized Mr. Trang, but it boiled down to the fact that Lan was left holding the bag. Poor Lan was so upset that Mr. Trang was afraid she was contemplating suicide. To keep her from taking her life, he presented her with enough money to pay off her debt. Lan's dark eyes filled with tears as her father told the story. "You can't trust a Vietnamese," concluded Mr. Trang bitterly, only to add cheerfully soon afterwards, "oh well, it's only money." A wan smile appeared on Lan's face.

To me Mr. Trang whispered: "I'll see you an hour from now in the restaurant next door to your hotel. Then we can down a cou-

NEW MEMORIES

ple of Heinekens." He glanced meaningfully at his wife, and I nodded knowingly.

At the appointed time Mr. Trang arrives at the air-conditioned restaurant just as I'm selecting a table. He's looking washed and scrubbed and the little hair he has left on his head is wet. He's wearing a spotless white embroidered shirt. I've never seen him looking so dressed up. He greets me with gallantry and gives our order to the waitress. "I told her to make sure the beer is ice cold," he says gravely. We take a sample sip and nod our approval: the temperature is just right.

"My wife has gone to bed with a headache," he informs me with feigned regret. "I've advised her to lie down and rest for a few hours."

The words are hardly out of his mouth before I recognize her gray hair in its characteristic chignon in the doorway. Mr. Trang also catches sight of her, and his eyes widen in shocked surprise. "*Ooh la la*," he mutters under his breath. She comes at us like a tornado. Mr. Trang hunches his shoulders as if to ward off a blow. A stern-faced Mrs. Trang seats herself next to her husband and begins scolding him in Vietnamese. Mr. Trang turns pale and has trouble maintaining his composure. With great dignity he summons the waitress and pays the bill.

"Excuse me," he says to me as he gets to his feet, "but my presence is required in the store."

I take his wife's hand in mine and say in French, which I know she understands a little: "Madame, you mustn't be angry. We were just sitting here talking." But her stony face doesn't relax. The deadly Vietnamese jealousy has struck again. I promise to stop by to say goodbye before I leave, and Mrs. Trang nods. I have her gracious permission to do that.

Left alone with my bewilderment, I order another beer and decide not to allow myself to be upset by this incident. After all, it's my last night in Vietnam, and I'm going to celebrate.

I go outside, cross the street and look for an empty table at Restaurant Thirteen. A gray-haired woman I remember meeting months ago comes and sits beside me. "I still haven't predicted your future," she says softly.

"That's true," I reply, "and I'm leaving tomorrow."

"Then this is your last chance." She holds a deck of cards in front of me, her face the picture of seriousness. "Take one," she says. It's a queen.

She reshuffles the cards. "Take another one." Again it's a queen. Alarmed, she spreads the cards on the table. The waitress respectfully sets my bowl of soup at the edge of the table and stays to watch, giving the cards her full attention. As I know from my experience at the Musicians' Union, the future is taken seriously in Vietnam.

"Beware of a woman," the fortune-teller hisses through her gold-capped teeth. "An older woman. She will be only a few years older than you. She will ask you to do her a favor, and you must refuse." She stares intently at me. "Don't accept her offer," she repeats. I hand her a stack of bills. She tucks them beneath her blouse, gets to her feet and goes to the bar next door in search of new customers.

Oh well, I think. Of course you should beware of women. Of men too. I pay for my soup and shake off a group of begging children who have attached themselves to me. I walk down Don Khoi Street, where the stores are closing their shutters for the night. I turn into a side street, passing Saigon's largest mosque, and enter Apocalypse Now.

Just as I did four months ago, I run into John the New Zealander. He's sitting at the bar, staring dejectedly into space. "How about a beer?" I ask. "You've sure lost a lot of weight!" I exclaim.

John gulps down the beer, as if it's the first thing he's had to drink for days. "Business isn't so hot," he admits. His ex-girlfriend, Miss Snow, went to the police and told them that John, a foreigner, is the real owner of the furniture factory, which is officially registered as a Vietnamese-owned company. Pending further investigation, they've seized his entire stock and all his equipment. At this point, he explains, he has no idea what the legal ramifications are going to be. "Now I understand how the Vietnamese won the war," he sighs. "They put up such a smoke screen that the Americans never figured out what was going on. All that confusion sapped their strength, and that's what did them in."

"And how're things going with your landlady's daughter?" I ask out of idle curiosity.

New Memories

John grins. "Well, I've got good news and bad news. The good news is that she's pregnant. The bad news is that her mother found out about our relationship three months ago and threw me out of the house, and her father has sworn to kill me." John took his threat seriously since the man has already been imprisoned once for aggravated assault.

"And to top it off I'm absolutely broke," he concludes. "Can you spare me a cigarette?"

I walk outside and buy a pack of Marlboro's from a woman in a nearby streetside stall. John avidly inhales his cigarette.

A new customer comes in. I remember seeing her the last time I was here, and she intrigued me then too. She's wearing sunglasses, even though the sun went down hours ago. She has on a cotton blouse, and her slender legs are encased in tight jeans. There's a silver chain around her neck and silver rings on her fingers. Her long hair keeps falling across her face. She reminds me of a hippie from the sixties.

"Most Vietnamese women like gold," I say, hoping to elicit an explanation for her appearance, "but you seem to like silver."

She nods and points to a large onyx ring. "An American friend of mine gave that to me years ago. He was a war correspondent." His name, she tells me, was Sean Flynn. One day Flynn took off for the Cambodian border and was never heard from again.

This explains her outfit: she's living in the past. I try to figure out how old she is. In her early forties? Is she the woman I'm supposed to be wary of? But she doesn't ask me to do her a favor. She does tell me her name. It sounds like "Jane" or something like that.

Gradually the bar begins to fill with people. I get to talking to an American nurse who's working for an international relief agency in Saigon. When I happen to mention that I'm flying to Bangkok tomorrow she says: "Oh, my sister lives there. Do you think you could give her a letter? The mail is so slow."

"Of course," I reply. "You can bring it to my hotel tomorrow morning. I'll be busy packing."

A Vietnamese of Chinese origin comes over and offers us a drink. He's wearing a gold chain around his neck and bragging about his many achievements. Suddenly I hear a scream and see a man with a bar stool in his raised hands. He slams it down on the Chinese man's head, and his crony kicks him in the stomach.

I take refuge under a table, along with Jane and the American nurse. We hear screams and shouts and see one of the waitresses standing on the bar crying. The two men run outside, and quiet is restored to the bar. We help the disheveled Chinese man to his feet. The nurse checks to see if anything is broken.

"I've never going to come here again," he moans. Suddenly he puts his hand to his neck: his gold chain is gone! "This city is full of thieves and murderers," he sobs. In the meantime the bar has emptied out. The injured man is helped into a waiting cyclo.

The next morning I take a taxi to the airport. I'm surprised that the nurse hasn't come to the hotel with her letter. But that's how things go, I think to myself. A lot of the plans made in bars never see the light of day.

As I lug my bags full of souvenirs into the departure hall, I hear the nurse shout my name behind me. "Hi," she says, "I've come to wave goodbye. Here's the letter for my sister in Bangkok. I've also made her a special kind of glutinous rice. It's one of her favorite dishes." She hands me a plastic bag.

I weigh the package in my hand and scan the departure hall. There doesn't seem to be a ladies' room where I can take a leisurely look at the contents. Why has she traveled all the way to the airport instead of dropping by my hotel? Is this really a specialty they don't have in Thailand?

Suddenly I feel absolutely sure: this is the woman the fortune-teller warned me about! Her glutinous rice is probably stuffed with drugs or diamonds. "I'm sorry," I say, "but I don't dare take something like that through customs."

She shoots daggers at me. "I just finished making it," she exclaims. "It's still hot."

Determined, I head for customs, where she can't follow me.

I only breathe normally again when I'm safely ensconced in the airplane, but my hands are still shaking. This incident has drained me of my last ounce of energy. I feel exhausted and empty. Maybe I'm only feeling this way because my long journey is at an end. Still, the prospect of leaving Vietnam doesn't make me happy.

New Memories

As far as I was concerned, life in Vietnam was one continuous stage play, with a cast of thousands. Some of the characters, like Mr. Trang, played many parts in the course of their lives. During my stay, I never managed to figure out exactly what the play was about or who the director was. But it didn't matter, since I was swept along by the play itself. One enchanting act followed another, and a host of elegant players moved on and off the stage.

New memories have replaced the bloody TV images and war movies that filled my head before I came to Vietnam. I long for the next act to begin.

The Gulf of Thailand shimmers below me. I try to picture Holland and realize I can't bear thinking of the tranquil life awaiting me there. I don't look forward to being in a country where everyone is merely playing himself. I've fallen in love with the cast of characters between the Mekong Delta and Hanoi. We haven't even landed in Bangkok, and already I'm homesick for Vietnam.